THE AUTOMOBILE INDUSTRY IN JAPAN
A STUDY OF ANCILLARY FIRM DEVELOPMENT

HD9710.J3

THE AUTOMOBILE INDUSTRY IN JAPAN

A STUDY OF ANCILLARY FIRM DEVELOPMENT

BY

KONOSUKE ODAKA

KEINOSUKE ONO

FUMIHIKO ADACHI

ECONOMIC RESEARCH SERIES
NO. 26
THE INSTITUTE OF ECONOMIC RESEARCH
HITOTSUBASHI UNIVERSITY
KUNITACHI TOKYO 186

KINOKUNIYA COMPANY LTD.

OXFORD UNIVERSITY PRESS

Printed in 1988

Published by Kinokuniya Company Ltd.
17-7 Shinjuku 3-chome, Shinjuku-ku,
Tokyo 163-91, Japan

Distributed in Japan by Kinokuniya Company Ltd.
Distributed outside Japan by Oxford University Press,
Walton Street, Oxford, OX2 6DP, England

ISBN 4-314-00487-8

Printed by
Kokusaibunken Insatsusha
Tokyo, Japan

PREFACE

This monograph tracks the spectacular growth of the automobile industry in Japan. Specifically, case studies of two assemblers and eight parts suppliers are presented.

The underlying thesis is simply that the formation and smooth functioning of a network of parts suppliers is an important condition for the development of machinery manufacturing in general, and the automobile industry in particular. Thus, this volume looks specifically for the factors that either contribute or hinder the growth of parts suppliers. The rationale as well as the basic premises of the study are explained in the introductory chapter.

The main body of the text (chapters 4 and 5) consists of the record of the authors' interviews at the ten companies, which took place rather intermittently between January 1976 and August 1979. Two interview sessions were held with each firm, each normally lasting for about half a day. In most cases the authors were able to talk with a wide range of company personnel, including the president, other executive officers, and engineers in charge. In addition, we had the opportunity to meet various experts directly responsible for the development of the parts supplier network in the Japanese automobile industry.

In the interviews, we tried to uncover whatever information we could on (1) the technological development of the firms, (2) interfirm linkages between assemblers and parts suppliers, and (3) policy implications. Needless to say, additional desk studies were conducted on historical and other background information. As early drafts of reports on the companies were completed, they were sent to the company concerned to ensure factual accuracy. Let it be clearly understood, however, that the views expressed are entirely ours, and none of the firms asked us to

PREFACE

change how we characterized it.

The study was undertaken as an integral part of the international joint project called "Ancillary Firm Development in Asia" (AFDA for short), which (excluding the Japan portion) was financed by the Council for Asian Manpower Studies (CAMS) during the years 1976–80. The project covered six countries: Indonesia, Japan, Korea, Malaysia, the Philippines and Thailand. Its final report was released in 1983 as *The Motor Vehicle Industry in Asia, A Study of Ancillary Firm Development*, edited by Konosuke Odaka and published by Singapore University Press. Space limitation could not possibly allow detailed country-by-country studies such as the present one.

This book thus constitutes a companion volume to the CAMS report, offering the reader detailed writeups of the case studies relating to the historical development of the Japanese auto parts supplier industry. These studies are summarized in Chapter 7 of the CAMS report. The basic framework of this study is perhaps best understood when placed in the context of the Asian industrialization process in general.

The individuals and organizations that came forward to help us complete the present study are too numerous to list exhaustively. Professor Shigeru Ishikawa was the source of constant inspiration and intellectual stimulus. In fact, he was the major source of energy that enabled us to push through to completion. Dr. Saburō Okita listened to our research proposal and introduced us to Mr. Shigenobu Yamamoto, then with Toyota Motor Company, who in turn made helpful arrangements with the company's Procurement Department. Mr. Yasurō Ito, then the department's director, personally arranged a series of interviews. Many executives and other employees at the ten companies gave generously of their time in meetings, sharing with us their knowledge and insights. Without their cooperation, this book would have been impossible to write. We also received valuable advice and support from Mr. Yoshihiro Ōkawara of the Japan Auto Parts Industries Association. Gratefully acknowledged also is financial assistance to Ono from the Japan Economic Research Foundation and from the Toyota Foundation during the academic years 1976 and 1978, respectively, and a research grant to Odaka from the Ministry of Education in fiscal years 1986–87 (Grant No. 6153024).

It is also pleasing to record our happy memories of camaraderie with the other researchers, with whom we labored for many years in the AFDA project. We got together on many occasions to discuss issues of mutual concern or to visit various machinery manufacturers, both in Japan and abroad.

Mrs. Aida Santos-Maranan provided editorial service while Odaka was stationed at the University of the Philippines (Diliman). Mr. Ronald Siani also came to our help at a later stage (in Tokyo). Mrs. Motoko Niimi typed most of the manuscript several times over efficiently and with much patience.

Finally, but not least, we thank Mr. Larry Meissner for editing the final version of the manuscript, which has improved immensely under his critical eye.

Spring 1987

The Authors

We wish to thank CAMS for granting us permission to make extensive use of text (with revision) and to reproduce several statistical tables and diagrams from Chapter 7 of *The Motor Vehicle Industry in Asia*.

CONTENTS

CONTENTS

CONTENTS

CONTENTS

Quality-First Policy (275)

EDITORIAL NOTE

In the text and footnotes of this volume Japanese surnames are listed first, in front of given names. Japanese rarely have middle names. Thus, for example, Yamada (surname) Tarō (given name).

Exceptions are the title page, the preface, and in some of the bibliographical listings (generally material in English, where we have followed the cited author's usage).

Chapter 1

INTRODUCTION

1.1   Purpose of the Study

This book examines the role of "ancillary firms" in the phenomenal growth of the Japanese automobile industry. An ancillary firm is either an independent or subcontracting manufacturer that supplies machine components or replacement parts to a primary firm, commonly called an assembler, which manufactures and markets the finished products under its name. The historical background of the industry as well as the growth process of two primary firms are also studied, inasmuch as they are related to the behavior of the ancillary firms.

A vertical division of work is a characteristic feature of the modern automobile industry. In other words, production of a large percentage of machine parts and components is carried out by ancillary firms (specialized manufacturers), whose products are later put together (assembled) by primary firms to form the final product (automobiles).

Figure 1.1 illustrates the structure of the automobile industry in postwar Japan. There were seven primary firms in 1950, fourteen in 1959, twelve in 1968, and eleven in 1987. Ancillary firms can be grouped into three layers. Those having direct contact with the automobile assemblers are labelled "first-tier" firms—some 1,500 in the mid 1970s, rising to 1,750 by the mid 1980s (see Appendix Table A-18). Approximately 300 to 350 of the firms in this category form an active industrial association, the *Nihon Jidōsha Buhin Kōgyō Kai* (Japan Auto Parts Industries Association, abbreviated JAPIA).

It is difficult to give an exact count of the "second-" or "third-tier"

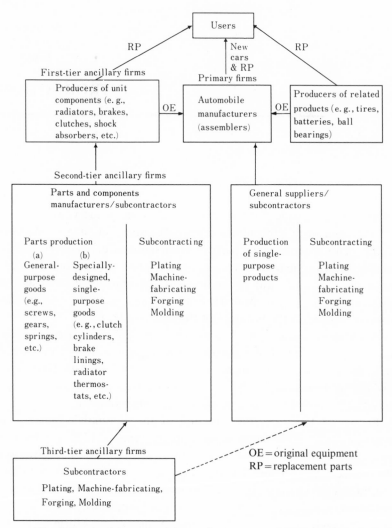

Fig. 1-1.   A Schematic View of the Japanese Automobile
Industry in the 1970s

Sources: Adapted from Jidōsha Buhin Kōgyō Kai (1968), pp. 301–02.

ancillary firms. According to a report from the Japan Development Bank (Nihon Kaihatsu Ginkō), the number of second- and third-tier firms in 1966 was approximately 1,000 and 3,000, respectively; in addition, there were about 4,000 suppliers/subcontractors working directly under the final assemblers (cited Kikai Shinkō Kyōkai 1975, p. 120). In any event, their number cannot exceed the total number of ancillary plants listed in the Census of Manufacturers (*Kōgyō tōkei hyō*), which includes both first-tier firms and the manufacturers of parts and components for motorcycles, in addition to the second- and third-tier firms. This source reports such plants increased from 778 in 1948, to 2,932 in 1958, to 11,311 in 1968, 13,662 in 1978 and decreased to 10,219 in 1984 (inclusive of chassis and body makers).

1.2 Why Study the Automobile Industry?

The automobile industry vividly illustrates the remarkable socio-economic transformation that accompanied the "high-speed growth" of the Japanese economy between the Korean War and the "Nixon Shock" of the early 1970s. (See, e.g., Nakamura (1981) and Kōsai (1986) for more on this.)

Self-propelled, high-speed vehicles excite the imagination. For many decades, tinkering with a motor car was a popular hobby for American boys; to many adults, posessing a fancy model—a "machine," it was called—was like a love affair. Auto mechanics courses were among the most crowded in official occupational training institutes in Japan during the rapid growth era after World War II. But this is not all of the story. The automobile industry became a sort of national status symbol, impelling many developing countries to launch production of their own nameplates.

Building the industry is complex, because the product is complex. An automobile has some five thousand components, which can be disassembled into over twenty thousand individual pieces. This complexity makes cars expensive and thus they do not sell well when per-capita income levels are low. On the supply side, production of automobiles requires the simultaneous (or, preferably, preceding) growth of supporting

3

industrial activities such as the manufacturing and processing of raw materials and the supply of various parts and components. Thus, the American automobile industry did not encounter any fundamental production difficulties in its early stages because it could draw technical leadership, plant facilities, and skilled labor from an existing machine tool industry. "The problems of large-scale automobile production involved the extension to a new product of skills and machines not fundamentally different from those which had already been developed for such products as bicycles and sewing machines. Underlying the discontinuity of product innovation, then, were significant continuities with respect to productive processes (Rosenberg 1963, p. 437)."

Not only could the fledging industry exploit the expertise accumulated in the economy over the years, but it achieved significant capital savings. Until well into the 1920s, the market for motor cars was in its infant stage, so the demand for auto-parts and components was also small. The average cost of production would have been much higher had the primary firms chosen to supply internally most of the required intermediate inputs. British firms opted for producing parts internally, and this decision is considered a reason why automobile output by the United States soon surpassed that of Britain, despite the fact the British were the first to engage in commercial production. (Shimokawa 1977, pp. 13–21; Maxcy and Silberston 1959, ch. 1). In the 1930s, subcontracting declined in the U.S., in part reflecting the consolidation of production into three major primary firms.

Before World War II, few countries had extensive machine tool industries, and thus lacked a firm foundation for the emergence of an automobile industry. In extreme cases, active support for automobile production by related industries was almost precluded. Without subcontracting or internal production, importation of the intermediate goods is the obvious and only alternative left to auto makers. But the final assembly operation alone is unattractive from a macroeconomic point of view, for it does not induce significant linkage effects in terms of employment, additional machinery demand, or the diffusion of advanced metal-working techniques.

WHY STUDY THE AUTOMOBILE INDUSTRY?

Primarily because the country had virtually no medium- and small-scale machine shops with appropriate technological experience, Hoshino (1966, pp. 45-47, 145-48) once remarked that the prospect for the autonomous development of the motor car production was extremely dim in prewar Japan. Manufacturers of parts and components were almost nonexistent in Japan in the early 1920s except for mudguards, a device road conditions made an absolute necessity. Similarly, during the early days of its development, Toyota found no domestic steel maker capable of supplying thin steel sheets with the desired specifications, and consequently resorted to foreign merchandise. Gradually, import substitution took place, probably due more to government encouragement than to market forces. Even at the time of the enactment of forceful protective measures for the domestic automotive production (the *Jidōsha seizō jigyō hō*, or Automobile Industry Act of 1936), the industry still relied heavily on imported parts and components (Table 1.1).

The status of the industry in the early days of its development may be understood more clearly when put in a comparative perspective. In phys-

Table 1.1. Source of Automobile Parts and Components, 1930s

Year	Domestic production (*Q*, in thousand yen)	Imported from abroad (*M*, in thousand yen)	M/Q
1930	4,494	19,765	4.40
1931	6,535	16,654	2.55
1932	6,096	11,927	1.96
1933	10,960	12,006	1.10
1934	22,736	28,945	1.27
1935	28,235	29,387	1.04
1936	33,398	33,445	1.00

Notes: Q is total value of shipments and is therefore over-estimated due to double-counting of subcontracting work.

Sources: Q: Shōkō Shō [Ministry of Commerce and Industry], *Kōjō tōkei hyō* [Census of Manufactures], various years;

   M: *Tōa jidōsha nenkan* [Tōa Automobile Almanac], 1941 edition.

ical volume of production, for instance, the size of the Japanese automotive industry in 1936 was less than 0.6 percent of that in the United States and some 6 percent of that in the United Kingdom. Similarly, average physical labor productivity of assembly operations in 1950 in Japan had barely reached the American standard of 1899. The gap in prime horsepower per employee between Japan and the United States is most striking, as seen in Table 1.2, although these figures cannot be

Table 1.2.　Prime Horsepower per Production Worker, Automobile and Automobile Parts and Components Industries, U.S. and Japan

United States

Year	Automobiles	Automobile parts and components
1904	0.734	1.353
1909	0.970	1.002
1914	1.324	1.421
1919	1.341	1.937
1923	1.805	2.599
1925	2.578	2.990
:	:	:
:	:	:
1954	7.233	

Sources: Seltzer (1928), pp. 76–77 and The U.S. Census of Manufactures, 1954.

Japan

Year	Automobiles	Automobile parts and components
1940	1.973	0.821
1948	0.990	1.496
1957	n.a.	1.967

Sources: Shōkō Shō [Ministry of Commerce and Industry], Kōjō tōkei hyō [Census of Manufactures] (prewar), and Tsūshō Sangyo Shō (MITI), Kōgyō tōkeihyō [Census of Manufactures] (postwar).

taken at face value because the U.S economy had been relatively more labor-scarce, and thus tended to substitute capital equipment for labor.

Cohen (1949, pp. 225–26) cited the difficulties the Japanese aircraft industry faced in connection with the production of parts for the war in expressing skepticism about the industry's postwar development. The difficulties included extremely poor interchangeability of parts, a high percentage of unusable machined parts, failure to meet delivery schedules, lack of adequate shop supervision, and shortage of skilled manpower. The dark postwar prospect for the industry culminated in a statement made in 1950 by Governor Ichimada Hisato of the Bank of Japan expressing serious doubts about pursuing automobile production. According to his view, it would be more consistent with Japan's comparative advantage to give up such capital-intensive operations as automobile manufacture (*Nihon Keizai Shimbun* (Japan Economic Journal), 13 April 1950). This opinion probably represented the feeling of a fairly substantial portion of the population at that time, including economists.

Things developed contrary to people's expectation. As described in Chapter 2, the postwar prosperity of Japanese car makers is obvious to anyone's observation, especially since the 1960s, suggesting the industry somehow overcame its deficiencies. In particular, this must imply that the country had succeeded in renovating the nature of supporting industrial activities for motor car production. A significant question, then, is how this change came about.

1.3   Managerial Reasons for Vertical Nonintegration

The vertically nonintegrated structure of the automobile industry is a consequence of the basic nature of machinery production. In general, the whole process of machinery production divides into processes that are self-contained and independent of each other. Such subsets consist either of the manufacturing processes of complete parts and components (e.g. bolts and nuts, shock absorbers, spark plugs, etc.) or of specialized processes engaged in the execution of well-defined industrial services (e.g. plating, painting, etc.). It is technically feasible, therefore, to break

7

down the entire process into a multiple of specialized operations.

These operations may be done either internally ("make") or subcontracted out ("buy"). For a network of ancillary firms acting as subcontractors to develop, however, certain prerequisites have to be met. For instance: various parts and components, although manufactured separately and independently, must be sufficiently homogeneous in quality and well-balanced in engineering precision; reliable delivery must be assured so the necessary quantity may be supplied at any time on request; and, the production technologies are subject to substantial economies of scale and thus are run most effectively by independent firms.

Aside from these conditions, however, subcontracting acts favorably to increase the economic efficiency of the primary firm, for instance through:

1. employing cheaper labor by taking advantage of a segmented labor market and thus avoiding an increase in the capital coefficient;
2. making fuller use of small-scale financial intermediaries with limited, but cheaper or easier-to-use credit resources;
3. achieving a higher rate of utilization of the given production facilities by changing the relative proportion of make and buy decisions and thus smoothing effects of demand fluctuations;
4. promoting competition among ancillary firms;
5. reducing inventory cost; and
6. economizing on investment as well as working capital—a consideration particularly relevant when capital is relatively scarce

(cf. Blair 1972, pp. 34–39; Williamson 1975, chs. 5–7).

In addition to these, the choice between "make" or "buy" is influenced by factors such as industrial secrets, specialized technology not elsewhere obtainable, etc. But most of such factors ultimately boil down to cost considerations in one way or another (cf. Culliton 1942).

1.4 Theoretical Orientation of the Study

At this point some reflections are in order on the factors that either promote or impede the development of ancillary firms in the machinery industry. (What follows draws heavily on Ishikawa and Odaka 1979.)

First, a brief explanation of a few essential terms. "Automobile" and "motor car" are used interchangeably to mean a vehicle powered by an internal combustion engine and equipped with three or more wheels, used primarily for transporting passengers or cargo of various kinds. By contrast, the term "motor vehicle" is much broader, including also motorcycles, tractors, bulldozers, and other special-purpose vehicles. In principle, therefore, the term "automobile" excludes motorcycles, although some of the data do not allow the separation of two wheelers. The manufacturers of complete automobiles are referred to as either assemblers, primary firms, or automobile manufacturers.

Firms producing or subcontracting automobile parts and components are referred to either as the manufacturers of automobile parts and components, or more simply as ancillary firms. They consist of producers of:

1. original equipment (OE), to be installed on the newly manufactured final product;
2. replacement parts (RP) or spare parts (SP), to be used for replacing worn-out parts; and
3. reconditioned parts, which are cheaper substitutes for RPs and SPs.

Normally, original equipment is manufactured according to the design and specifications required by the primary firm and thus supplied directly from ancillary to primary firms. By contrast, the other categories are sold in the open market. It is easy to see that the market size of the RPs (or SPs) is subject not only to the demand for the final product, but also to the durability of the part in question: the more quickly it wears out, the larger its market.

The terms "parts" and "components" are not differentiated except that the phrase "unit component" is reserved for an automobile part that forms a self-contained system by itself and which can be regarded as an independent product, such as carburetors, spark plugs, etc. Note, however, that tires and batteries are for some reason traditionally

9

classified as "related products," and not included in automobile parts in the strict sense of the term. On the other hand, chassis and bodies may be regarded as automobile parts in a broad sense, but are often listed separately in statistics.

Now we suggest that the following four factors should be taken into consideration in evaluating the development of ancillary firms: the conditions of markets for outputs, inputs, and intermediate products; the technological level; managerial capabilities; and the extent of government intervention.

Market Conditions

Market conditions refer to the degree of market development, factor endowment, the structure of commodity prices, market performance (competitiveness, etc.), and organizational efficiency. In particular, a crucial factor in ancillary firm development is the size of both domestic and foreign markets.

The vertically nonintegrated structure of the machinery industry comes as no surprise to those familiar with the concept of the division of labor. According to George Stigler (1951), who related it to the industry, a network of ancillary firms will remain underdeveloped in the early stages of the machinery industry because the size of the market for its product is relatively limited; instead, industrialists would manufacture necessary parts and components inside their own firms. However, as the market for the final product eventually expands, the vertical nonintegration of discrete processes becomes not only feasible but highly essential in realizing economies of scale.

Pertinent to this proposition are the following four conditions:
1. the degree of market fragmentation, due for instance to excessive product specification;
2. the limited size of the spare parts market, which is largely determined by the durability of the product in question;
3. the opportunity for ancillary firms to serve more than one group of industries or to export their products; and
4. the possibility of developing a new type of product that is not

only sufficiently attractive to create a domestic market, but is also shielded from international competition.

Obviously, factors (1) and (2) work negatively, while (3) and (4) work positively for the development of ancillay firms.

Technology

Independent of the condition of the market, the level of technological capabilities is clearly related to the development of ancillary firms. The term "technological capabilities" is defined here as the capacity to comprehend, adapt, improve, apply and develop technological knowledge. It may refer either to that of a firm, an industry, or the economy as a whole.

Technological knowledge (or, simply, technology) may be classified into two broad categories: capital-embodied and labor-embodied. Capital-embodied technology is intrinsic to various production processes such as casting, forging, metal-cutting, welding, pressing, etc. Also included here are technologies relating to process and quality controls. On the other hand, labor-embodied technology includes (1) skills and know-how in the operation of specific processes, (2) the ability to understand capital-embodied technology—that is, (on an elementary level) the ability to maintain and repair machines and equipment, and (on a more advanced level) the ability to devise alternative processes and equipment in response to various economic and engineering needs, (3) the capacity to design or redesign products, processes and plants, and (4) the ability to innovate and to develop new production techniques.

Given the economy's level of technological capabilities, one may then classify the production processes and the final products of a branch of the machine-building industry into three types.

Type 1, those simple enough to allow indigenous varieties to be devised by way of imitation;

Type 2, those amenable to adaptive application after taking into consideration local conditions of resource endowment and product design; and

11

Type 3, those so advanced that there is no other choice than simply borrowing it from abroad.

The larger the proportion of type 2 and (especially) type 3 processes and products that an industry can undertake successfully, the more technologically sophisticated the industry.

Relevant to this idea is a classification of agricultural machinery using these three levels of technological development, as suggested by a Regional Advisor of Transfer of Technology from ECAFE/ILO (Lalkaka 1974). The first level covers items manufactured in small artisan shops such as hand tools, hand-operated machines and animal-driven implements; the second refers to items that are imitations of foreign products with or without some adaptation, manufactured by use of relatively less sophisticated equipment but incorporating standard components procured abroad (e.g., power tillers, diesel engines, pump sets, tractor-drawn implements); and the third includes those requiring importation of product designs, skills in management, marketing and maintenance, such as heavy tractors and combines.

For firms engaged in any of these activities to emerge and grow, demand must have reached a threshold. The equipment required for preparing dies, moldings, machine tools, etc., is relatively expensive. Only when the size of the market is sufficiently large is it feasible for independent firms to specialize in die-making, casting, machine-tool manufacturing, etc. However, the minimum scale of operation varies according to the level of technolgical development. In the experience of Japan, for instance, the average scale for these basic processes was very modest until around the 1960s, so that firms specializing in these basic trades were mostly small or medium-sized firms. (This observation is based on Tsūshō Sangyō Shō 1960, vol. II and Chūshō Kigyō Chō 1969, pp. 74ff.)

But the arrival of the high-growth era of the 1960s fully supported the development of the machine-building industry. It seems that the minimum scale of operation in the basic activities has considerably increased through the years, side by side with the noticeable upgrading of technological capabilities in the industry. Pertinent in this context are the following two questions:

First, given the type and the quality of products and parts to be manufactured, what is the prospect for the substitution of labor for capital equipment? Is it possible for some manufacturing methods, particularly those commonly done with automated transfer machines in the advanced countries, to be replaced by an alternative, labor-intensive technology that is not only adaptable to low production volume, but also capable of realizing internationally competitive prices?

An interesting case of technological adaptation is described by Baranson (1967 and 1976). Komatsu Manufacturing (Japan) acquired a license for a component of Cummins' diesel engine (a T-shaped crosshead valve), the production of which was later subcontracted to Tsuzuki, a small establishment. Surprisingly, Tsuzuki succeeded in producing it in small quantities—only 1 to 2.5 percent of the volume produced by the U.S. factory—but with comparable price and quality. The task was accomplished by substituting 22 labor-intensive processing stages for an automated transfer line. The capacity to devise a new product design with suitable material specifications, a high standard of machining operations, and adequate quality controls were major contributing factors.

The second question is whether it is possible to develop a meaningful formula for the choice of techniques in the machine-building industry while keeping in mind that the industry consists typically of firms characterized by multiple processes with a variety of production equipment, and by many kinds of products. How can the formula (if any) be employed to determine the optimum technique for a typical firm in a certain specific branch of the machine-building industry?

In the earlier discussion on the relation of the cost of machine products to the volume of production, an implicit assumption was made that there is only a single technique that can be used in manufacturing a specified product. But the discussion on the relationship between technological capabilities, type of products, and cost of production points to the possibility of a set of alternative production techniques. Capital-intensive technology may be fitting for a system of mass

13

production, but a labor-using alternative (if such exists) may be more suitable in a situation that calls for production in samll quantities (cf. Saxonhouse and Ranis 1985). The actual question facing the machine-building industry is how to choose a particular combination of products, processes and equipment.

In studying the prevailing circumstances of the machine-building industry, one often comes across a case where machines and equipment in use are of a much inferior quality by world standards, but where the products (machinery or otherwise) are quite competitive vis-à-vis similar products made by the standard machinery and equipment, so that the former's low prices compensate sufficiently for their lower quality (Ishikawa 1979, pp. 92–103).

Managerial Capabilities

The term managerial capabilities means the ability to plan, initiate, co-ordinate, and execute corporate activities in the areas of production, marketing, finance and organization-building.

To carry out production activities, the firm must be equipped with material and intermediate inputs, capital equipment, a work force, technological know-how and other managerial resources. Managerial capability is the ability to procure the required inputs described above, to coordinate them as efficiently as possible, and to promote sales of output to achieve the highest possible rate of growth of the firm.[1]

Although the role of specific individuals is undoubtedly a critical factor in determining the economic performance of a firm, the definition of managerial capabilities pertains to much broader issues—the admin-

---

[1] "Managerial resource" refers to the entire set of endowments that the firm may avail itself of in executing its day-to-day operations, consisting of (1) accumulated labor-embodied knowledge and experience concerning managerial controls, production engineering and marketing, (2) the power to influence the market in procurement, finance and sales, and (3) organizational set-ups to collect pertinent information and to promote R&D. The term was coined originally in connection with discussions of foreign direct investment and multi-national corporations. Therefore, its main emphasis has been on the more sophisticated sides of managerial practices. In the present context, however, the term refers more to basic principles and practices of modern management.

14

istrative practices of the company as a whole as it undergoes the process of organizational growth.

Managers are either company founders (and families) or people hired from outside the family. Historically, the pattern of where they come from has undergone three distinctive stages. At the relatively early stage of industrialization, a firm generates its own managerial resources or imported them from abroad. Later, a class of non-owning managers emerges to offer its services to the owners. At a still later stage, the supply of certain managerial resources may again be entrusted to nonmarket mechanisms (cf. Arrow 1974).

For follower nations, most large and medium-sized companies initially rely heavily on managerial resources imported from developed countries. Methods are devised whereby in-plant training is provided to prospective managers and professional engineers; alternatively, the candidates may be sent abroad and enrolled in formal training courses.

The diffusion of managerial resources to small machine shops and ancillary firms, on the other hand, takes place largely through occupational or social mobility. In the experience of Japan, the degree of intra-generational mobility has not been particularly high. It has been especially difficult for a person of middle age and over to experience any upward mobility. However, there is some evidence that a form of downward mobility has been extensive. Thus, ex-employees (e.g. skilled workers) of primary firms sometimes quit their jobs to establish themselves as heads of small machine shops (see Odaka 1984, ch. 2). Occasionally, primary firms send ex-managers to assume executive positions in subcontracting firms that are close allies.

Before World War II, Japan had a hybrid form of managerial recruiting. The historical custom of adopting a male heir (often a son-in-law) was used. A succeeding generation of managers marrying into a firm was of course not uncommon in Europe and the United States.

Government Policies

The technologies used in the metal-working and machine-building industries are characterized by a high degree of transferability and wide applicability. Consequently, their spread is likely to foster growth in the entire economy. One could thus make a case for protecting these industries, provided such a choice is feasible and the prospect for the industries' growth is reasonably bright.

However, like any infant industry, the emphasis on development entails economic costs. High import tariffs on basic parts and components for machinery production as well as the introduction of domestic content programs are both likely to push up the prices of manufactured products in the domestic market.

A protection policy should be evaluated, therefore, in reference to the economy's tolerance for the cost vis-à-vis the benefits. Attempts have often been made to alleviate cost pressures by stressing the need for achieving international competitiveness at some point—often by encouraging the industry to achieve competitiveness in the unprotected markets of other countries.

Import substitution may lead to higher price levels, if it implies straightforward, direct adoption of imported technologies with no modifications to reflect the country's factor endowment, technological and managerial capabilities, market size, etc. High-cost industrialization is in part a consequence of the rapid and massive introduction of highly sophisticated commodities, whose production requires the use of equally expensive machinery and other production facilities, including equipment and tools, parts and components.

The undesirable consequences of import substitution can be alleviated if the country develops products similar to the imported ones, but cheaper and simpler. Compared with other manufacturing activities, the machinery industry in fact permits wider room for such adjustments. Along with this line of thought, therefore, the government may render effective service leading eventually to the faster growth of ancillary firms.

As a summary expression of the state of ancillary firm development in the industry, one may employ a diagram that relates the (relative) cost of production to the degree of domestic content for a given volume of production, such as drawn in Figure 1.2.

The cost is measured (on the vertical axis) in terms of the production

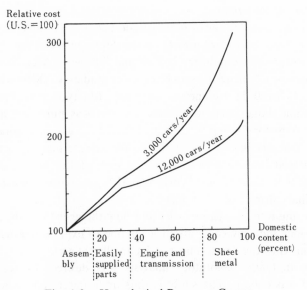

Relative cost
(U.S.=100)

300

200

3,000 cars/year

12,000 cars/year

100

20	40	60	80	100
Assem-	Easily	Engine and	Sheet	
bly	supplied	transmission	metal	
	parts			

Domestic
content
(percent)

Fig. 1-2.　Hypothetical Baranson Curves

Sources:　Adapted from Baranson (1969), pp. 30–31.

cost of the same commodity in a reference country such as the United States, whereas the domestic content ratio is expressed (on the horizontal axis) as the proportion of domestically manufactured goods in the total output value of the completed machine product. This diagram is called the Baranson curve, as it was introduced by Jack Baranson (1969).

The Baranson curve illustrates a claim that, given the technological and managerial capabilities, and the limited size of demand for the machine product in the country, either the proliferation of models and plants or progressive import substitution by way of raising domestic content will result inevitably in cumulative increases in the domestic cost of production relative to that in a more advanced nation. It is quite noticeable that the curve shifts downward as the volume of production increases, and as technological and managerial capabilities improve.

17

1.5 Plan of the Study

The present study was originally undertaken as an integral part of a larger, international joint project on the development of ancillary firms in the motor vehicle industry in East and Southeast Asia. The project, sponsored by Council for Asian Manpower Studies (CAMS), was carried out in 1976–80 in Indonesia, Thailand, Malaysia, the Philippines, Korea, and Japan, and its summary report was published as Odaka (1983). A major finding of the study was, contrary to original expectation, that ancillary firms in the motor vehicle industry were quite undeveloped in Southeast Asia at the time of the survey, making a contrast to the case of post-World War II Japan, where a mushrooming of ancillary firms had taken place.

Inquiring into the reasons why and how the growth of the Japanese automobile industry came about leads one to explore the factors that contributed to the development of its ancillary firms.

Since in-depth exploratory analysis was desired, the case study method was chosen. The study is thus quite micro, and considerable space is allotted to report the results of a field survey. It focuses on ten representative concerns, two primary and eight ancillary firms. The particular corporations included have been selected more by chance than design, as their names were suggested by several experts and representatives of various organizations (firms, industrial associations, research centers, etc.). For this reason, observations made in the present volume do not necessarily warrant wide generalization.

Nonetheless, the authors believe the eight ancillary firms reported herein are representative, and thus reasonably illustrate the major characteristics of the development process of parts and components suppliers in postwar Japan. In fact, when additional interviews were conducted, the authors discovered the same characteristic features began to repeat themselves despite vast differences in the environment in which the individual corporations originated and grew.

It should be noted, moreover, that a substantial part of the investigation was conducted in the period of 1976–79 and that the major emphasis was placed on the historical experiences of the firms until

PLAN OF THE STUDY

around the time of the two oil embargoes. Little attempt has been made to update the information acquired through the interviews and review of other sources, as the object of study has never been to present a source book of up-to-date, comprehensive industry information.

The next chapter presents a short historical summary of the Japanese automobile industry, followed in Chapter 3 by a quantitative overview of the Japanese automobile parts and components industries. Chapters 4 and 5, the main body of the book, are devoted to the reports of the field surveys of the two primary firms and the eight ancillary firms, respectively. The final two chapters offer a summary.

Chapter 2

A SHORT HISTORY OF THE
JAPANESE AUTOMOBILE
INDUSTRY, 1900–71

2.1 Before World War I

In 1900, in commemoration of the wedding anniversary of the Crown Prince, Japanese residents in San Francisco presented him with an electric automobile. This was the first automobile in Japan. Subsequently, foreign residents in Yokohama and other metropolitan areas established several automobile sales agents which imported American and European CBU (completely built-up) cars. At the beginning of the century, automobiles were imported by foreign commercial firms that had been engaged in the import and sale of other machinery. The market was quite limited. Only a handful of wealthy people, such as foreign residents, peers, big merchants, and industrialists, could afford to own a car. Selling a car took more than mere sales promotion because it often entailed training drivers in both mechanical handling and driving techniques. Furthermore, in terms of transportation economy, automobiles could compete neither with railways for long distance transportation, nor with rickshaws and bullocks for short distant travel. For the same reason, trucks were regarded more as moving billboards than as a practical means of transportation.

Although the exhibition of imported and locally produced cars at domestic industrial expositions, held frequently in various parts of the country, had a strong demonstration effect on the potential innovators

21

and users, it was not until the importation of the Ford Model T that a single model began to sell in large volume(At the end of 1912 there were 521 automobiles in use, mostly in major metropolitan areas.)

At the same time, quite a few enthusiastic tinkerers and inventors initiated trial manufacture of autos. For the most part, these men were not business-minded entrepreneurs. Even when they made economic calculations, they were too optimistic to take market and technological constraints into serious consideration. By contrast, the case of Hashimoto Masujirō stands out clearly among all the owner-cum-engineers of the day, because he not only had outstanding engineering expertise but also practical management experience. To give a flavor of these early endeavors, we will describe three of them briefly.

Yoshida Shintarō, an owner of a bicycle shop in Tokyo, brought back two gasoline engines from his trip to the United States in 1902. Deeply impressed by the extent of modernization in that country, he decided to attempt the manufacture and sale of motor cars in Japan. As an assistant, Yoshida employed Uchiyama Komanosuke, then an engineer at the Communications and Electricity Laboratory (Teishin Shō Denki Shikenjo).

In his youth, Uchiyama had worked in Vladivostock for a machine factory that had an automobile. While helping with its repair and maintenance, he learned how it worked and how to drive it. Within a few months, Uchiyama completed a car by mounting a body on a chassis and using the engine Yoshida had brought home. This was the first automobile ever assembled domestically. Later, in 1907, Uchiyama built the first local gasoline engine. Ironically, however, this technological advancement was in sharp contrast to the deteriorating financial condition of the company. (For further details, see Jidōsha Kōgyō Kai 1965, pp. 170–210.)

Having witnessed an automobile in action at the Fifth Domestic Industrial Exhibition (*Naikoku kangyō hakuran kai*) held in Osaka, Mori Funazō and Kusunoki Kentarō of the Okayama district thought of operating a bus line. They placed an order for a bus with an iron works in Osaka which, however, proved unable to build it. This did not, however, dampen their enthusiasm. They next asked Yamaba Torao, an engineer who owned a small electrical repair shop, to experiment and complete a bus. Yamaba was initially reluctant, but being an inventor by nature, he was gradually drawn in because of curiosity. He sought technical advice from an Italian engineer who worked for an automobile importer in Kōbe. Within a year, Yamaba completed (in 1904) the first steam-powered automobile ever produced in the country. The chain-driven, ten-passenger bus was immediately given a test drive. Unfortunately, the experiment failed because of the poor quality of the tires; solid tires bolted on the wheel rims loosened while running on a rough road. The trouble was quite unanticipated and seemed insurmountable with the prevailing technology. The initial bus enterprise was a failure (Jidōsha Kōgyō Kai 1965, pp. 210–24).

In 1911, Hashimoto Masujirō, a mechanical engineer with an academic background, established Kwaishinsha Motor Car Works in Tokyo with the hope of manufacturing local automobiles. In this venture he followed the advice of Ōkura Kiichirō, a well-known industrialist as well as car enthusiast and a patron of another automobile company, who told him that the time was not quite ripe for the domestic production of automobiles because of the technological gap between the required sophistication and the low level of general industrial arts in the country. Hashimoto thus opted for a gradual domestication scheme, beginning with the assembly of imported CKD (completely knocked-down) packages and repair operations. Because Kwaishinsha figures in the history of Nissan, we will return to the company's story in chapter 4.

In addition to these, a host of other attempts was made to turn trial production into continuous business. Most failed within a few years because of insufficient funding, immature technology, and the lack of market. The ones that survived were those that confined trial manufacture to a fraction of their diversified business activities. Sales of imported cars, manufacturing and mounting of bodies on imported chassis, spare parts production, repairs, and car rental business were the dominant and substantial aspect of their business. Enterprising as it was, trial manufac-

23

ture was pursued only to the extent that profit from other lines of business could compensate for the loss from automobile production.

After the Russo-Japanese War (1904–05), the Japanese Army realized the strategic value of motor vehicles in warfare. Through intensive testing of imported trucks, the Army came to the conclusion that trucks could be utilized as an effective element in a war. Because most sophisticated machine tools were concentrated in arsenals in those days, it was not long before the Osaka Arsenal turned out two experimental military trucks. Their satisfactory performance convinced the military officers of the value of manufacturing military trucks. The remarkable contribution of these trucks in the Tsingtao operation in China in 1914 further reinforced the Army's conviction (Jidōsha Kōgyō Shinkō Kai 1973, p. 26).

An Investigation Commission on Military Vehicles (*Gunyō Jidōsha Chōsa Iinkai*) had been established in 1912 to inquire into the requisition policies of military vehicles in European countries, and to work out appropriate policies for the promotion of the local automobile industry. The activities of this Commission culminated in the promulgation of the Act to Aid the Production of Military Vehicles (*Gun-yō jidōsha hojo hō*) in 1918, which is discussed later.

The most distinct technological characteristic of the Japanese automobile industry in its infant stage was the low level of technology of the industry itself and of the supporting industries, especially metalworking and machine-building. This meant most of the Japanese assemblers and manufacturers had to answer for themselves questions western suppliers answered for their customers. In face of the fierce worldwide arms race in the first decade of the 20th century, the military boosted the production capacity of its arsenals, and terminated subcontracting practices (except in the shipbuilding industry) that had been giving the private sector experience with machine tools. Consequently, the former subcontractors lost a very effective channel of technological upgrading (Hoshino 1978, pp. 82–86).

Under such unfavorable conditions, domestication efforts moved slowly, and took various forms. Simplification of imported models was

Table 2.1. Parts and Components by "Make-or-Buy" Classification[a]: Tokyo Automobile Works (Jidōsha Seisaku Sho)[b], 1907–08

Make[c]	cylinder, piston, piston ring, connecting rod, crank, crank case, flywheel, transmission, transmission drum, transmission case, sprocket gear, differential drive gear, pinion, rear shaft, wheel, wheel hub, steering knuckle, steering wormgear, front axle, frame assembly
Buy (1): Subcontract	casting—cylinder, piston, piston ring, crank case, flywheel, timing gear cover, transmission drum, transmission band gears—timing gear, transmission gear, differential pinion gear sheet metal—fuel tank, radiator, head lamp, gas generator, window frame heat treatment and forging—frame, front axle forging, steering knuckle forging forging—crankshaft, con rod, front axle, rear spring arm painting—body painting springs
Buy (2): Purchase	driving chain, ignition coil, distributor, speedometer, battery

Notes:
[a] This table is not meant to be exhaustive, being based on the simple recollection of a retired employee.
[b] The number of employees and major facilities of the factory were as follows. The number of employees: usually 26 or 27. Major facilities: lathes (7), milling machine (1), boring machine (1), grinder (1), slotting machine (1), fixture (1), fan (1), forges (2), 3 hp motor (1) (Jidōsha Kōgyō Kai 1965, pp. 200–205).
[c] Including parts and components whose casting and forging were subcontracted, whereas machine fabricating, finishing, and assembly were done inside the factory.

Sources: Jidōsha Kōgyō Kai (1965), p. 207.

attempted, for instance by omitting some non-functional parts, modifying design, adjusting jigs and fixtures to the needs of the simplified models, etc. Assemblers continually sought existing (or potential) subcontractors to supplement their own skills. One example was the subcontracting of automobile bodies to horse-drawn coach manufacturers or (in the case of buses) to railway carriage producers. Generally, major functional parts and components such as cylinders, pistons, crankshafts, etc., were manufactured by the primary firm itself. Table 2.1 depicts a make-or-buy classification of parts and components by a representative firm.

For the subcontractors, as with the assemblers, involvement with automobiles was usually only a fraction of their business. The fact that tires were the first item mass produced in Japan for motor vehicles suggests the importance of market size.

2.2 Transition to Factory Production: 1917–35

The boom during World War I gave an impetus to the hitherto stagnant automobile market. As a result, certain forward linkages emerged, such as the increase in the number of taxicab companies, gas stations, automobile insurance companies, parking lots, and garages for rent.

After a series of trials by individuals and small firms, most of which ended in failure, several larger firms joined the business: mostly shipbuilders and machine-building companies that had been engaged in arms manufacture during World War I. Entry was led by the Japanese armed forces, which wanted a stable domestic supply of trucks, and had finally secured the backing of the central government through the Act to Aid the Production of Military Vehicles of 1918.

In addition to a guaranteed market, these firms received encouragement and assistance from military arsenals, while supplying their own capital and a variety of manufacturing equipment. The close ties between the arsenals and private automobile manufacturers were of the utmost importance in facilitating technological diffusion. For one thing, the arsenals then occupied a dominant position in the use of the most sophisticated imported machine tools.

While the 1918 Act was under preparation, military arsenals extended various technolgical assistance to potential military manufacturers, because the arsenals did not have the capacity to produce trucks by themselves. For example, when the Osaka Arsenal recommended that Tokyo Gas and Electric try manufacturing trucks, it provided the company with basic materials, forging dies, and cast items as well as detailed blueprints and technical advices. Furthermore, the Arsenal bore the expenses of the trial run. Later, when a production line for the Datsun was introduced by Kwaishinsha, the Osaka Arsenal decided to establish a full-fledged local automobile plant. It was in such a tech-nological environment that in 1918 Kwaishinsha opened Japan's first factory equipped with machine tools specifically designed for auto-mobile production (Jidōsha Kōgyō Kai 1967, pp. 314–15).

The Kantō Earthquake in 1923 triggered a surge in demand. Tokyo's railway and streetcar networks were virtually destroyed, which created a demand for buses, and trucks were needed to help in the city's rebuilding. To promote reconstruction by strengthening transportation capacity, the government removed import tariffs on automobiles. This led to the number of imported CBU (completely built-up) units more than doubling, to over 4,000, between 1923 and 1924. With promptly-delivered, high quality imported vehicles for no more (if not less) money than a domestically made car, it is no wonder domestic makers received little benefit from the demand. In 1924, a four-wheel, four-seater called the Rilah sedan was sold in Osaka for 2,000 yen and 1,755 yen for a wagon. By comparison, the standard imported Ford four-passenger model was 1,700 yen.

Ford and GM decided to built assembly plants for CKD (completely knocked-down) units to capitalize on the popularity of their cars. The Ford plant opened in 1925 in Yokohama, and a Chevrolet plant in 1927 in Osaka. Subsequently, in 1930, a Japanese-controlled firm, Kyōritsu Jidōsha, began assembling CKDs for Plymouth and Dodge.

The rapid increase in the number of motor cars in use and the domestic purchase of parts and components by Ford and GM enlarged the spare parts market as well as the original equipment market, opening an opportunity for development of ancillary firms. By contrast, local motor vehicle assemblers, knowing they were unable to compete with Ford and GM, either had to withdraw from automobile production or build noncompetitive products, that is, military trucks or small passenger vehicles. Table 2.2 shows the number of automobiles in use in the 1910s and '20s.

Table 2.2. Number of Automobiles in Use at Year End (1912–31)

Year	Units
1912	512
1913	892
1914	1,066
1915	1,244
1916	1,648
1917	2,672
1918	4,533
1919	7,051
1920	9,998
1921	12,117
1922	14,886
1923	16,476
1924	27,233
1925	31,881
1926	40,070
1927	51,762
1928	66,379
1929	80,730
1930	88,708
1931	97,256

Notes: Trucks included.
Sources: Jidōsha Kōgyō Kai (1967), p. 25.

An interesting aspect of motorization in the late 1920s and '30s was the production of three-wheel trucks to meet demand from medium- and small-sized firms. Compared with four wheelers, three wheelers were much cheaper and technologically less sophisticated, being similar to a motorcycle with a carrier. It was not difficult to manufacture their functional parts and components. Consequently, the local three-wheeler industry experienced a boom during the mid-1930s (Amagai 1982, pp. 61–65). Ishikawa (1979) has emphasized the importance of this experience in terms of the choice of appropriate technology and product, as is discussed in Chapter 3.

Technological Advances

Two major factors contributed to the technological upgrading of the infant industry, and both are related to government policies. One was the assistance extended by the arsenals, already discussed, and the other involved the establishment of CKD assembly plants by Ford and GM.

Not long after they opened their plants, Ford and GM were asked by the Japanese government to use more locally-made parts and components. This was partly due to the effect imports of CBU and CKD autos were having on the trade deficit. The "Buy Japanese" campaign led to the growth of some 30 subcontractors, who had achieved output standards acceptable to the two American companies.

These firms, in turn, fostered a second tier of subcontractors in such specialized fields as casting, forging, sheet metal processing, and plating. The development of this subcontracting network laid the foundation for the development of a full-scale domestic industry in the 1930s (Amagai 1982, pp. 65–66).[1]

Government Policies

The military had become interested in vehicles after using them in the

[1] Information on parts and components suppliers in the 1920 s is based on Fukushima (1929, pp. 347–60). According to the same source (p. 350), there were 18 automobile maintenance shops in Tokyo in 1917, and 65 in 1928. By 1930, however, the number of factories in Japan engaged in the production of parts and accessories was about 143, which increased to 351 by 1935 (Jidōsha Mondai Kenkyūjo 1940, p. 31).

A SHORT HISTORY OF THE JAPANESE AUTOMOBILE INDUSTRY

Russo-Japanese War, and not long afterward the Osaka Arsenal had succeeded in building two trucks. Still, it was 1912 before the next major step was taken: formation of a commission to study the matter of military vehicles, including how they were being used and acquired by European armies. Ultimately, in 1918, an act to promote production of

Table 2.3. Subsidies Available under the Act to Aid the Production of Military Vehicles as of 1918

(In yen per vehicle)

Type and size of vehicle (in metric tons)	Production subsidies			Purchase subsidy	Maintenance subsidy
	Four wheelers	Six wheelers	Additional subsidy		
Trucks					
(A) 0.75–1 t.	400	1,400	500	1,000	400
(B) 1–1.5	750	1,750	500	1,000	500
(C) 1.5 and over	1,250	2,200	500	1,000	600
Applied vehicles					
(A) 0.75–1 t.	250	1,250	375	750	300
(B) 1–1.5	500	1,500	375	750	400
(C) 1.5 and over	800	1,800	375	750	500

Notes: 1. Production subsidy and additional subsidy were subsidies for producers. The additional subsidy was paid when producers used vehicles.
2. Purchase subsidy and maintenance subsidy were subsidies for purchasers-cum-users.
3. Production subsidy and purchase subsidy were paid in a lump sum at the time the vehicle was completed or purchased.
4. The additional subsidy and maintenance subsidy were disbursed annually for up to five years.
5. Six wheelers were added to the list from March 1930.
6. Applied vehicles refer to those which could be remodeled for military use.
7. Presumably total susidies would roughly equal price differentials between foreign- and domestically-made cars. Amagai (1982, p. 34) cites the case of Buick and Hudson selling for 6,000–7,000 yen as against a locally assembled trial model of the Wolseley A9 costing over 10,000 yen.
Sources: Jidōsha Kōgyō Kai (1967), p. 174.

Table 2.4. Production of Military Vehicles, 1918–24

(In units)

Year	Planned	Actual
1918	15	4
1919	10	3
1920	100	22
1921	73	28
1922	—	3
1923	—	16
1924	—	84

Notes: Vehicles include both trucks and cars, though virtually all of the vehicles were trucks.
Sources: Nissan Jidōsha (1965), p. 8.

military vehicles by Japanese companies passed the Diet.

Among other things, the 1918 Act involved subsidies. These were necessary because imported trucks were cheaper than locally produced ones, and transportation by horse carriage was less expensive than by truck. Table 2.3 shows the subsidy levels.

Only three companies successfully met the Act's standards to become registered truck makers: Ishikawajima Shipbuilding, Tokyo Gas & Electric, and Kwaishinsha (though not until 1924). Their production under the Act is shown in Table 2.4.

It is clear that the Act failed to promote production as much as intended. There are several reasons for this failure:

1. the product design and production techniques of the local automobile industry were still quite underdeveloped;
2. the amount of subsidy per truck was insufficient to make the product competitive with imported models in terms of sales price plus operating cost;
3. the total amount of the subsidy was limited by the government budget (this did not apply to the first few years when actual units of production were far less than prescribed, but it certainly did in

31

the mid-1920s when the production of military trucks increased);
4. the administrative procedure to receive the subsidy was very cumbersome; and
5. the military-purpose trucks were unsuitable for private use, because of their size and the ban on remodeling.

But the ultimate failure came on the battlefields of the Manchurian Incident in 1931. The government requisitioned civilian Ford and Chevrolet trucks assembled in Japan, and they proved superior to the trucks built specifically for the military, to its specifications, by domestic producers.

There were, however, some positive aspects to the 1918 Act as far as several specific firms were concerned. The wave of imports after the Kantō Earthquake washed away many companies, but those with subsidies from their truck building operations survived, to be folded during the 1930s into companies that exist today (Iwakoshi 1968, pp. 248–49).

The government had established an advisory board to the Ministry of Trade and Industry (*Shōkō Shō*) in 1926, called the Committee for the Promotion of Local Industry (*Kokusan Shinkō Iinkai*), and it had, in turn, formed a Special Commission on the Feasibility Study of the Automobile Industry (*Jidōsha Kōgyō Kakuritsu Chōsa Iinkai*), which released its findings in 1931.

The report emphasized four points. (1) The number of motor vehicles˙ had increased from about 15,000 in 1923 to about 80,000 in 1929, and annual demand was estimated to be in excess of 30,000 units and rising. (2) Annual local production was under 500 units, with imports providing the rest, at a cost of over 40 million yen a year in foreign exchange. (3) Establishment of a domestic auto industry offered various benefits. These included improvement in the balance of trade, linkage effects that would promote other industries, and the strengthening of defense. (4) Because the primary reason for the stagnation of the domestic auto industry was relatively high production costs, which related to low production volumes, adequate promotion policies would revive the infant industry.

Based on these points, the Committee made a number of specific recommendations and practical observations.

1. Place priority on the production of a single model of midsized (1.5–2.0 ton) trucks and buses. This would avoid the costs imposed by model changes for passenger cars.
2. Encourage production with subsidies, while reducing the user tax and raising the import tariff.
3. Organize an efficient production system under centralized control.
4. Encourage subcontracting as a way of utilizing existing production capacity, including excess capacity in the shipbuilding, ironworking, casting and forging shops that could produce parts and components for vehicles.
5. Although full domestication was desirable, it was going to be necessary to rely on specific imported materials and parts, as well as foreign designs and methods of production.

The committee felt part of the problem was too many firms making too few of too many different models. Their recommendations dealt very directly with this, and thus was conceived the production of the "domestically-manufactured standard model (*kokusan hyōjun jidōsha*)."

Accordingly, a cartel (*Kokusan Jidōsha Kumiai*) was formed in 1932 among the top three manufactureres at the time—the registered truck makers: Ishikawajima Shipbuilding, Tokyo Gas & Electric, and DAT (who had succeeded to Kwaishinsha's license). (The three companies were merged in 1937 to form Tokyo Motor (*Tokyo Jidōsha Kōgyō*)). The Ministry of Railroads (*Tetsudō Shō*), which used many imported buses for the bus lines it operated, supported the program by placing a purchase order with the cartel, as well as extending technical assistance. Prototypes were completed in 1932.

At this point, the government did not intend to promote domestication of passenger vehicle production. However, the government did raise the tariff on imported cars and in effect disapprove (in 1934) Nissan's plan to conclude a licensing agreement to produce Chevrolets, and Ford was prevented (in 1936) from expanding its Yokohama assembly plant. To encourage buying small vehicles, in 1933 the government allowed driving vehicles with engines smaller than 750 cc without a license. Table 2.5 summarizes the supply of vehicles during this period.

Table 2.5. Supply of Four Wheelers[a] (1916–35)

Year	Local production[b]		CBU import	CKD assembly
1916	294		218	—
1917	250		860	—
1918	195		1,712	—
1919	60		1,579	—
1920	45		1,745	—
1921	4		1,074	—
1922	—		752	—
1923	—		1,938	—
1924[c]	—		4,063	—
1925[d]	—		1,765	3,437
1926	245		2,381	8,677
1927[e]	302		3,895	12,668
1928	347		7,883	24,341
1929	437		5,018	29,338
1930	458		2,591	19,678
1931	436	(2)	1,887	20,199
1932[f]	880	(184)	997	14,087
1933	1,681	(626)	491	15,082
1934	2,787	(1,710)	896	33,458
1935[g]	5,089	(3,908)	931	30,787

Notes: [a] Trucks and cars included.
　　　　[b] Small cars in parentheses.
　　　　[c] Kantō earthquake spurs demand.
　　　　[d] Ford plant opens in Yokohama.
　　　　[e] Chevrolet plant opens in Osaka.
　　　　[f] Import tariff raised.
　　　　[g] First Datsun sedan produced.

Sources: Production: Ozaki (1966), pp. 305–06 (1916–21 figures) and Jidōsha Kōgyō Kai (Japan Automobile Manufactures Association), *Jidōsha tōkei nempyō* [Automobile Statistical Yearbook], 1953, p. 3; CBU import and CKD assembly: Nissan Jidōsha (1965), p. 16.

2.3   The Establishment of Domestic Manufacturing: 1936-45

In 1936, the government initiated a full-scale local manufacturing program for the automobile industry. The Automobile Industry Act of November 1936 (*Jidōsha seizō jigyō hō*) introduced various restrictive conditions to be met by the industry (such as majority ownership and control by Japanese nationals, obedience to the government's operational orders, etc.), while extending various economic incentives (such as five-year income tax holidays, tariff exemption for the importation of specified machinery and materials, etc.) to the officially-recognized local manufacturers. Registered firms were required to buy as much as possible from domestic sources, something they already were committed to. Non-registered manufacturers were allowed to continue their operations so long as they had no expansion plans. After 1936, output at Ford and General Motors was thus limited to 12,360 and 9,470 units, respectively.

As the decade progressed, import tariffs were raised again, the yen was devalued against the dollar, making imports more expensive, and, in January 1937, a foreign exchange licensing system was implemented. A concerted effort was made to force Ford and GM out of Japan, and it succeeded. By 1939 the domestic production of four-wheelers came to be in the hands of three local manufacturers: Nissan, Jidōshà Kōgyō (which became part of Isuzu), and Toyota. It is perhaps ironic that even as the Japanese were pushing American cars out of Japan, Nissan was busy importing an entire factory from a failing U.S. company.

During the early period of regulated production, automobile manufacturers were permitted to import production facilities, functional parts, and special steel materials in order to get the mass-production system going as soon as possible. In the meantime, however, they strove to establish domestic sources. Accordingly, they manufactured some parts and components within their own plants, and also sought to increase the subcontracting of parts and components by forming a network of subsidiary or cooperative ancillary firms.

By the late 1930s, the parts and components market had expanded to such an extent as to allow the local manufacture of all the parts and components used on small trucks. Tokyo Motor assembled over 100 small trucks between 1934 and 1938 with only about 30 employees, procuring almost all the parts and components from subcontractors. Companies that had begun making the relatively simple parts moved on to producing even the ones involving sophisticated skills and complex machine tools. Manufacturers of spare parts mushroomed in the Osaka area, where there were numerous cars in use but few leading motor car manufacturers or assemblers. However, quality and efficiency problems remained.

Nonetheless, in the early 1940s, the effect of the mass production of trucks was already felt in the supporting industries such as special steel production, stamp forging, casting, and pressing. The introduction of special purpose machine tools and improved jigs and tools increased the efficiency of machine processing (Jidōsha Kōgyō Shinkō Kai 1979, pp. 79–95).

Under the umbrella of the 1936 Automobile Act, officially registered automobile producers, especially Toyota and Nissan, made various efforts to establish a mass-production system. Since there was a significant technological gap between Japan and the United States, it is understandable that when Nissan decided to initiate mass production of small passenger vehicles, it purchased a whole set of second-hand production equipment and model engine blocks from Graham-Paige Motor Company. To Nissan, this purchase, in 1936, seemed the best way to avoid technical problems in the commercial manufacture of passenger cars. Within two years the company attained a monthly production level of 1,000 units. On the other hand, Toyota in 1938 built a brand new plant in Koromo (now Toyota City) with a monthly production goal of 500 passenger cars and 1,500 trucks. By the end of the war, the plant had built over 94,000 trucks.

Along with efforts to increase production, the institutional environment for technological upgrading was also improved. In 1933, the Society of Automotive Engineers (Jidōsha Gijutsu Kyōkai) was organized as a consultative body of the government for motor vehicle administration. The Ministry of Trade and Industry established a

Committee on Automotive Engineering (*Jidōsha Gijutsu Iinkai*) in 1939, while the Government's Murayama Automobile Experiment Station, in cooperation with private motor vehicle manufacturers, initiated intensive research on the improvement of production techniques. This station put special emphasis on the development of efficient and durable trucks and diesel engines, as well as on the standardization and quality improvement of parts and components, and on cost reduction.

Managerial Factors

During this stage the government's policy to protect and foster the industry emerged mostly from the demands of the military. This was a demand first for trucks. Nevertheless, Nissan and Toyota chose to make passenger cars as well. As the linkage effects of this became clearer, the government moved to promote their endeavors.

Nissan had undergone a series of plant constructions before the demand for military vehicles increased after the Manchurian Incident. The production capacity of the plants, however, was not enough to fill the needs of the expanded market. Nissan, accordingly, rented the whole of Ford's assembly plant and subcontracted the assembly of imported parts and components for which Nissan had acquired import licenses. Thus, without investing much in new facilities or plants, between April 1939 and March 1940, Nissan acquired annual production capacity of 5,000 units. A similar policy of subcontracting an assembly system was again adopted in Manchuria, when Nissan rented a plant from Do-Hwa Motor in order to assemble CKD packages exported from Nissan in Japan (Amagai 1982, pp. 50–51).

In the case of Toyota, its fundamental production management policy was embodied in the various devices adopted in its new Koromo plant. For example, most of its special-purpose machine tools were of the adjustable variety; that is, they were not only more efficient than general-purpose machine tools but were more easily adaptable to changes in design than special-purpose machines. In addition, the working process was standardized for each part or component, and, where necessary, a conveyor flow production system was introduced. By avoiding the

37

premature introduction of all-out flow production with special-purpose machine tools, which is appropriate only for a monthly production of tens of thousands of units, Toyota realized a less expensive, intermediate production technology.

The government-formed cartel could not cope with the competition posed by Toyota and Nissan, because the 1936 Act reinforced their position. The government thus forced a merger of the cartel companies in 1937, creating Tokyo Motor. The new company concentrated on "standard models" and diesel engines, which were more appropriate for large-vehicles and offered more fuel economy. Later, with the participation of a few other diesel engine manufacturers, Tokyo Motor turned into Diesel Motor (renamed Isuzu in 1950) and was given the status of officially authorized producer in 1940.

Government Policies

The Automobile Industry Act of 1936 was a major driving force of the automobile industry's development in the late 1930s. It is evident that the Act violated the principle of free trade, and the Legislation Bureau of the Ministry of Foreign Affairs expressed apprehension when the Act was under preparation. The first section spells out the government's rationale: "This law, in anticipating *the needs of national defense* and the development of manufacturing, aims to design the establishment of automobile manufacturing in the Empire" (italics added). In short, the Act aimed to promote the local automobile industry and thereby to aid the growing militarization of the country.

The Ministry of Trade and Industry followed up on the Act in 1938 by issuing Regulations on the Registration of Qualified Auto Parts and Materials (*Yūryō jidōsha buhin oyobi jidōsha zairyō nintei kisoku*). The auto parts industry was thus formally recognized as an important sector of the machinery industry. The regulation was intended to promote interchangeability of parts and components by their standardization and improved quality.

Supported by the Act and the Regulation, annual volume of truck production reached 42,000 units in 1941. However, as the government tightened control over manufacturing production during the war, the industry was directed to utilize its production facilities for the manufacture of airplanes and their parts and components.

2.4 Rehabilitation and Improvement: 1946–60

The war left the industry with ragged, half-wrecked production facilities and almost no market. Except for meeting the limited demand for trucks by the Occupation Army, resumption of operation was out of question, despite discussions among government officials and even in the National Diet regarding Japan's commitment to a domestic motor car industry. When production resumed, automobile producers suffered from serious deficiencies of just about everything: capital, machines, experienced labor, and parts and materials.

The government finally designated the industry as one of the high priority industries in its economy reconstruction program. Some companies soon started car assembly, while others ventured into the manufacture of auto parts. In general, however, the automobile industry suffered seriously from excess capacity.

It was only with the special procurement demand brought on by the Korean War, and the establishment in August 1950 of the Police

Table 2.6. Domestic Supply of Four-wheeled Passanger Vehicles, 1951–53

(In number of units)

| Year | Local | Imported | | Total |
		New	Second-hand[a]	
1951	3,611	—	1,650	5,261
1952	4,837	4,700	5,476	15,013
1953	8,789	5,170	13,467	27,426

Notes: [a] Mostly sales by the Occupation Army and foreign residents.
Sources: Tsūshō Sangyō Shō, Jūkōgyō Kyoku (1960), II, p. 514.

Reserve Force (*Keisatsu yobi tai*) that the Japanese automobile industry experienced a recovery. The Japanese market was, however, dominated by American and European brands, with the exception of a small segment for low-priced, small commercial vehicles. The weak position of Japanese manufacturers was manifest in all aspects: design, production technology, and performance. Foreigners were able to sell the cars they imported, and this was a major source of supply during the Korean War years. Table 2.6 summarizes this.

Faced with such difficulties, local manufacturers .took a series of drastic actions to modernize their production systems and to upgrade their technological levels. A number of new machines were imported and foreign production technologies were actively sought. In the area of passenger cars, in particular, most of the car assemblers decided to go into licensing agreements with European counterparts for the assembly of European models from imported CKD packs. With these measures, production efficiency increased remarkably during the 1950s. For example, labor input per unit of small truck decreased from 293.3 hours in 1954 to 128.6 hours in 1958 (Hoshino 1978, p. 241). This helped cause a relative decline in automobile prices, a precondition for later acceleration in the growth of domestic demand. By 1960, the licensees of the European models were ready to introduce their own models.

Throughout this period, the government provided protection and encouragement by way of tariffs and import quotas, discounted commodity taxes, restrictions on foreign capital participation, loans and subsidies, accelerated depreciation, and special measures for the importation of technology and of specialized machinery.

Market Factors

Fortunately for the Japanese automobile industry, the General Headquarters of the Occupation Army recognized the importance of the transportation industry for the reconstruction of the war-ravaged country, and permitted the industry to resume truck production within weeks of the surrender. More than a thousand units were completed within a year, using the unfinished chassis and bodies at the undamaged plants (Jidōsha Kōgyō Shinkō Kai 1979, pp. 140–47). Machine tools disposed of by the arsenals aided production at these plants during the late 1940s. The recovery slowed in 1949, however, because of the policies adopted to combat severe inflation and deficits in the balance of trade.

The early 1950s witnessed an interesting development in the automobile market and the concomitant shift of demand by type of vehicle. At the outbreak of the Korean War, military procurement demand for medium trucks expanded, triggering the revival of the previously registered truck manufacturers. In 1954 production (exclusive of three wheelers) finally surpassed the previous high of 46 thousand units reached in 1941. Vehicle production is summarized in Table 2.7 (see also Appendix Table A-12).

As reconstruction of the economy proceeded, the production of three-

Table 2.7.   Production of Automobiles by Type, 1950–85

(In thousand units, except the last column)

Year	Passenger cars (A)	Trucks (B)	Buses (C)	Subtotal[a] (A)+(B) +(C)	Three wheelers	Exports[b] (D)	Ratio (D)/{(A) +(B)+(C)}
1950	2	27	4	32	35	—	—
1955	20	44	5	69	88	1	1.8%
1960	165	308	8	482	278	39	8.1
1965	696	1,160	19	1,876	43	194	10.3
1970	3,179	2,064	47	5,289	14	1,087	20.6
1975	4,568	2,338	36	6,942	—	2,677	38.6
1980	7,038	3,913	92	11,043	—	5,967	54.0
1985	7,647	4,545	80	12,271	—	6,730	54.8

Notes: [a]   Columns (A)~(C) do not necessarily add to the subtotal because of rounding.
   [b]   Four wheelers only.
Sources: Nihon Jidōsha Kōgyō Kai (Japan Automobile Manufacturers Association), *Jidōsha tōkei nempō (nempyō)* [Automobile Statistical Yearbook], various issues.

wheeler trucks was boosted by the increasing transportation demand from medium- and small-scale establishments. This, in turn, was followed by expanding production of small four-wheeler trucks, and passenger cars. Postwar motorization in Japan began with the popularization of trucks and three-wheelers catering to the needs of the military and small enterprises. Small passenger cars were produced simply by mounting bodies on truck chassis (Ōshima 1973, pp. 24–26). In the meantime, the market for regular-sized passenger cars was made up of business enterprises and a limited number of the relatively well-to-do, and was dominated by imported European models.

The government policy to promote domestication of passenger vehicle production, coupled with tightening import restrictions on CBUs, began to take effect around 1953. The move was not welcome by consumers, as they were now supplied with more expensive, locally-produced European models instead of imported CBUs. Price competition in the passenger car market came to the fore when the slowdown in 1954 brought financial difficulties to companies that operated taxis and automobiles for hire. These two industries had accounted for over 80 percent of passenger vehicle demand. From the middle of the 1950s, Toyota took the initiative in a series of price reductions to attain price leadership, thereby getting ahead of the three licensees of European makes: Nissan, Hino and Isuzu. Fierce price competition ensued in the early 1960s.

Technological Factors

Fuji Motor was established in 1948 to contract with the United States Armed Forces in the repair and recondition of used military trucks and jeeps. The company reconditioned over 200,000 units before it closed in 1958 (Amagai 1982, pp. 91–93). This experience had two important implications. First, it suggests the United States Army recognized the value of the repair technology of a Japanese firm. Second, this experience must have had a learning-by-doing effect which later diffused among Japanese car makers.

The Korean War generated a massive demand for trucks, enabling the producers to accumulate tremendous profits, which they reinvested in (mostly imported) new machines and plants. The investment fund was initially expended on multipurpose machines to expand the production capacity of trucks. Both ordinary and small trucks could now be turned out from the same production line. Although this was inefficient compared with a fully specialized production line, the government protection tolerated such inefficiency under the guise of "achieving automobile self-sufficiency" in a quasi-closed economy. Moreover, in an effort to attain the quality standard set by the United States military, the assemblers sold their used equipment at nominal prices to their parts and components suppliers. Thus rationalization of the production system for trucks was realized because of the enormous military procurement demand generated by the Korean War.

Licensing

As gradual liberalization of imports proceeded, 1952 and 1953 witnessed a rapid increase of imported motor cars, which naturally was a threat to the local automobile manufacturers. MITI (the Ministry of International Trade and Industry), having estimated that Japanese producers were twenty to thirty years behind their U.S. and European counterparts, concluded that the best alternative for remedying the situation in the shortest possible time was to arrange technical tie-ups between domestic and foreign manufacturers.

Licensing agreements with European firms ushered in an era of technological upgrading of passenger vehicles. Nissan concluded a technical tie-up with Austin Motor in 1952, Hino with Renault, and Isuzu with Rootes Motors (Hillman) in 1953. In this regard, Toyota is often cited as not entering licensed production because of nationalistic enthusiasm. The fact is, however, that Toyota failed to reach an agreement with Ford and was obliged to promote domestication on its own. The Japanese assemblers concentrated their efforts on establishing mass production lines for small passenger vehicles by such measures as automation of multi-purpose machines, the introduction of special-purpose machine tools and transfer machines, the multiplication of press and boring machines, and so forth. Along with the upgrading of production facilities, plant layout was redesigned and operations were standardized, leading to the establishment of flow production by means of a conveyor system (Hoshino and Sakisaka 1960, pp. 92–94).

In retrospect, the nature of cooperation from the licensor has apparently affected the later growth of the licensee. For instance, the tie-up of Nissan with Austin, which was the most cooperative among the European counterparts, was an important element in the subsequent development of Nissan. In the meantime, the primary firms transmitted their technological know-how to their subsidiary manufacturers, resulting in the strengthening of the primary-ancillary relationship.

As a result of the all-out effort to absorb the borrowed technology, the production of parts and components was gradually domesticised and, within five years (by 1958), all three companies had completed full domestication of passenger cars and were ready to develop their own models.

After 1955, in anticipation of the advent of an era of mass-ownership of passenger vehicles, the primary firms, especially Toyota and Nissan, took a step forward by increasing their production capacities of small passenger cars. Furthermore, as part of their efforts to strengthen international price competitiveness, they built new plants for passenger car production in which the so-called "Detroit Automation System" was introduced (Iwakoshi 1968, p. 270). Well-timed managerial decisions were essential in coping with changing market demand and in thus pushing both Toyota and Nissan to dominant positions in the industry. The key decisions were

1. to shift the major production line from ordinary trucks used by relatively large enterprises to small trucks demanded by medium and small establishments, and
2. to switch from trucks to passenger vehicles, which offered a huge potential market (Okumura, Hoshikawa, and Matsui 1965, pp. 240–41).

Government Policies

In the initial phase of the postwar development of the automobile industry, a comparative-advantage versus infant-industry controversy took place. Those who supported the principle of comparative advantage advocated the gains from an international division of labor. On the other hand, the Ministry of International Trade and Industry (MITI, or Tsushō Sangyō Shō) took up the infant industry argument, maintaining that promotion of the industry would serve as a springboard for industrial development in general. In the end, the automobile was chosen as a strategic target for the government's industrial policy, together with such industries as synthetic fibers, petrochemicals, and electronics.

Even prior to the decision, the Regulation on the Registration of Qualified Auto Parts (*Yūryō jidōsha buhin nintei kisoku*) was promulgated (in 1947) to discourage the sales of inferior products and to give incentives to auto parts producers for installing improved manufacturing facilities and technologies. Between 1948 and 1953, 351 plants and 673 items were qualified under the Regulation, establishing the relative superiority of former government licensees and their subsidiary parts makers.

Immediately after the Korean War, local manufacturers were fully occupied in the production of military trucks and small trucks. Importation of passenger vehicles increased, so the market share of locally produced passenger vehicles declined from 69 percent in 1951 to 32 percent in 1952.

The government then issued guidelines for licensing agreements involving passenger vehicle production, intending to encourage technical tie-ups, as described earlier. When passenger car production by the foreign licensee companies got under way, the government pushed for domestication of parts and components through gradual reduction of foreign exchange allocations. The program was based on a detailed deletion schedule. Consequently, all three licensees (Nissan, Isuzu, and Hino) achieved complete domestication of the particular models they were making and by 1958 were ready to develop their own license-free

45

models.

In the meantime, MITI announced, in May 1955, the "Citizens' Car Project" aimed at accelerating motorization by providing consumers with small, inexpensive passenger cars. The basic philosophy of the project was that the government would subsidize the manufacture of automobiles satisfying the following specifications:

1. four-wheel passenger car with a speed of 100 km/hr or over,
2. fuel efficiency of 30 km per liter of gasoline when driving at 60 km/hr,
3. an engine capacity of 350–500 cc, and
4. a unit production cost of ¥150,000 and unit market price of ¥250,000 at a production rate of 2,000 units per month

(*Nihon Keizal Shimbun* (Japan Economic Journal), 18 May 1955). Although the Ministry's rigid specifications (particularly for fuel efficiency) precluded the completion of even a single unit, the plan triggered popularization of light passenger vehicles with engine capabilities below 360 cc (Okumura 1960, pp. 340–45).

By this time, the automobile industry together with other machine-building industries was recognized as a promising candidate for an export-oriented industry. In 1956, the Provisional Act for the Promotion of the Machinery Industry (*Kikai kōgyō shinkō rinji sochi hō* or *Kishin hō* for short) was promulgated with the aim of further promoting the development of the machinery industry. An official Auto Parts Committee (*Jidōsha-yō Buhin Bukai*) was set up, consisting of 30 representatives from the government and the academic community, as well as car makers and auto parts producers, and was made responsible for the implementation of the Act as applied to the auto parts industry. The Committee first selected specific auto parts to be the concerted targets of assistance, and endorsed applications from the makers of prescribed products, who would then be eligible to receive low-interest financing for renovating their production facilities. Loans were made by the Japan Development Bank (Nippon Kaihatsu Ginkō) and the Small Business Finance Corporation (Chushō Kigyō Kinyū Kōko). In addition, the Act authorized MITI to encourage mergers in some cases in order to hasten "rationalization" of production.

The Act undoubtedly contributed to the reduction of the cost of auto parts and components through rationalization, export promotion, technological upgrading, and materials procurement. It is conceivable, moreover, that the Act widened the gap between the relatively large subcontracting parts makers and the remaining smaller firms. However, such a selective promotion policy was probably inevitable in the period of advancing technological innovation (Okumura 1960, p. 362).

2.5   Achieving International Competitiveness: 1961–71

With the rapid growth of the domestic market, the automobile manufacturers decided to make heavy investments in order to expand their production capacities. A major portion of the investment was expended on the establishment of mass-production facilities designed specifically for small passenger cars. While production capacities were increased, extensive efforts were made to improve product quality and lower price.

Gradually, the export of Japanese cars gained momentum. By the late 1960s, Japanese automobile manufacturers, who had started with simple imitation of foreign models, were generally state-of-the-art (in their price range) even in the areas of emission control and safety devices, which were considered new dimensions in automotive technology.

Market Factors

The rather coercive domestication program directed by the government in the late 1950s was complemented by unprecedented rapid economic growth and the spread of private car ownership in the following decade. Market development became evident when the Income Doubling Plan (*Shotoku baizō keikaku*) was launched in 1960, and within the next ten years real income per capita more than doubled. The increase in demand enabled producers to take advantage of the economies of mass production. In a competitive setting, cost reduction led to falling prices, which, in turn, brought another surge of demand.

The relative price of automobiles vis-à-vis the consumer price index declined by as much as 8 percent per annum in the period 1960 to 1970. Admittedly, the price factor plays a far less important role than the income variable in determining the level of automobile demand. Suppose, for the sake of illustration, that automobile prices, deflated by the consumer price index, decrease by 7.9 percent per annum, while per-capita real personal disposable income increases by 9.6 percent per annum, as they actually did in the 1960/1970 period. Using price and income elasticities for automobile demand of −0.53 and 1.60, respectively, the above changes in price will generate 4.2 percent annual increase in the demand, only slightly over a quarter of the newer demand created by the change in income levels.[2]

If the rapidly declining trend in automobile prices had a relatively minor impact on domestic demand for new automobiles, it must have had a far-reaching consequence in enhancing international competitiveness. In this regard, the fixed exchange rate served as an additional, big plus factor. The ratio of the price of Japanese passenger vehicles of all kinds (four wheelers only) to that of American makes, both expressed in current yen, showed an unmistakable sign of a downward movement in 1960, followed by a very fast, continuous decline through 1969. Taking the 1960 level as the base (100), the ratio was 102 in 1951, peaked at 120 in 1957, and then went down on a long down slide, hitting a trough of 60 in 1969. After 1969, the relative price ratio went up again, reaching 69 in 1975.[3]

A result of the mutually reinforcing cumulative process was the arrival

[2] Per capita domestic automobile sales increased by 19.6 percent per annum during the 1960 s. Of this, price decline and income growth accounted for 21 and 79 percent, respectively, using the elasticity figures given in the text (cf. Ueno 1970, pp. 91–92). Note, however, that the estimated demand function for new automobiles was derived from the estimated demand for automobile holdings. Actually, therefore, these elesticity values relate only indirectly to the demand for new cars. This is ignored in the text because we are interested only in the relative magnitudes of the elesticity figures, and the approach used provides good estimates for this purpose.

[3] Both the Japanese and U.S. data are net of taxes, duties, etc. For the moment, we avoid all complications arising from quotas, import duties, insurance fees, transport costs, other government regulations and what-not.

of rapid motorization. On the other hand, the heated price competition resulted in the formation of an oligopolistic market structure dominated by the two giant primary firms, Toyota and Nissan.

The few years just after 1960 saw the opening of an entirely new era for the Japanese motor vehicle industry, as the export demand for automobiles began to gain momentum, first to Asian countries and then to North America and other regions. The proportion of exported cars in total production increased from a meager 0.6 percent in 1955 to 10 percent in 1965 and then 39 percent in 1975 (see Table 2.7, last column).

The export drive became particularly pronounced in the 1970s when the rate of growth of the domestic market began to slow down. As of 1971, the sales price of the Nissan Bluebird (1,600 cc) and Nissan Sunny (1,200 cc) in the U.S. were $2,120 and $1,736 respectively, whereas the Chevrolet Vega (2,300 cc) was $2,091 and the Ford Pinto, $1,919. Because the unit prices of Japanese models included accessories that were usually not standard equipment on American models, the price differences are somewhat overstated (Ōshima 1980, pp. 73–74).

The quadrupling of oil prices in 1973 drew the world's attention to the fuel-efficient, small cars Japanese makers had been building for their domestic market. With a head start, they quickly demonstrated superior technological position and comparative advantage.

Technological Factors

The early 1960s witnessed the multiplication of plants specially designed for the production of passenger cars and equipped with special-purpose machine tools and transfer machines. The sophisticated production technology, coupled with scale economies, strengthened the price competitiveness of Japanese motor cars in the international market. The export of four-wheelers increased by about 30 times, from 39,000 units in 1960 to over a million in 1970.

In the 1970s, when the public became increasingly intolerant of automobile accidents and environmental pollution, representatives from the government, primary firms, and ancillary firms organized a joint research group to study safety standards and emission control. The government, for its part, set a rather strict standard on emission levels, which forced the manufacturers to design new devices to qualify. Unwittingly, the devices later helped them acquire non-price competitive strength in the international market.

The phenomenal growth of the automobile industry was sustained by high levels of investment by parts and components manufacturers as well as the assemblers. For example, investment in equipment by primary firms increased from 4 billion to 24 billion yen between 1955 and 1971, and the corresponding increase in the annual volume of production was from 73,325 to 5,883,526 units. In a similar manner, auto parts makers carried out a large-scale investment program to renovate their production equipment. As a result, machinery less than five years old accounted for 57 percent of the total in 1968, whereas equipment over ten years old had amounted to 55 percent in 1955 (Ueno and Mutō 1970, p. 443; cf. Appendix Table A-4).

Managerial Factors

Two policies were adopted by the primary firms to combat liberalized trade and capital transactions. First, amalgamation and business cooperation took place among major primary firms in the late 1960s. Nissan absorbed Prince in 1966 and Fuji Heavy Industries in 1968, and Toyota acquired partial ownership of Hino in 1966 and of Daihatsu in 1967. Business cooperation was realized in such fields as product design, technological upgrading, the procurement of parts and components, and export promotion as well as production and sales assistance.

Second, the primary firms rationalized their subcontracting practices in the following ways:

1. They extended generous assistance to affiliated parts makers to upgrade their technological and managerial capabilities through equity participation, dispatch of managerial staff, equipment disposal, provision of materials, etc.
2. In a few cases the primary firms encouraged ancillary firms to initiate dealings with other primary firms in order to achieve scale economies that would enable further reduction in unit cost. (The

only exception was (and still is) that the Toyota affiliated subcontractors were never allowed to produce parts and components for Nissan, and vice versa.)

3. For the same reason, the primary firms tried to limit the number of ancillary firms supplying them with parts and components.

In the process, the Japanese automobile industry established its own unique system of mass production, which accomplished much more than mere scale economies (Tomiyama 1973, pp. 22–23). Under the system, parts and components manufacturers were categorized as:

1. independent firms whose products were more or less standardized and sold in a wider market outside the auto parts market (e.g., glass, tires and tubes, batteries, bearings, and electrical parts), or

2. semi-independent firms that produced pistons, piston rings, manifolds, radiators, spark plugs, wheels, shock absorbers, brakes, frames, carburetors, or

3. subcontractors who were closely affiliated with the assemblers.

Government Policies

In the early 1960s Japanese-made automobiles were not competitive. But the government regulations pretty much kept foreign cars out of Japan, and those that landed had what should have been a price advantage turned into a substantial premium. This is illustrated in Table 2.8 for 1962.

In the 1960s, the government maneuvered to delay as long as possible the liberalization of international trade and capital transactions. By the same token, it directed its efforts to protect and promote the motor car industry so that whenever a barrier was lifted on the importation of foreign cars or components, local manufacturers would be sufficiently competitive to maintain their position in the domestic market. Eventually the import of commercial vehicles (buses and trucks) was liberalized in 1961, that of passenger vehicles in 1965, and foreign capital participation in 1971.

Regarding the policy to promote the domestic manufacture of parts and components, the terminal date of the Provisional Act for the

Table 2.8.   Japanese-Built vs. Foreign-Built Automobile Prices, 1962[a]

(In percent)

Vehicles size by engine cc	Price ratios	
	In country of origin[b]	In Japan [c]
1900	130	82
1500	116	62
1000–1200	124	63
800	120	57
400–500	110	—

Notes: [a] Arithmetic means of representative models.
[b] Ratio of the sales price of Japanese models in Japan to the sales price of comparable models in their country of origin, both net of sales taxes, value added taxes, and the like.
[c] Ratio of the sales price in Japan of a Japanese car to the price of an imported comparable model, inclusive of duties, taxes, etc.
Sources: Tokyo-to Keizai Kyoku (1963), p. 124.

Promotion of Machinery Industries was extended three times (up to 1971) to ensure the expansion of the scale of operation of the individual companies and to reinforce their technological capabilities. In 1971 the Act (*Kishin hō*) was repealed and replaced by the Machinery and Electronics Industries Act (*Kikai denki sangyō hō*, or *Kiden hō* for short).

These policies have revolved around two basic orientations: first, to limit the number of promoted firms and thus to help them realize scale economies in order to improve production efficiency; second, to avoid excessive competition among Japanese firms by the so-called "one-source, one-licensee principle," which was probably also instrumental in introducing foreign sophisticated technologies into the country (Japan External Trade Organization and Japan Auto Parts Industries Association 1979, p. 21). If anything, the government policy was conducive to promoting the standardization and mass production of parts and components, which were manufactured by a few, increasingly oligopolistic suppliers, supported by smaller, third-tier ancillary firms.

Chapter 3

THE ROLE OF ANCILLARY FIRMS IN THE DEVELOPMENT OF THE JAPANESE AUTOMOBILE INDUSTRY

3.1 Some Characteristics of Parts Suppliers

Subcontracting is a feature of automobile manufacturing regardless of geographic location. However, for reasons to be explored later, the Japanese industry is characterized by a higher rate of subcontracting than its western counterparts. To see this, one need only glance at the cost structure of representative primary firms. As an indicator of the role subcontracting plays in assemblers' production budgets, the percentage of gross value in net sales is given in Table 3.1.

One finds a similar situation in other countries where the history of automobile production is relatively short. According to comparative data compiled by Baranson (1969, p. 41) for January 1969, the proportion of expenditures on parts and materials in total production cost was 46 percent in the United States, whereas it was 71 percent in Brazil, 74 percent in Argentina, and 75 percent in Mexico. Although these countries have even newer auto industries than Japan, because of active involvement by foreign firms, these percentages are lower than Japan's in Table 3.1, column five.

The ratio varies from one company to another. Among the four American assemblers, for instance, the indicator was as high as 67

ANCILLARY FIRMS IN THE JAPANESE AUTOMOBILE INDUSTRY

Table 3.1. "Make" or "Buy" in Automobile Manufacturing:
An International Comparison[a]

(In percent)

Year	Purchased inputs to net sales				Goods and services purchased/ production cost
	U.S.A.[b]	West Germany[c]	France[d]	Japan[e]	Japan[e]
1955	58	n.a.	n.a.	72	87
1960	47	n.a.	n.a.	78	83
1965	53	63	53	73	82
1970	57	61	n.a.	77	81
1975	61	59	n.a.	80	81

Notes: [a] Straight international comparisons are subject to some qualifications. For one thing, the figures ought to be adjusted for different tax systems, production subsidies (if any), and so on. In the present table, no such adjustments have been attempted.
[b] 1955–65: weighted averages of G.M., Ford, Chrysler and American Motors (the 1955 figure is a geometric average of the four corporations, making use of a 1953 figure for A.M.C.); 1970–75: weighted averages of G.M., Ford and Chrysler.
[c] Weighted average of Volkswagen and Benz, except for 1970 where the Volkswagen figure is not available.
[d] Figure for Renault.
[e] Weighted averages of seven to eleven corporations. Note that the numerator includes materials cost.
Sources: Japanese figures are from Nihon Ginkō (Bank of Japan), Hompō shuyō kigyō keiei bunseki chōsa (Analysis of Financial Statements of Main Industrial Corportaions in Japan); others are from Tsūshō Sangyō Shō (MITI), Sekai no kigyō no keiei bunseki [Survey on Financial Statements of Major Corporations in the World], 1964 ed. pp. 93–95, 150–56 and 1968 ed. pp. 69–73, 1973 ed. pp. 147–49, 1978 ed. pp. 151–53, and Kikai Shinkō Kyōkai (1975), p. 78 (1955 figure only).

percent for American Motors (1962), the smallest U.S. firm, but only 49 percent for General Motors (1960), the largest (Kikai Shinkō Kyōkai 1975, p. 78). Similarly, in 1954 the two British companies Maxcy and

Silberston cite (1959, ch. 2, sec. 4), purchased parts and raw materials comprised 55 percent in one case and 75 percent in the other.

Note also that the figures in Table 3.1 include not only the cost of parts and components but also that of materials. According to a separate questionnaire survey of six Japanese car manufacturers, the proportion of purchased parts and components in the total production cost for fiscal year 1965, excluding materials cost, ranged from 50 to 85 percent, with an average of 72 percent (Kikai Shinkō Kyōkai 1975, p. 165). These data suggest that the relative magnitude of the cost of parts and components to that of materials is approximately 7 to 1.

It seems not unreasonable to assume, then, that an increase in demand

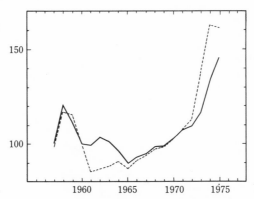

Fig. 3.1. A Comparison of Two Price Indices for Automobile
Parts and Components

KEY ——: price index of selected automobile parts and components (1960 = 100)
------: value of output of parts and components to be assembled on four wheelers, excluding replacement goods, divided by physical units of automobile production (1960 = 100)

Notes: A great deal of change actually takes place in the field of parts and components production. Old parts are improved in weight, size, cost, and performance, while entirely new products are introduced. The use of totally new materials is also quite important. Our conjecture here is simply that all these factors are happily cancelled out to make the physical quantities of parts and components per vehicle more or less constant.

Sources: Appendix Tables A-12, A-14 and A-16.

for automobiles generates an approximately equal rate of expansion in the demand for parts and components. As indirect evidence for this assertion, Figure 3.1 demonstrates that an independently estimated price index of parts and components displays a highly consonant movement with an index of the values of parts and components installed on a complete motor vehicle. This suggests a complete motor vehicle, whether new or old, is equipped with constant physical quantities of parts and

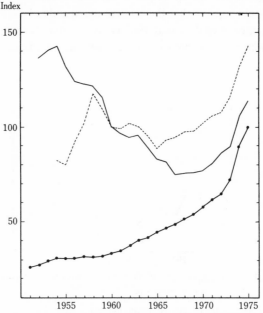

Fig. 3.2. Automobile Prices in Japan, 1951–75

KEY ——: implicit output price (1960 = 100) of passenger vehicles produced domestically

------: price index (1960 = 100) of selected automobile parts, components, and steel sheet

——•——: consumer price index (1975 = 100)

Notes: The price series for completed motor vehicles is simply output deflators, which are naturally affected by the changing compositions of different types of vehicles. This fact has been ignored for simplicity's sake.

Sources: Appendix Table A-16.

components.

Quite clearly, then, cost-saving by ancillary firms contributes directly to improvement in the competitive position of primary firms. As an historical example, Japanese parts and components manufacturers managed to reduce their output prices after 1960, as Figure 3.2 indicates. This contributed to lowering automobile prices and increasing the domestic content of Japanese automobiles.

Periodization of the Industry's Performance
What factors underlie this splendid performance? An increase in

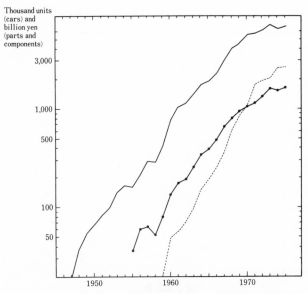

Fig. 3.3.   Production of Automobiles and Parts, 1948–75

KEY ——: production of three and four wheelers of all kind
       ------: exported three and four wheelers
       —•—: production of parts and components (for use in three and four wheelers, in 1960 constant prices)
Notes: Vertical axis is logarithmic.
Sources: Appendix Tables A-12 and A-14.

productive efficiency is an obvious answer. Four charts present indicators of the overall development in automobile and automobile parts and components production. They cover physical output (Figure 3.3), labor inputs (Figure 3.4), average physical labor productivities (Figure 3.5), and the index of domestic content ratio defined as the ratio of import to total domestic production (Figure 3.6).

One may draw some inferences from these figures. First, it seems feasible to break the entire period, 1930–70, into four major sub-periods by the characteristic performance of each variable. Table 3.2 below is the result of such an attempt, with the first two demarcations (I and II) more or less conjectural. Note especially the contrasting performances be-

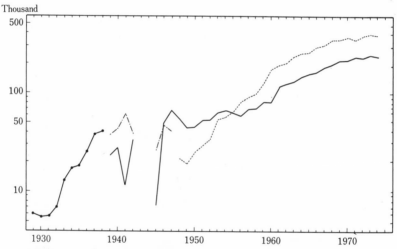

Fig. 3.4. Employment in the Automobile Industry, 1929–74
(Two, Three and Four Wheelers)

KEY ———: assemblers (primary firms)
———: assemblers, and parts and components manufacturers (primary and ancillary firms)
------: parts and components manufacturers
– · –: parts and components manufacturers plus chassis manufacturers
Notes: Vertical axis is logarithmic.
Sources: Appendix Tables A-13 and A-15.

tween primary and ancillary firms in reference to periods III and IV. Ancillary firms lagged behind in period III in improving their productive efficiency, although they soon succeeded in overtaking the primary firms in period IV. This is reflected in the poor performance of the price variables in period III.

Second, it is significant that the direction of the relation between relative prices and the domestic content ratio reversed between periods III and IV, going from positive to negative. Baranson (1969, pp. 31–40)

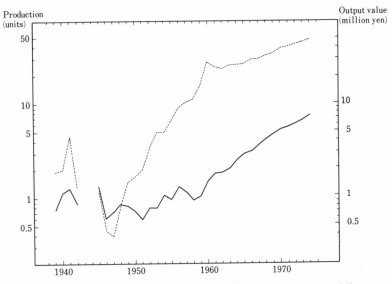

Fig. 3.5. Average Labor Productivity in Automobile Production, 1939–75

KEY ———: annual output, in 1960 prices, of parts and components per employee (for use of two, three and four wheelers), in million yen (right scale)

------: units of two, three and four wheelers produced per year per employee (left scale)

Notes: In order to obtain output series of parts and components in real terms in the earlier decades, the Bank of Japan's wholesale price index (machine and equipment) has been linked at 1953/54 with the authors' price index of parts and components. Vertical axis is logarithmic.

Sources: Appendix Tables A-13 and A-15.

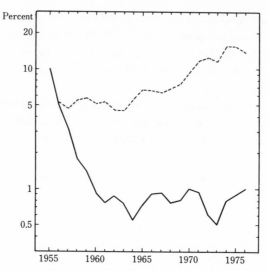

Fig. 3.6. Degree of Dependency on Foreign Markets, Automobile Parts and Components Manufacturing, 1955–75 (Parts for Two Wheelers Inclusive)

KEY ———: imports as a percentage of domestic production, excluding electric and miscellaneous parts

------: exports as a percentage of domestic production, inclusive of parts for two wheelers

Notes: This relates only to the value of manufacturing activities of automobile parts and components makers, excluding electric parts. Vertical axis is logarithmic.

Sources: Appendix Table A-14.

remarked, on the basis of experiences in India, New Zealand and some Latin American countries, that (1), given the scale of output, the cost of motor vehicle production is an increasing function of the domestic content ratio, and (2) the whole function shifts downward as the market expands. (See also Jenkins 1977, ch. 8.) In view of this thesis, one may note that the cost of Japanese automobiles kept increasing during period III *in spite of* the gradual expansion of the market. In other words, the second part of the Baranson thesis failed for this period. By contrast,

Table 3.2. A Periodization of the Development Path of the Automobile Industry in Japan

Rate of change in	I 1930–40		II 1940–50		III 1950–60		IV 1960–70	
	Primary firms	Ancillary firms	Primary firms	Ancillary firms	Primary firms	Ancillary firms	Primary firms	Ancillary firms
Physical output	+ +	+ +	(0)	(0)	+ +	+ +	+ +	+ +
Labor input	+ +	+ +	+	+	+	+ +	+ +	+
Average physical labor productivity	+	(+)	−	−	+ +	0	+	+ +
Output price divided by consumer price index	?	?	?	?	+	+	−	−
Domestic content ratio	+ +		(+)		+ +		+	

Notes: + stands for a modest, and + + for a marked rate of increase. Similarly, − signifies negative growth, and 0 no visible change in either direction. Parentheses indicate uncertainty.

Sources: Derived from Figures 3.1–3.6.

during period IV, the industry escaped the dismal prediction of the first part of the claim, thanks to the rapid growth of both domestic and overseas markets. In any event, these findings invite a closer examination of the years around 1960—a topic taken up in Section 3.2 below.

Division of Work

In Chapter 1, some theoretical reasons were given as to why subcontracting is beneficial to primary firms in the machinery industry, in general, and in the automobile manufacturing industry in particular.

One may also look at the issue from an ancillary firm's point of view.

Faced with a critical decision whether or not to engage in the production of automobile parts and components, the firm will weigh several factors carefully;

1. Whether the part is mechanically independent of other components so that it warrants a sufficiently integrated operation
2. Whether it allows the firm to realize comparative advantage (vis-à-vis the primary firms) by utilizing its expertise or specialized equipment
3. Whether it makes use of a production technology that is manageable by the ancillary firm, both in terms of labor skills and capital requirements
4. Whether it comprises a so-called "fast-moving" part so that the firm can count on the growth of a sizable spare parts market
5. Whether it is subject to significant economies of scale
6. Whether it calls for a relatively labor-intensive operation—a consideration acutely relevant under the conditions of abundant labor supply and of relatively high elasticity of substitution between capital and labor

Factors (1)-(3) relate mostly to the nature of the product, and (4)–(6) to the type of production process. Positive reactions to these items are, *ceteris paribus*, favorable to ancillary firm development, with the sole exception of item (5), whose effect by itself is adverse to it. Purely engineering matters such as (1), (2) and (3) cannot be adequately dealt with in the present framework. Accordingly, they will not be explored any further.

Item (4), like (5), deals with scale economies. The existence (or the potential) of replacement demand is certainly a factor that will invite development of smaller ancillary firms, including "backyard operators," although it does not necessarily exclude the possibility of the entry of primary firms into the market.

On the other hand, the extent of scale economies differs from one operation to another. For instance, consider the following five major production processes, commonly found in automobile manufacturing plants: assemblying, casting, forging, machine fabricating, and stamping (see Appendix Figure A-1). A study conducted by Toyota in 1960 found that economically desirable scales of operation (in two shifts), as measured by the number of completed motor vehicles, were as follows (in thousand units per month):

assemblying	8–15
machine fabricating	10–20
forging	15–30
casting	30–40
stamping	40–50

Of the five operations, stamping displayed the most conspicuous and far-reaching decline in unit cost as the scale of output expanded. (Three figures agree with those cited in Jidōsha Gijutsu Kai 1976, p. 13–2.)

Such findings are dependent on the type of machinery adopted, as optimum size depends in part on the capacity of the equipment utilized. By way of illustration, the economic scale of machine-fabricating processes grows steadily, while the minimum unit-cost level keeps declining, when general-purpose machines are replaced first by special-purpose machines and then by transfer machines. Putting this in reverse, the size of the market determines the type of machinery that can be effectively adopted (assuming, of course, that suitable machinery is physically available).[1]

The Toyota study concluded that the desirable monthly output level of automobiles at a plant was in the neighbourhood of 50,000 units (using two shifts). Obviously, the scale economies of the stamping process were a key element in deriving this figure. Moreover, this 600,000 annual output level is in basic agreement with the number suggested by Bain (1956, p. 245) on the basis of his 1951–52 questionnaire survey in the United States. Note, however, considerably larger figures are indicated by a more recent estimate: White (1971, ch. 4) argued that the minimum efficient size of operation in the American

---

[1] The Toyota study suggests the following optimum levels of machine fabricating operations in the production of engine blocks: about 4,500 units/month using general-purpose machine tools; about 9,000 using special-purpose machine tools; and 15,000–20,000 using transfer machines. (See also Jidōsha Gijutsu Kai (1976), p. 12–2.)

automobile industry was approximately 800,000 units annually (in two shifts) as of the late 1960s and that the number cited by Bain was outdated. Considering these figures, one may infer that by 1960 the engineering and economic environment for Japanese automobile production, at least at the primary-firm level, had probably become roughly comparable to that prevailing in the United States in the late 1940s or in the early 1950s.

Clearly related to the consideration of the size of the operation is the degree of ease in substituting between capital and labor. Surely, a production process more open to factor substitution is likely to be more suitable for medium- or small-scale operation, provided labor is sufficiently cheap to compensate for the relative inefficiency resulting from the use of a technology geared toward small-scale production (item (6) above). According to extensive research by Ozaki (1976, pp. 104–07), metal-working belongs to a cluster of industries where not only highly labor-intensive, traditional technology dominates, but scale diseconomies exist with respect to capital inputs. Note also that various empirical studies suggest there is considerable room for substitution between capital and labor in machinery production (see White 1979).

Judging from the patterns of employment distribution in the first-tier ancillary firms, which were extensively surveyed in 1956, machine fabricating is a process that is relatively more congenial than others to the nature of small business (Figure 3.7).

The same survey has also found that the degree of capital intensity (fixed tangible assets per production worker) is lowest in machine fabricating, while it is highest in the manufacturing of springs. Surprisingly, the ranking order changed considerably within the three-year period 1952–55, as shown in Table 3.3.[2]

All three factors (replacement demand, scale economies, and factor substitution) work together to contribute at least partially to the choice of which parts and components are manufactured by ancillary firms.

---

[2] The result of the 1956 survey of first-tier ancillary firms is reported in Jidōsha Buhin Kōgyō Kai (JAPIA) and Nihon Kikai Kōgyō Kai (1957). For the data referred to in the text, see *ibid.*, vol. 2, pp. 581 and 605.

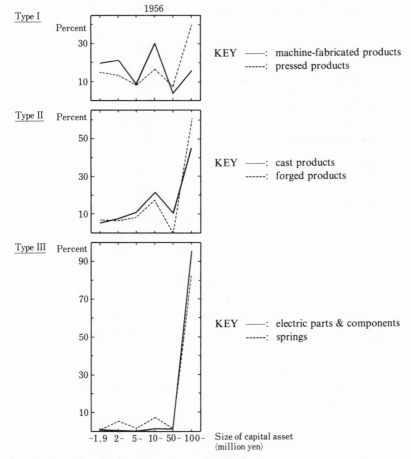

Fig. 3.7. Distribution of Employment by Size of the Firm, the Automobile Parts and Components Industry (JAPIA Members)

Sources: Computed from Jidōsha Buhin Kōgyō Kai and Nihon Kikai Kōgyō Rengō Kai (1957), vol. 2, p. 24.

Table 3.3.   Fixed Tangible Assets per Production Worker

(Thousand yen)

Type of product	1952	1955
Machine-fabricated products	73	149
Automobile tools	107	178
Automobile accessories	120	208
Pressed products	167	245
Forged products	210	262
Cast products	165	297
Unit components	123	322
Electric parts	147	323
Springs	160	373
Weighted average	135	288

The upward trend in ancillary productivity beginning in 1960 is an indication that the scale factor had by then begun to function effectively for the development of ancillary firms. If anything, the growing market size provided a momentum for further growth of the industry.

Vertical Integration, Japanese Style

In visualizing the inter-firm relations in the Japanese automobile industry especially during the era of "high-speed growth," it is important to realize that quite a few parts producers, especially at the first-tier level, have maintained steady and long-lasting trading relations with a particular assembler. The primary firms were in fact supported by networks of their own ancillary firms, commonly referred to as *Kyōryoku Kai*. Thus, the Toyota group of ancillary firms formed *Kyōhō Kai*, the Nissan group *Takara Kai*, and so on (see Table 3.4). Some parts manufacturers kept plural ties. One example, Yazaki Sōgyō, a producer of wire harnesses and meters of various kinds, is discussed in Chapter 5. However, this is a minority.

The notable features of the relations between primary and ancillary

SOME CHARACTERISTICS OF PARTS SUPPLIERS

Table 3.4. Associations of Ancillary Firms, 1968

Primary firm	Association	Number of member firms
Daihatsu Kōgyō	Daihatsu Kyōryoku Kai	73
Fuji Heavy Ind.	Shinwa Kai	98
Hino Motors	Hino Kyōryoku Kai	79
Isuzu Motors	Isuzu Kyōryoku Kai	228
Mitsubishi Motors	Mitsubishi Kashiwa Kai	67
	Mitsubishi Kyōryoku Kai	289
Nissan Motor	Nissan Motor Takara Kai	107
	Nissan Motor Shōhō Kai	34
Toyota Motor	Kyōhō Kai	182
Toyo Kogyo	Tōyū Kai	54
	Tōkō Kai	45

Sources: Chūshō Kigyō Kenkyū Center (1968), pp. 62–66.

firms varied from one case to another. Some ancillary firms were very independent from, while others were more dependent on, the decisions their "parent" assemblers made. The nature of the relationship was determined to a large extent by historical circumstances. The majority of first-tier ancillary firms had started as small producers of some simple components. They succeeded in gaining the confidence of the primary firms owing to their unique know-how or specific lines of operations and, in many cases, reinforced this confidence with close personal ties, including family relationships, and gradually transformed themselves into larger corporations. On the other hand, there were examples of firms that had started as a section of an assembler, but later were separated to form independent corporations. Whichever was the case, the primary firms took utmost care in keeping good, cordial relations with their associates. As the declaration of the Toyota Motor Company's procurement policy (*Kōbai kitei*, 1939, Article 4) put it, "once affiliated, an ancillary firm shall be regarded as an organic part of the (Toyota) corporation; in principle, therefore, standing purchase orders shall be maintained with the firm, and as much assistance as possible will be extended to improve its performance." Similarly, each of such first-tier ancillary firms in turn kept its own group of "relative" companies, which again organized some form of semi-institutional ties among themselves.

Group formation of this kind was hardly a mere social affair for the parties concerned. To begin with, the primary firm took a very active interest in leveling up the economic and engineering capabilities of the parts manufacturers, offering advice of various kinds. Furthermore, ancillary firms themselves were highly motivated in seeking better achievement, for the primary firm usually dispatched purchase orders to two (but not more than two) ancillary firms, with the explicit aim of pushing them to strive for lower prices and better product quality. In some cases, a portion of the order was placed with a branch factory of the primary firm itself. The market mechanism was effectively utilized in this fashion to enhance the economic efficiency of the network as a whole.

Within-industry associations also played a not insignificant role in this regard. For example, *Kyōhō Kai*, the organization of Toyota associates, sustained the primary firm's concern to spread the practice of stricter cost accounting ("value analysis") and of quality control, e.g., by establishing "QC circles" among its member companies. The association also served as an information clearing house, and as a means to keep up the morale ("we" feeling) of the member firms. In short, these inter-company ties substituted in part for formal, vertical integration.

3.2 Factors Contributing to the Growth of Ancillary Firms

Differential Structure[3]

The presence of a differential structure in factor markets must have been an important element in fostering the growth of ancillary firms in Japan, leading to a relatively higher rate of subcontracting work. Table 3.5 examines, on the basis of data drawn from three industrialized

---

[3] Some reasons for a differential structure are suggested in Odaka (1984). The term was coined by Ohkawa and Rosovsky (1965, p. 52).

countries in the 1950s, the extent to which workers' earnings and average value-added labor productivity differed among automobile and automobile parts manufacturers of varying sizes (see also Appendix Figure A-3).

Note especially that in Japan the magnitude of differentials in average productivity surpassed that in wage earnings. Whatever reasons there were for the earnings defferentials, they contributed to a reduction of the unit labor cost for the smaller firms and thus compensated in part for their economic inefficiency. The smaller ancillary firms took advantage of the relatively cheap labor available to them, substituting as much labor as possible for capital equipment. The other side of the coin was that their capital turnover ratio (output divided by tangible fixed assets) was higher (Appendix Table A-3).

Figure 3.8 (panel A) examines Japan's differential structure by utilizing a slightly different method; it compares the relative economic

Table 3.5. Differentials in Labor Productivity and in Earnings by Size of Establishment, Automobile and Automobile Parts and Components Industries, U.K., U.S. and Japan[a]

Size of establishment by employment	Value added per employee			Average earnings		
	U.K. (1958)	U.S.A. (1954)	Japan (1958)	U.K. (1958)	U.S.A. (1954)	Japan (1958)
5– 49	72.2[b]	73.0	26.8	72.2[b]	77.1	42.2
50– 99	76.3	71.4	32.5	76.9	84.6	47.1
100–499	77.7	80.2	48.9	82.6	90.1	59.5
500–999	85.9	82.2	66.2	86.5	95.4	74.7
1000–	100.0	100.0	100.0	100.0	100.0	100.0

Notes: [a] Expressed in index numbers, taking the value for the biggest class as 100.
[b] Data for establishments with 25–40 employees.

Sources: U.K.: *The Report on the Census of Production for 1958*, pt. 63, p. 9; U.S.A.: *1954 Census of Manufactures*, vol. 1, p. 203–86; and Japan: Tsūshō Sangyō Shō (MITI), *Kōgyō tōkei hyō* [Census of Manufacturers], 1958.

(A) Parts and components manufactures at large, 1957

Index (largest class=100)

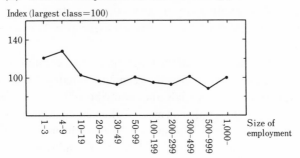

(B) Members of JAPIA, 1955 and 1966

Index (largest class=100)

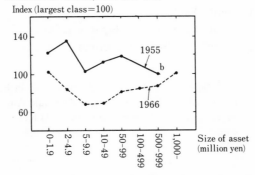

Fig. 3.8. Total Factor Productivity in Automobile Parts and Components Production[a]

Notes: [a] Total factor productivity index for class i (P_i) may be expressed as

$$P_i = a(Y/L)_i + (1-a)(Y/K)_{i'}$$

where Y/L and Y/K stand for labor and capital productivities, respectively (all expressed in index forms), and a for the relative labor share. Two different values of a have been used as explained in the text. By construction, this computation procedure assumes constant returns to scale.

[b] The 1955 data are classified into six (instead of eight) classes, the largest of which covers firms with capital asset of ¥100 million or more.

Sources: Appendix Table A-3.

Table 3.6. Indicators of Differential Structure in Automobile
Parts and Components Production, 1953–68 (Index
Numbers, Smallest Establishment = 100)

Size of establish-ment by employment	Monthly wages per employee			Value-added per employee		
	Annual average of:			Annual average of:		
	1955–59	1955–64	1960–68	1953–59	1955–64	1960–68
4– 49	100	100	100	100	100	100
50– 99	116	112	111	133	126	118
100–199	131	120	117	156	151	133
200–499	159	137	121	181	163	140
500–999	170	157	132	225	218	175
1,000–	225	198	160	237	257	203

Notes: The data cover two, three and four wheelers.
Sources: Tsūshō Sangyō Shō (MITI), *Kōgyō tōkei hyō* [Census of Manufacturers],
various issues.

efficiency of firms of varying sizes by computing the index of total factor
productivity. Taking the largest class of firms as the standard point of
reference, two types of productivity index have been computed, corresponding to two sets of weights, one employing the income shares in
the standard class, the other those in the size group with which a
comparison is made vis-à-vis the standard class. Subsequently, the two
values have been averaged geometrically. The result of the computation
confirms that in the mid 1950s medium- and small-scale firms were at
least as efficient as larger ones, although the smallest size class seems to
be an exceptional case.

It should not escape one's attention, however, that the smaller firms'
advantage in labor cost deteriorated after the mid-1960s, as a tighter
labor market began to work against them (Table 3.6). The squeeze in the
wage differential structure forced the ancillary firms to "modernize"
themselves through bigger investment in physical equipment. Some of
them lost ground or disappeared from the scene, perhaps contributing to

a gradual increase in the average size of the firms. The chart in panel B of Figure 3.8 supports this interpretation by showing that the smaller firms' superior position had been eroded by the middle of the 1960s, although here again the smallest group presented itself as an exception to the rule.

Technological Upgrading

There was remarkable growth of average physical labor productivity in the ancillary firms after around 1960 (Figure 3.5 above). The most

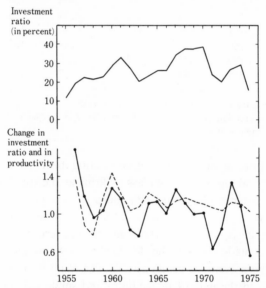

Fig. 3.9. Investment and Productivity Changes in the Production of Automobile Parts and Components, 1955–1974 (Two, Three, and Four Wheelers)

KEY ——: investment ratio (gross capital expenditure (inclusive of land procurement) divided by value added)

——•—: annual rate of change in the investment ratio (as defined above)

– – –: annual rate of change in average labor productivity in real terms

Notes: It is envisaged here that the growth rate of average labor productivity is positively related to the growth rate of the investment ratio.

Sources: Computed from Appendix Tables A-15 and A-17.

fundamental factor underlying the change was the active capital formation that took place in the industry. The rates of change in the investment-income ratio demonstrate a fairly high degree of correspondence to the rates of growth in average physical labor productivity, as shown in Figure 3.9.

In order to understand the actual transformation that occurred in the years around 1960, however, a more careful investigation is necessary. The following is a first step in this direction.

In 1956, the Ministry of International Trade and Industry (MITI) commissioned a group of professional engineers from various parts manufacturers to investigate the engineering characteristics of several key automobile components commonly available both in Japan and abroad (mostly the United States). Presumably, the aim of the research was to locate Japan along the international spectrum of engineering capabilities and to make an objective evaluation of the prospects for the growth of parts manufacturing in the country. A total of 25 items were selected, for each of which a detailed report was prepared after careful analyses were made. Commonly observed by the separate investigating teams in this project were:

1. The quality of raw materials was superior in some foreign components
2. Japanese parts reflected minute and equal attention to both functionally essential *and* non-essential elements
3. By contrast, the foreign components demonstrated concentrated care in processing vitally important areas while neglecting functionally incidental operations such as exterior polishing
4. Despite minor deficiencies which were spotted, the engineering performance of the Japanese products was at least on par with the foreign counterparts

Table 3.7 summarizes the comparisons. It is significant that essentially no Japanese products were technically inferior to the imported ones, unless one was exceptionally particular about some details. The logical conclusion of this finding, coupled with the earlier observation that Japan had been ill prepared to launch into the mass production of motor

73

Table 3.7. A Comparative Analysis of Domestic and Foreign
Automobile Parts and Components, 1954–55

Parts and components tested	Purely engineering traits			Economic aspects of production engineering	
	Domestic superior	No difference	Foreign superior	Domestic part costly owing to small production lot	Foreign part showing signs of intensive cost-saving measures
Cast parts					
Pistons	(×)[a]	×			
Piston rings		×		yes	
Intake exhaust bulb guides	×				yes
Wheel hubs & brake drums	(×)[a]	×			yes
Forged Parts					
Intake & exhaust bulbs	(×)[b]	×			yes
Tie rod ends	(×)[c]	×		yes	yes
Rear wheel axles			×	yes	yes
Knuckle supports	(×)[b]	×			yes
Universal joints			×		yes
Machine-fabricated parts					
Piston pins		×	(×)[d]		yes
King pins		×	(×)[e]		yes
Unit components					
Fuel pumps		×	(×)[f]		
Clutch discs			×	yes	yes
Oil seals		×		yes	yes
Brake linings		×		yes	yes
Water pumps		×			yes
Brake cylinders		×	(×)[g]	yes	
Electrical parts					
Spark plugs		×			

Table 3.7. (continued)

Parts and components tested	Purely engineering traits			Economic aspects of production engineering	
	Domestic superior	No difference	Foreign superior	Domestic part costly owing to small production lot	Foreign part showing signs of intensive cost-saving measures
Spark coils	×				yes
Condensers		×	$(\times)^c$	yes	
Distributors		×	$(\times)^h$		
Generators & regulators		×			yes
Body parts					
Back mirrors		×			
Electric windshield wipers			×	yes	
Switches			×		
Total					
No functional differences	2	18	5	9	15
No functional differences, but superiority in a non-functional aspect	7	7	11		

Notes: In 11 cases there is no functional difference but the domestic or foreign component excels in at least one aspect; this is noted by (×) in the appropriate superior column.
    [a] Exterior finish.
    [b] Precision.
    [c] Less dispersion.
    [d] Hardness.
    [e] Heat treatment.
    [f] Performance at high speed.
    [g] Quality of die-casting, pressing, etc.
    [h] Quality of materials.
Sources: Derived by Odaka from Jidōsha Gijutsu Kai (1955).

Table 3.8. The Role of Second-Hand Machinery in Fixed and Components Production, 1960

Size of establishment in terms of employment	Total value of newly acquired machines and equipment (million yen)			
	(A) Machine tools[a]	(B) Secondary metal forming and cutting machinery[b]	(C) Machines and equipment other than (A) and (B)	(D) Total of (A)~(C) and others
10– 19	104	33	196	1,364
20– 29	120	40	213	386
30– 49	149	94	324	619
50– 99	182	123	472	1,082
100–299	630	230	1,453	2,898
300–490	329	150	731	1,385
500–999	471	137	1,424	2,112
1,000–	4,751	1,469	10,267	14,299[c]
Total	6,736	2,276	15,080	24,145

Notes: [a] Consisting of lathes, drilling machines, boring machines, milling machines, planers, grinding machines, gear cutting and finishing machines, etc.
[b] Consisting of bending machines, hydraulic presses, mechanical presses, shearing machines, forging machinery, wire forming machines, manual presses, etc.

vehicles in the prewar days, is that technological upgrading must have taken place between 1945 and 1955.

Observations such as (2) and (3) above are obviously consistent with the basic difference in resource endowment between Japan and other countries, especially the United States. At the same time, however, many examiners detected overall *economic* inefficiency in the Japanese production lines (see the last two columns of Table 3.7). This implies that cheap labor alone could not overcome the effects of other factors (small-

FACTORS CONTRIBUTING TO THE GROWTH OF ANCILLARY FIRMS

Capital Formation, Automobile and Automobile Parts

	Of which the proportion of second-hand machines and equipment (in percent)		
(A)	(B)	(C)	(D)
65.7	27.2	53.2	86.6
60.3	21.4	51.2	39.4
49.8	20.9	38.5	35.8
46.2	20.9	29.5	24.9
34.8	19.2	21.2	19.1
13.9	7.5	11.3	8.4
21.7	46.5	13.6	10.0
6.9	0.6	4.1	5.0
14.7	8.3	9.9	14.2

Notes: ᶜ The sum of (A)~(C) exceeds the value given in (D); the reason for the discrepancy in the source is not clear.

Sources: Computed from Tsūshō Sangyō Shō (MITI), *Kōsaku kikai setsubi tō tōkei chōsa hōkoku* [Report on Statistical Research on Machine Tools, etc.], 1960.

lot production, among others), resulting in costlier Japanese products. In fact, an independent survey of first-tier ancillary firms in 1956 revealed that the prices of Japanese automobile parts and components could hardly compete internationally. According to this survey, Japanese parts were anywhere from 20 to 100 percent more expensive than the foreign equivalents:

| electrical parts | 80–100 percent |
| pressed and forged parts | 60 percent |

unit components   40 percent

cast parts   20 percent.

(Jidōsha Buhin Kōgyō Kai and Nihon Kikai Kōgyō Rengō Kai 1957, vol. 1, p. 39).

Turning Point in Technological Upgrading

There was little or no sustained upward trend in average labor productivity in real terms prior to 1960. The best explanation for this somewhat surprising fact is that technological upgrading in the late 1940s and the 1950s was of such a nature that it either improved the product quality or increased capital efficiency, or both, without significantly affecting the standard of labor efficiency. Statistical evidence such as that presented in Table 3.8 indicates that as of 1960 the smaller firms expended proportionately more for the purchase of second-hand machine tools. Qualitative information from other sources support the hypothesis. Not too many years after World War II, some major primary firms sold portions of their used equipment at nominal prices to their associated ancillary firms. Some parts manufacturers were even more fortunate, obtaining high quality machine tools from the Army or Navy Arsenals. In addition, some aeromechanic engineers and other specialists returning from their military duties joined the industry and thus strengthened the basic engineering capabilities of the ancillary firms.

A transformation came about sometime in 1960. Parts manufacturers were actively engaged in the installation of newly-developed machinery, of which an increasing amount was domestically made. As a consequence, the age structure of machine tools declined rapidly after that (see Figure 3.10).

Not only did the medium- and small-scale firms increase the capital intensity of their production facilities, but they pushed it much further than the larger corporations. Data in Table 3.9 bear beautifully on this point. Note, first, that the number of machine tools per employee is consistently larger for the smaller firms and, second, that it shows a clear upward trend over time. The implication is that the smaller firms had

Table 3.9. Number of Machine Tools per Employee, Automobile and Automobile Parts and Components Manufacturers, 1960–73

Size of establishment, in terms of employment	Machine tools[a]				Secondary metal forming and cutting machines and equipment[b]				Total of two types listed herein and all others			
	1960	1963	1967	1973	1960	1963	1967	1973	1960	1963	1967	1974
30– 49	0.55	0.67	0.73	—	0.14	0.17	0.25	—	0.69	0.84	0.97	—
50– 99	0.42	0.49	0.57	—	0.11	0.14	0.19	—	0.53	0.63	0.76	—
100–299	0.32	0.39	0.47	0.52	0.09	0.10	0.12	0.14	0.42	0.48	0.59	0.66
300–499	0.42	0.28	0.31	0.31	0.08	0.10	0.10	0.09	0.49	0.38	0.41	0.40
500–999	0.37	0.31	0.28	0.36	0.05	0.06	0.08	0.11	0.43	0.37	0.36	0.47
1,000–	0.39	0.29	0.25	0.24	0.04	0.03	0.04	0.05	0.43	0.32	0.29	0.28
Average	0.40	0.35	0.34	0.30[c]	0.08	0.07	0.08	0.07[c]	0.47	0.42	0.42	0.37[c]

Notes: [a] Consisting of lathes, drilling machines, boring machines, milling machines, planers, grinding machines, gear cutting and finishing machines, etc.
 [b] Consisting of bending machines, hydraulic presses, mechanical presses, shearing machines, forging machinery, wire forming machines, manual presses, etc.
 [c] Average of establishments with 100 employees or more.

Sources: Computed from Tsūsan Shō (MITI), *Kōsaku kikai setsubi tō tōkei chōsa hōkoku* [Report on Statistical Research on Machine Tools, etc.], various issues.

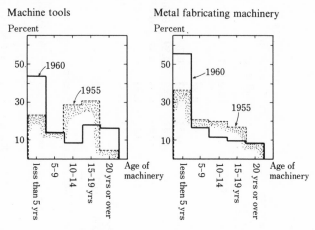

Fig. 3.10. Distribution of Machine Tools and Metal Fabricating Machinery by Age in the Automobile Parts and Components Industry (JAPIA Members)

Sources: Appendix Table A-4.

striven harder to renovate themselves through the process of capital deepening.[4]

This is supported by the data in Table 3.10, which reports the number of foreign technologies introduced by the automobile parts and components manufacturers. An unmistakable shift occurred after 1963, when the number jumped to a new high and then was maintained

[4] The cross-section comparisons are subject to some reservations. The following are two such examples: (1) The denominators are inclusive of both production and office workers, and the proportion of office workers is likely to be higher for larger firms. (2) The ratios are expressed in terms of units of machine tools irrespective of their size or economic value. Accordingly, the numbers may overestimate the significance of smaller-sized, cheap machines. In presenting Table 3.9, it is assumed that the degree of bias created by these factors remains more or less constant over time, so that intertemporal comparisons are not affected.

It may be pointed out in this connection that the number of newly installed machine tools *per company* presents an entirely different picture from the one suggested by Table 3.9, as it is smaller for the smaller firms. Furthermore, it shows a clear increasing trend regardless of size classes. See Appendix Table A-5.

throughout the decade.

The findings thus far conform to the notion that technological transformations succeeded one after another in various branches of the machine-tool industry after 1960. First, the engineering standard in machine fabricating improved around 1960. As a consequence, by 1963, the quality of general-purpose machine tools caught up completely with that in more advanced, industrialized countries. Subsequently, the technological levels in stamping and forging operations went up significantly around 1965 (die-making was also one of the most sophisticated

Table 3.10. Introduction of Foreign Technology in the Automobile Parts and Components Industry, 1951–68

Year	Number of foreign technologies introduced
1951	1
1952	1
1953	1
1954	0
1955	5
1956	2
1957	0
1958	0
1959	8
1960	3
1961	9
1962	4
1963	17
1964	14
1965	11
1966	32
1967	26
1968	66

Sources: Nihon Jidōsha Buhin Kōgyō Kai (JAPIA), *Jigyō hōkoku sho* [Annual Report of Activities], 1965 ed., p. 337, 1968 ed., p. 313.

operations in machinery production). A few notable exceptions to this statement were gear cutters, gear finishers, and screw grinders. Transfer machines were first adopted by the industry in the early 1960s, and shortly thereafter achieved great popularity. (For a general account of the postwar technological progress in the Japanese machine tool industry, see Tomiyama (1973, pp. 75–96) and Kikai Shinkō Kyōkai (1968)).

One should not overlook the changes both in the quality and the type of basic materials utilized in the automobile production. These include the effective use of lower-grade specialty steel, the substitution of ordinary steel for specialty steel, the replacement of steel parts by those made of nonferrous metals such as aluminum, the introduction of artificial rubber, the increasingly frequent use of plastic, and so on. The changes resulted in a reduction of automobile weight and thus contributed to better fuel economy.

The years following 1965 witnessed greater emphasis on improvement in organizational efficiency: the introduction of the idea of quality control and various production control ideas such as value analysis. Perhaps the standard of hardware technology had reached a saturation point, at least for the time being.

The average size of ancillary firms gradually increased over the period. For instance, the distribution of employment among the first-tier ancillary firms, classified by the size of employment, shifted to larger numbers as time went on: median employment was up from 82 in 1956 to 167 in 1960, 252 in 1965, 336 in 1970, and 417 in 1974, although the mode of the distribution remained in the range for middle-sized firms (those with 100 to 299 wokers) except in 1956, when the mode was in the smallest class (see Appendix Figure A-4). Although not so clear as this, a similar trend is observable from the data covering all ancillary firms, inclusive of the manufacturers of two-wheeler parts (See Appendix Table A-8).

All these findings lead to the conjecture that technological innovation in the automobile parts manufacturing industry was more of a capital-augmenting kind through the 1950s, after which it switched to more of a labor-augmenting variety.

FACTORS CONTRIBUTING TO THE GROWTH OF ANCILLARY FIRMS

Expanding Market

There are a number of critical factors that have contributed to the expansion of the domestic market for motor cars. To begin with, note that the role of the spare parts market was relatively greater in the earlier stage of the growth of the industry, until domestic demand for automobiles gained momentum. In other words, the so-called "fast-moving" parts must have presented a relatively promising avenue of development, especially in the early decades. As time went on, however, its significance seemed to have declined slowly while the relative importance of the export market rose (Table 3.11).

The most fundamental constraint to the development of ancillary firms was found in the technological aspects of automobile production. In contrast, the growth of the automobile market helped the parts manufacturers realize economies of scale. In the early stage of its postwar development, the industry was forced to concentrate on the manufacture of commercial vehicles (mostly trucks, as seen in Table 3.12). As the engineering specifications for trucks were not so stringent as those for passenger cars, one would have imagined (and rightly so) that this factor was a big plus in mobilizing and upgrading the technological potential of the ancillary firms.

Table 3.11.   Replacement and Export Markets in Total Output, Automobiles Parts and Components, 1956–75

Average of:	Shipment of replacement goods as percentage of total output of auto-mobile parts[a]	Exported parts as percentage of total output of automobile parts, inclusive of parts for two wheelers[a]
1956–65	22.9[b]	5.3
1961–70	17.1	6.4
1966–75	15.4	10.3

Notes: [a] Underlying data are in value terms.
          [b] Substituting 1955 figure for 1956 figure, as source data are incomplete.
Sources: Nihon Jidōsha Buhin Kōgyō Kai (JAPIA), *Jigyō hōkoku sho* [Annual Report of Activities], various issues (see Appendix Table A-14).

83

Table 3.12.   Distribution of Output by Type of Vehicle, 1946–75

(In percent)

Average of:	Passenger vehicles	Trucks	Buses
1946–55	10.1	83.0	6.9
1951–60	23.6	70.0	6.5
1956–65	30.7	67.0	2.4
1961–70	40.9	58.1	1.0
1966–75	56.5	42.7	0.7

Notes: Underlying data are the number of each vehicle type.
Sources: Computed from Jidōsha Kōgyō Kai (Japan Automobile Manufacturers Association), *Jidōsha tōkei nempō* [Automobile Statistical Yearbook], 1966, 1973 and 1976.

Toyota produced essentially only two or three varieties of passenger car engines until 1955. Moreover, a considerable percentage of larger models (e.g., Crown and Corona) were marketed for use as taxi cabs. Equally important, until 1960, more than 40 percent of the domestic production of motor vehicles, excluding two wheelers, were three wheelers, except during the war years 1939–46 (Figure 3.11).

Three wheelers in fact played an essential role in sustaining the demand for parts and components while per-capita real disposable income hovered at too low a level to support much demand for four wheelers. This point has been emphasized by Ishikawa (1979) as a factor favoring the dynamic development of ancillary firms. True, not all the car assemblers went into the manufacture of three wheelers. Therefore, the first-tier ancillary firms with strong ties with such assemblers never benefitted from the demand for tricycles. Nevertheless, the presence of the tricycle market must have been quite beneficial for the automobile parts industry as a whole.

Institutional Driving Forces
Finally, a big push came from government agencies and from

industrial associations. Shortly after World War II, MITI conceived of a long-range development plan for Japanese industries, in particular the production of automobiles. In June 1956, special temporary legislation was enacted to encourage the development of machinery industries (*Kikai kōgyō shinkō rinji sochi hō*, or *Kishin hō* for short: The Provisional Act for the Promotion of Machinery Industries), which was kept effective through March 1971 (Nihon Kikai Kōgyō Rengō Kai 1983, pp. 3–11). The legislation designated automobile parts and components production as one of the most important target industries for active promotion. Under the Act, the purchase by ancillary firms of specified machine tools and of testing devices was encouraged; special loans were extended through the Japan Development Bank (Nihon Kaihatsu Ginkō)

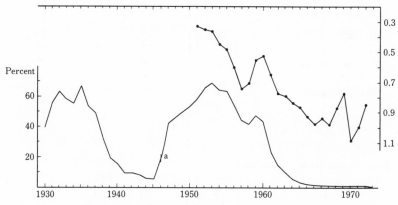

Fig. 3.11.   Three Wheelers vs. Four Wheelers

KEY ——: Ratio of three-wheel truck production to total truck production (left scale)

——·——: Relative price (reversed scale) of three-wheel to four-wheel trucks (right scale)

Notes: Computed on fiscal-year basis.

    [a] Prior to 1946 bus production is included with truck production in the available data sources. This leads to an understatement of three-wheeler share of several percentage points in the 1930s, but few buses were produced after war began in 1937.

Sources: Appendix Tables A-12 and A-16.

Table 3.13. Planned New Investment Expenditures in Automobile Parts and Components Manufacturing, Expressed as Percentages of the Industries' Total Annual Projected Capital Formation

Parts and components	Annual average[a]			Proportion of replacement goods in total production[b]
	1956–60	1958–62	1961–65	
Type I: with a declining trend				
Pistons, pistons pins, piston rings & cylinder lines	11.2	9.8	4.5	39
Fuel injection systems	10.4	6.8	4.6	22
Speedometers & other meters	8.3	7.4	1.4	9
Lamps	6.3	5.4	4.4	18
Chassis springs	5.7	4.1	2.3	42
Oil seals	4.1	4.8	2.7	36
Clutch systems	4.1	4.3	3.6	24
Frames & axle housings	3.9	1.6	0	0
Coil springs	2.7	1.9	0	1
Window frames	2.7	2.3	1.3	1
Carburetors	2.6	2.5	1.8	14
Power steering systems	2.1	1.2	0.8	5
Oil pumps & water pumps	1.4	0.9	0.4	7
Type II: with an increasing trend				
Electric parts	9.3	9.8	12.2	32
Pressed parts	0	3.5	9.4	?
Wheel discs	3.0	4.8	7.6	15
Connecting rods	2.6	3.9	5.9	31
Brake systems	5.0	5.6	5.9	49
Radiators	1.7	2.7	4.0	5
Vibration-proof rubbers	0	0.4	3.2	55
Steering handles	1.1	2.0	2.6	2
Intake bulbs & exhaust bulbs	1.3	2.3	2.6	36
Seats	0	0.6	1.9	2

FACTORS CONTRIBUTING TO THE GROWTH OF ANCILLARY FIRMS

Table 3.13.   (continued)

Parts and components	Annual average[a]			Proportion of replacement goods in total production[b]
	1956–60	1958–62	1961–65	
Type III: with little changes over time				
Fuel strainers & oil filters	2.9	3.2	2.7	22
Shock absorbers	2.3	1.4	2.1	24
Switches	1.9	1.9	1.7	28
Windshield wipers	1.4	1.4	1.0	27

Notes: [a] There are cases where no expenditures were planned for the year. The value of zero was assigned to such cases in carrying out the computation.
[b] As of the second half of fiscal year 1960 (see Appendix Table A-11).
Sources: Computed from Nihon Jidōsha Buhin Kōgyō Kai (JAPIA), *Jigyō hōkoku sho* [Annual Report of Activities], various issues.

and also from the Small Business Finance Corporation (Chūshō Kigyō Kinyū Kōko). Each year the association of parts manufacturers, JAPIA, composed a formal rationalization plan for the industry, the relevant portion of which was duly submitted to the financial institutions for approval.

In drawing up the rationalization project, JAPIA put forward its own guidelines, justifying its organized endeavor. Accordingly, some 80 parts and components were selected as the objects of rationalization, 60 of which received financial assistance at one time or another under the Act. A part was selected on the basis of three criteria. (1) It served an independent and integrated operation. (2) It could expect a growing demand from the spare parts market. (3) It needed specifically designed facilities, special materials, or unusual production methods. (For more on the basic guidelines, see Jidōsha Buhin Kōgyō Kai (JAPIA) 1956, pp. 36–57 and 1961, pp. 230–35.)

Table 3.13 shows how much the respective components weighed in terms of their relative importance in this project, by computing the average percentage of investment funds allotted to each of them. This table should be read with care, as it presents *planned* figures. The data therefore suggest which components were considered vital in the development of the parts manufacturing at different points in time. (The record of actually appropriated amounts is given in Appendix Table A-10 and the manner of its allocation in Appendix Table A-11.)

It was estimated that, owing to these rationalization projects, the average production cost of eleven key parts and components went down by approximately 25 percent between 1956 and 1960, and another 26 percent between 1960 and 1965. The items are: pistons, piston rings, intake and exhaust bulbs, fuel injection systems, radiators, connecting rods and bushes, electric parts, shock absorbers, and window frames (Jidōsha Buhin Kōgyō Kai (JAPIA) 1959, pp. 153–55 and 1966, p. 362).

Various scientific and engineering projects were sponsored by the government and related agencies. For example, as early as 1940 a section on automobile research was added to the Engineering Laboratory (Kikai Shikenjo), a public organ attached to the Ministry of Commerce and Industry (Shōkō Shō). After the War, the Ministry of Education (Mombu Shō) awarded a scientific research grant in 1950–53 to promote a joint industry-university group to study the elimination of automobile vibrations. In the same vein, MITI commissioned a number of experimental investigations that had bearing on the improvement of automobile performance. For instance, a study on improving vehicles by use of special springs was undertaken by the Society of Automotive Engineers of Japan (Jidōsha Gijutsu Kai) in 1952–53.

Many other public and private undertakings contributed to the growth and the levelling up of automotive technology. Even commercial events such as automobile shows, competition meets, and international rallies found their place in this venture.

Such a list is merely a sample of institutional measures for the encouragement of automobile parts production. A more thorough evaluation of such policies will be the topic of a separate investigation.

Chapter 4

SELECTED PRIMARY FIRMS

4.1 Nissan Motor Company, Ltd.[1]

4.1.1 Company Profile

Founded	:	December 1933
Origins	:	1911
Production	:	2.3 million units
Sales	:	¥2,332 billion
Profit net of tax	:	¥65 billion (2.8% of sales)
Vehicle types	:	passenger cars, trucks, buses
Other products (10% of sales)	:	textile machinery and rockets
Number of employees	:	55,747
Number of domestic factories	:	8
Number of domestic dealers	:	272
Overseas importers and distributors	:	151
Overseas assembly plants (1974)	:	28

All data are for the fiscal year ending March 1979, except as noted.

In 1979 Nissan Motor Company was the second largest automobile

[1]   The analysis in the section is based on the authors' interviews with Nissan officials, former Nissan personnel, and materials in Industry Research System (1977), Jidōsha Kōgyō Kai (1965, 1967), Nihon Jidōsha Kōgyō Kai (1969), Nissan Jidōsha (1965, 1975), and Wada (1937).

maker in Japan, after Toyota, and the fourth largest in the world. That year, Nissan accounted for about one-fourth of Japan's production, with almost half of its output going to exports. Table 4.1 shows Nissan's growth since the early 1930s.

Nissan had 53 core ancillary firms. Characterized by strong personnel and financial ties with the primary firm, these were called the Nissan Group. In-group firms and major subcontractors were grouped into three cooperative organizations. Figure 4.1 shows the distribution by paid-in capital and the number of employees of the first two groups.

Takara Kai includes 109 firms that make major parts and components. Their output is regarded as quasi-in-plant production by Nissan.

(1) Distribution of paid-in capital

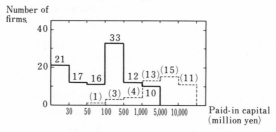

(2) Distribution of number of employees

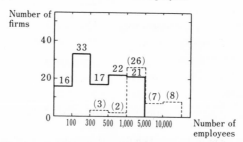

Fig. 4.1. Profiles of Nissan-Related Ancillary Firms

Notes: ——: Members of Takara Kai.
              –––: Members of Shōhō Kai.

90

Table 4.1. Growth of Nissan Motor: 1933–79
(In thousand yen: 1933–46, and in million yen: 1946–79)

Fiscal year[a]	Sales	Net profit[b]	Fixed assets	Number of employees
1933[c]	238	15	3,621	500
1934	2,443	96	9,348	1,900
1935	6,192	811	11,554	1,900
1936	6,577	1,060	22,725	3,800
1937	28,403	1,229	30,357	7,700
1938	69,300	3,665	35,495	10,300
1939	83,676	3,736	33,503	8,000
1940[c]	72,847	3,305	41,987	7,400
1941	117,763	4,228	48,748	7,700
1942	95,235	4,820	58,194	7,700
1943	66,658	5,786	79,085	n.a.
1944	60,363	7,952	97,194	n.a.
1945	56,111	− 13,886	106,051	7,400
1946[d]	115,793	5,547	108,945	9,000
1946–50[e]	13,365	20	351	8,400
1950[c]	1,754	114	1,535	6,600
1951	11,367	897	1,604	6,700
1952	12,488	946	1,752	6,900
1953	14,990	944	4,755	7,700
1954	14,247	1,025	5,147	7,000
1955	17,356	1,182	5,784	6,700
1956	30,893	2,806	8,194	7.700
1957	38,673	2,583	10,913	7,800
1958	40,049	3,151	10,953	7,800
1959	54,801	5,097	12,129	9,400
1960	83,321	8,064	19,719	11,900

Table 4.1. (continued)

Fiscal year[a]	Sales	Net profit[b]	Fixed assets	Number of employees
1961	120,064	11,164	31,769	14,200
1962	148,081	14,338	38,629	16,100
1963	184,587	18,036[b]	55,168	18,400

1964	213,419	10,371	88,333	21,248
1965	214,927	10,713	94,164	22,591
1966	302,266	14,578	121,955	34,443
1967	421,448	19,550	160,538	40,174
1968	556,133	21,529	208,280	46,307
1969	669,050	24,835	260,231	47,454
1970	799,316	28,487	233,689	48,608
1971	981,812	33,692	356,534	50,430
1972	1,176,425	48,032	410,044	51,395
1973	1,270,833	41,422	466,411	52,819
1974	1,429,637	18,800	507,273	51,612
1975	1,770,198	52,214	537,822	51,454
1976	2,024,624	85,292	599,116	52,577
1977	2,246,393	80,680	664,039	54,411
1978	2,306,685	65,465	745,337	55,747
1979	2,738,868	87,457	803,191	56,702

Notes: [a]   Fiscal years varied over time.

Fiscal year	Began	Ended
1933	26 December 1933	30 April 1934
1934–39	1 May	30 April
1940	1 May 1940	31 March 1941
1941–45	1 April	31 March
1946	1 April 1946	10 August 1946
1946–50	11 August 1946	29 December 1950
1950	30 December 1950	31 March 1951
1951–79	1 April	31 March

b   Net profit before tax from 1933 to 1963; net profit after tax from 1964 to 1979.
c   Short year—see note (a).
d   Fiscal year less than five months. The large sales and profit figures reflect rapid inflation. Fixed assets and employees are as of 31 March 1947.
e   Sales and net profits are for the four years and five months from 11 August 1946 through 29 December 1950. Fixed assets and employees are as of 31 March 1949.

Sources: Nissan Jidōsha (1965), Appendix and Ōkura Shō (Ministry of Finance), *Yūka shōken hōkokusho sōran* [Report on Corporate Securities], various issues.

Shōho kai covers 47 large companies that supply parts to Nissan as only one aspect of their business. They are thus largely independent of the primary firm in terms of decision making.

Kōhō Kai is an organization of 21 die and jig makers.

4.1.2   Historical Development

Aikawa Yoshisuke is considered the founder of Nissan. Born in Yamaguchi Prefecture, the southwestern Honshū island, in 1880, he graduated in engineering from Tokyo Imperial University (now the University of Tokyo) in 1903 and went to work for Shibaura Manufacturing (Shibaura Seisakusho), a manufacturer of electrical machinery, for two years.

At Shibaura, he decided, unlike most university graduates, to start at the bottom to learn the details of the job. He worked first as a finisher, and became a caster in his second year. He made it a rule to visit as many factories as possible on Sundays, his day off. From these visits, he learned that the successful manufacturers of the day depended heavily on imported technology. This made him decide to go to the United States to master malleable casting.

His experience in a foundry in the U.S. affirmed his confidence that, in spite of technological inferiority, Japan could excel the West in labor efficiency by utilizing what he felt was an innate dexterity and alertness. This confidence was so firm, it became a part of his business philosophy.

On his return from the United States in 1910, Aikawa established the

Tobata Casting Company (Tobata Imono) to produce malleable cast iron. He received financial support from Inoue Kaoru, also from Yamaguchi, and an important figure in politics since the Meiji Restoration, as well as in business circles. Gradually, the company diversified to include malleable parts for motor cars. We will return to Aikawa and Tobata again, after tracing two other companies that are part of Nissan's early history.

Kwaishinsha Motor Car Works, started in 1911 in Tokyo by Hashimoto Masujirō, is one of these. Hashimoto was a graduate of Tokyo Technical High School (now known as the Tokyo Institute of Technology) and worked for an iron foundry and as a mine engineer before tackling the manufacturing of automobiles. He also had practical training working with a steam engine manufacturer in the United States as an overseas trainee dispatched by the Ministry of Agriculture and Commerce (Nōshōmu Shō).

Ōkura Kihichirō, a pioneer in the auto industry, suggested to Hashimoto that making parts and components was more profitable than production of complete vehicles, as there was not yet sufficient demand for vehicles because of the low level of general industrial development and income.

Hashimoto therefore decided to repair and assemble imported cars while designing cars for domestic production. He initially had seven employees. In 1914 he completed the first trial model, after overcoming various technical difficulties, especially the casting of an engine block. He named the car DAT, the initials of his three financial supporters: Den Kenjirō, Aoyama Rokurō, and Takeuchi Meitarō. A remarkable feature of this car was that all the functional parts, except such items as wheels, tires, magnetos, spark plugs, and ball bearings, were locally produced. Thus he continued to accumulate automobile production experience on an experimental basis for the next few years, until in 1918 he decided to reorganize his private company into a corporation in order to initiate full-scale production of the DAT. He was helped in this by the Osaka Arsenal, which undertook to provide specialized tools. When the production line opened, it was Japan's first to have tools specifically designed for automobile production.

But the company soon faced financial difficulty because of stagnant sales. Passenger vehicles were considered a luxury item, so only the wealthy could afford them, hence the market was rather small. Production was difficult and costly, which made the cars expensive relative to imported models. Moreover, there was a snob appeal attached to owning a foreign car. And, the World War I boom had busted.

Military procurement almost saved the company in the 1920s. In 1918, after observing their usefulness in World War I, the Japanese government promulgated a plan to promote domestic manufacturing of military vehicles. By 1920 Kwaishinsha had remodeled a DAT car into a one-ton truck, and applied for inspection by the Army. However, the nuts, bolts, and several other items were not up to military standards and the application for entry on the procurement list was rejected. It was not until 1924 that the company became a registered truck manufacturer. But by then Kwaishinsha was too weak to exploit it, and the company was finally dissolved in 1925.

William R. Gorham's activities form another thread in Nissan's story. Gorham was an American aircraft engineer who arrived in Osaka during World War I with the intention of building aircraft. This idea did not take off, so he turned his attention to the production of small-sized trucks, and the motorization of rickshaws, with the help of four American engineers who had worked under him in the United States. This also failed.

Nonetheless, he kept at it and soon had completed a three-wheeled two-seater by mounting a body on an imported Harley Davidson motorcycle engine. This was called the Kushi car after his manager, Kushibiki Yumito, to whom the car was presented. The car was intended to replace rickshaws, but to initiate commercial production, financial supporters were badly needed. They approached Kubota Gonshirō, president of Kubota Ironworks, and his son-in-law Kubota Takujirō. The Kubotas persuaded their colleagues to join in the enterprise, and Jitsuyō Motors (Jituyō Jidōsha Seizō) was established in

1919.

A license was purchased from Gorham for 100,000 yen, and he was employed as chief engineer at the then-handsome salary of 1,000 yen a month. Gorham and his three fellow American engineers drew factory layouts, and imported production equipment, parts, components, and basic materials from the United States. At the end of 1920, the most modern automobile plant of the time in the country was completed, and production started with some 140 workers, including skilled labor from the Osaka Arsenal. In 1921, the three-wheeler, two-seater came on the market priced at ¥1,300.

However, the vehicle was not successful against the rickshaw, as it was simply too expensive. At the other end of the market, the Ford Model T was a much better vehicle for not much more money. Faced with financial difficulty, the company could no longer afford to pay Gorham and the other Americans. So in 1921 two Americans (Gorham and Albert N. Little) transferred themselves to Tobata Casting, where they directed the manufacture of motors for agricultural equipment and fishing vessels. Gorham had earlier become acquainted with Aikawa, who paid a visit to the former's factory in 1920 and was impressed by Gorham's bright outlook on the Japanese machine industry. In the mid 1920s Jitsuyō established an auto repair section and later began making machined axle-shafts, pins and U-bolts for the Chevrolet assembly plant in Osaka. Other diversifications included producing engines for naval craft.

DAT Motors was established as a limited partnership by Hashimoto to continue production of DAT cars after Kwaishinsha was dissolved. DAT also had a license to produce trucks for the military, and this attracted Jitsuyō's attention. After extensive discussions, in 1926 the two firms combined. Although Jitsuyō was the stronger company, the new company was called DAT Motors.

In 1931, DAT developed a new four-wheel, two-seater initially called the Datson. The name was subsequently changed to Datsun. The company planned to manufacture 100 units a year and sell them for 1,150 yen. In comparison, the imported Austin 7 was 1,600 yen and the

Morris Minor was 1,900 yen. At the low end of the market was a domestically manufactured three wheeler at 600 yen, which had established itself in the niche Gorham had originally targeted.

The Creation of Nissan

Tobata Casting entered the automobile industry in 1931. Aikawa Yoshisuke, Tobata's president, established an automobile department in

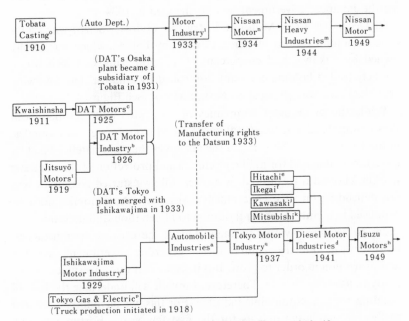

Fig. 4.2. Nissan and Isuzu Family Trees, 1910–49

Notes: Japanese names of the companies:
a) Jidōsha Kōgyō, b) DAT Jidōsha Seizō, c) DAT Jidōsha Shōkai, d) Diesel Jidōsha Kōgyō, e) Hitachi Seisakusho, f) Ikegai Jidōsha, g) Ishikawajima Jidōsha, h) Isuzu Jidōsha, i) Jitsuyō Jidōsha, j) Kawasaki Sharyō, k) Mitsubishi Jūkōgyō, l) Jidōsha Seizō, m) Nissan Jūkōgyō, n) Nissan Jidōsha, o) Tobata Imono, p) Tokyo Gas Denki Kōgyō, q) Tokyo Jidōsha Kōgyō.

the Osaka plant and began producing parts for Ford and Chevrolet. These included original equipment front and rear wheels with brake drums, hubs, and spring brackets for Ford and replacement U-bolts and axle shafts for Chevrolet. The company also made front yokes for Harley Davidson motorcycles.

Discussions were held with General Motors beginning in 1932 about building Chevrolets under license, as part of GM's plans to expand production in Japan. However, the military's desire for greater control of vehicle production in the wake of the Manchurian Incident ultimately led the Japanese government to veto the idea in 1934.

In December 1933, Motor Industry Inc. (Jidōsha Seizō) was established as a joint venture 40 percent owned by Tobata, which was wholly owned by Aikawa, and 60 percent by Nippon Sangyō, which was a publicly-traded holding company controlled by Aikawa. The following year the name was changed to Nissan Motor (see Figure 4.2).

While the predecessor companies of the 1910s and '20s had been thinly capitalized and faced stiff competition from foreign automobiles, in the 1930s the new Nissan had the resources that, ultimately helped by government demand for military vehicles and protection of the domestic market, allowed it to succeed. But when Aikawa started Nissan, he was not depending on such government assistance. "Automobiles must be produced in quantities of ten thousand to fifteen thousand units a year in order to become a viable business. Under the existing circumstances, however, the industry requires rather generous government subsidies and protection in order to grow. But it seems that our government is not ready to assume this role. Therefore, I myself will undertake the task of building a viable automobile industry. For this, we have to be prepared to face accumulating deficits for the first few years. Fortunately, this deficit will be offset by the profitable sectors of the Nissan concern. I think this is a contribution to the country, and we should be proud of undertaking a venture that will be useful for the people and society." Thus spoke Aikawa in 1934 (Nissan Jidōsha 1965, pp. 39–40).

Nissan realized it was pointless to compete with Ford and Chevrolet head on, so it sought to fill what it perceived as a gap between the three wheelers and the full-sized American cars. This is also what the new Datsun was intended to do, and rather than develop an automobile internally, Tobata had arranged to take over production of the Datsun from DAT Motors by buying the latter's stock in 1931.

Nissan soon realized it could not produce the new car in the DAT plant and meet its price objectives. So it was decided to build a new plant in Yokohama that utilized a mass production system comparable to prevailing systems in the United States. Imported production equipment was used, and Gorham directed the plant layout. Little and four other American engineers were invited to provide technical assistance in such specific fields as machining, pressing, forging, body assembly, and die making. They also trained workers in these areas and oversaw the installation of machinery. The American also argued for single-purpose machines as more appropriate than general-purpose ones. Although this involved greater investment, it was agreed that increased efficiency and quality justified the expense. Work on the plant began in May 1934, and in April 1935, the first Datsun sedan came off the line.

When Nissan initiated mass production of the Datsun, the company promoted sales in several ways. A network of exclusive agent was spread across the country, each restricted to sales activities in a specific territory. The agents sponsored driving classes and excursions for owner-drivers, and female demonstrators were employed to attract potential drivers among housewives. To advance the sales of trucks as well as passenger cars, the Datsun Truck Sales Company was formed. The Sales Company provided monthly-installment financing of all Datsun vehicles. The *Nissan Graph* was published to attract potential buyers. These efforts were so successful that "Datsun" became almost synonymous with "small car."

Both passenger cars and trucks sold well, and Nissan's share of domestic production by Japanese firms improved from 32 percent in 1933 to 73 percent in 1935. Within two years of completion of the first Datsun at the Yokohama plant, over 10,000 had been made. In adopting the American idea of the continuous flow method on a conveyor line

(Ford's innovation in 1913), Nissan had established the technical basis of mass production, and thus of mass distribution. Japan had stepped into the age of mass-merchandised, mass-produced consumer durables, though the war delayed further progress another two decades.

In 1936, Nissan registered under the newly passed Automobile Industry Act, which aimed at aiding domestic automobile makers. One of the conditions imposed was to make the utmost effort to procure materials and parts domestically, something the company was already committed to.

At the time, Nissan had been planning to add a mass-produced economy car to its line. As part of this, two managing directors were sent to the United States to study the latest developments in automobile technology. While they were in the United States, the president of Libbey Owens Glass was in Japan, and he met with Aikawa, president of Nissan. Aikawa asked about possible sources of technical help and was given the name of the Graham-Paige Motor Company, which was a Libbey customer. The two Nissan men in the States were immediately instructed to meet Joseph Graham, GP's president.

GP was an outgrowth of the Graham Comany, established in 1903 by the Graham brothers. They took over Paige Detroit Motor Car in 1908, and initiated production of passenger vehicles. In the 1920s, the company's cars were noted for their sportiness and quality. At its peak in 1929, GP employed about 5,000 workers and turned out 62,600 cars, making it 14th among American auto makers, with about $1\,^1/_2$ percent of total production. GP was in financial difficulties when Nissan came calling, having over-invested in passenger car capacity. The company had already sold a manufacturing license for trucks to Dodge.

Nissan liked GP's engine blocks, as they could be used for both commercial and passenger vehicles. GP was ready to deal, and an agreement was reached without any difficulties. Nissan purchased and shipped from the United States to Japan a manufacturing line for the engine blocks, including machinery, tools, dies, gauges, jigs, mills, and shapers. Also acquired were newly designed prototype engine blocks and cab-over trucks that Nissan could produce in the future, and blueprints for a casting plant to make cylinder blocks, cylinder heads, and manifolds.

Other purchase contracts and technical tie-ups were concluded with GP's ancillary firms so that Nissan could absorb the technology as rapidly as possible. Besides engine blocks, sophisticated manufacturing technology in the areas of axles, transmissions, and propeller shafts was acquired. Engineers and foremen from GP came to Nissan to direct installation and help initiate production. Nissan engineers who received training at the GP factory were deeply impressed by the open-minded, cooperative attitude of all the GP employees.

This introduction of advanced American technology was mainly responsible for the development of all types of Nisssan vehicles—cars, trucks, and buses—and it was widely publicized at the time. The new economy car, named the Nissan Car, came on the market in May 1937. Graham Paige was absorbed by Kaiser Frazer after World War II.

When the American companies were forced out of Japan in 1939, Nissan rented Ford's plant. After Pearl Harbor, Nissan, like the other auto makers, was put under the Automobile Control Commission (Jidōsha Tōsei Kai), and the company began producing aircraft engines. Production of private passenger cars was banned during the war.

Postwar Recovery

In the immediate postwar days, it was evident that the reestablishment of transportation was urgently needed to break distribution bottle-necks and thus help stabilize the supply of daily necessities. On 25 September 1945, Nissan acquired permission from General Headquarters (GHQ) to resume production. The company temporarily dismissed all its employees and then reemployed about one-third of them (some 3,000) to resume operations. Because of the requisitioning of land and many factory buildings by GHQ, however, production efficiency was extremely low. Furthermore, an insufficient supply of food, as well as shortages of materials, coal, electricity, parts and components, kept production targets from being met. To cope with these difficulties, Nissan engaged in the repair of old Datsun and Nissan vehicles, including special repair orders from the Occupation Army.

The postwar hardships facing the company worsened in 1949–50 under the anti-inflationary policies of the Dodge Line. Inventories rose because of the drastic decrease in demand. Fortunately, the recession did not last long. The outbreak of the Korean War in June 1950 brought massive U.S. military procurement orders. Nissan received an order for about 5,000 motor vehicles during the space of a year. Inventory accumulated during the recession was sold, overtime continued day after day, and production efficiency, in terms of labor hours required to complete a standard chassis, improved by 20 percent. Furthermore, the Bank of Japan had adopted generous financing policies for recipients of special procurement orders. Nissan, like its competitors, thus invested aggressively. Previously, they had been limited to buying or leasing equipment from the military arsenals—these were sophisticated machine tools, some in good working condition.

Achieving International Competitiveness

In the early 1950s the Ministry of International Trade and Industry (MITI) had concluded that the best way to improve the domestic auto industry was by encouraging the firms to seek technical tie-ups with foreign firms. Thus, in 1952, Nissan reached an agreement with Austin Motor of England. There were many reasons for this choice. Austin was the oldest auto maker in England, it produced reliable cars—over a thousand were in use in Japan, enjoying a good reputation, the Americans considered the Austin to be the best car produced in Europe, and the engine was superb in terms of fuel economy. But, above all, the Datsun was in fact a copy of the Austin, so Nissan engineers were already familiar with its mechanical aspects. The major points in the agreement concluded on 4 December 1952 are listed below.

1. Nissan Motor would import KD (knocked-down) packs of the Austin A 40 Sommerset Saloon for assembly
2. Parts and components of the KD packs would be gradually replaced by domestically made products so that complete domestication would be achieved in three years

3. Austin would extend any technical assistance necessary for the assembly and domestication of parts
4. Nissan could freely use the parts and components of the Austin A 40 for any other models
5. The exchange of engineers and other personnel would be conducted whenever necessary
6. Nissan would pay royalties to Austin Motor from the second year of assembly (two percent of the ex-factory price of assembled cars in the second year, and 3.5 percent the third year and onwards)
7. The contract period would be for seven years

The domestication of parts and components began immediately. Moreover, Article 4 enabled use of the Austin engine in Nissan Junior trucks, contributing to the development of Nissan's own models. This process led to development of the Datsun Bluebird in the late 1950s.

Under the agreement, extensive efforts were made to establish a mass assembly system, including building a new plant. Operations began with SKD (semi knocked-down) assembly and gradually proceeded to CKD (completely knocked-down) assembly. In addition to domestically produced tires, batteries, and flat glass, which were already being used, over 200 items were domesticated within a year. By August 1955, domestic content was 25 percent for the body (scheduled to be completely domestic by March 1956), 80 percent for chassis parts (to be 100 percent by October 1955), and 100 percent for the rear axle and transmission. In August 1956, installation of a transfer machine allowed mass production of cylinder blocks and cylinder heads, thus achieving complete domestic content. It had taken just 45 months. During the process, Nissan absorbed valuable technical know-how in precision work, maintenance, processing, inspection, and cost control, among others.

In 1959, Nissan announced a new subcompact called the Datsun Bluebird as a successor to the Datsun. Sporting improved performance and refined styling, the new model quickly won a nationwide reputation and within a few months it had become the largest selling model in the market. The age of the family car had begun in Japan. In 1964, monthly production of 10,000 units of a single model was attained for the first time by a Japanese company. By 1968, one million Bluebirds had been sold.

Building Relationships with Ancillary Firms

While Nissan was striving to introduce modern management techniques, it was also working to spread industrial engineering techniques (IE) and quality control (QC) among its subcontractors. At the same time, the company sought to strengthen cooperative ties with its ancillary firms to cope with ever-increasing price competition. Purchased parts and components accounted for 60 to 70 percent of Nissan's production costs, so controlling Nissan's costs meant helping suppliers control theirs.

Centralized purchasing of materials was extended to include ancillary firms. This meant larger volume discount from material suppliers, such as steel companies. It also allowed greater synchronization of production throughout the system, including better control of overall inventory levels.

Responding to administrative guidance from MITI, Nissan absorbed Prince Motor Industry in 1966. This was followed by mergers and reorganizations among the ancillary firms.

Some examples of how Nisssan and some specific ancillary firms dealt with each other are given below.

Minsei Diesel was an independently owned supplier of chassis for Nissan vehicles, although some of the executives of the company, including the president, had come from Nissan Motor. In 1953, Nissan bought newly-issued Minsei stock to help finance diesel engine development. The two companies also cooperated to establish a sales company to market new diesel trucks.

Tokyo Sokuhan Company was a producer of gauges, jigs, tools and micrometers, and was supplying gauges to Nissan. When the company experienced financial difficulties in 1952, Nissan provided it with short-term loans and later bought shares of stock. In addition, Nissan dispatched a research staff member to the company to assume the post of managing director.

Nissan bought sixty percent of Nihon Radiator and, to promote rationalization, transferred its own production machinery to the company. With the first purchase order from Nissan came a managing director.

In order to rationalize transportation of parts and components among its own plants and subsidiary companies, Nissan and three other companies established the Yokohama Unsō Company.

Both the Tokyo Seikōsho plant (steelworks) and the Atsugi plant (which made bolts and nuts) were spun off as independent firms. Atsugi Motor Parts later diversified into propeller shafts, borrowing processing machines from the primary firm.

Nissan Kōsaikai was established as part of the post-retirement employment program. Its employees engaged in such light work as duplication of blueprints and repair of parts and components.

Modernization of Personnel Management

In 1950, Nissan decided to study and introduce American personnel management systems in order to increase labor productivity. The major points of the plan adopted under the new policy were:

1. A personnel evaluation system for the purpose of hiring, promotion, transfer, training, etc.
2. Establishment of working efficiency standards and job analysis in order to rationalize the production process, and to put the right man in the right place
3. Training within the industry (TWI), which aimed at the re-education of production department section chiefs, as well as basic courses for improving the technical skill of young workers who had graduated from junior high schools
4. Publication of *General Affairs Weekly*, which contributed to the exchange of information between the main office and the nine plants
5. Publication of *Nissan News* to keep employees and their family members informed of company activities

6. Campaigning for improved efficiency so as to be able to cope with the severe market competition among domestic automobile manufacturers

In 1955, the Japan Productivity Organization (Nihon Seisansei Hombu) dispatched a study-tour to the United States by representatives of various automobile manufacturers. Headed by Nissan's Iwakoshi Tadahiro, the mission's major purpose was to learn methods of modern business administration in such fields as industrial relations, wage systems, welfare policies, and so forth. As a result, over the next few years another round of personnel management changes took place at Nissan.

First, elements of incentive wages were introduced into the seniority wage system. Job evaluation was applied to determine wages so that the basic wage reflected the nature of the job, i.e., the required ability, contribution, etc.

Second, the company instituted a system of encouraging employees to make suggestions on how to improve their work and environment. Employees who made effective proposals received prizes according to the level of contribution.

Third, personnel training programs were diversified and systematized to cover the following programs:

1. Training programs for managers and supervisors, which included training within the industry (TWI) for section chiefs and foremen, management training programs (MTP) for managers of departments, and job specific training (JST) for clerical employees
2. Education courses on production technology
3. Overseas training
4. Courses in industrial relations

In addition to these, the all-out introduction of quality control (QC) started in 1956, leading to winning the Deming Prize (awarded to companies with outstanding quality control activities) in 1960.

4.2   Toyota Motor Company, Ltd.[2]

4.2.1   Company Profile

Incorporated	:	August 1937
Origins	:	1930
Production	:	2.9 million units
Sales	:	¥3,310 billion
Profit net of tax	:	¥144 billion (4.4% of sales)
Vehicle types	:	passenger cars and vans (1000–3400 cc), gasoline-engine trucks (1200–2000 cc or 0.75–2 t), diesel-engines (3600–6500 cc or 3.6 t), and others (land-cruisers, micro-buses, etc.)
Number of employees	:	47,064
Number of domestic factories	:	9
Number of domestic dealers	:	253
Overseas importers and distributors	:	156
Overseas assembly plants	:	12

Data are for the year ending June 1979. In the same year, Toyota Motor Sales earned a profit of ¥34 billion and employed 4,992 men and women. TMS was an unconsolidated but wholly owned subsidiary of Toyota that handled all Toyota sales.

Throughout the 1970s Toyota Motor Company was the largest automobile manufacturer in Japan, and also ranked third in the world in terms of number of cars produced, after General Motors and Ford. Although the company's product line ranged widely in size and type, the majority of its total production and sales consisted of medium- and small-sized passenger cars. In 1976, the company sold about 1.4 million

[2]   This section draws on Kimoto (1968), Mainichi Shimbun Sha (1971), Nikkan Kōgyō Shimbun Sha (1980), Ozaki (1955), Toyota Jidōsha (1958, 1967), and Yamamoto (1978).

Table 4.2.   Growth of Toyota Motor: 1937–80

(In million yen, except the last column)

Fiscal year[a]	Net sales	Net profit		Fixed assets[b]	Number of employees[b]
		Before tax	After tax		
1937	8	−0	n.a.	14	n.a.
1938	24	1	n.a.	33	4,065[c]
1939	59	3	n.a.	42	5,348[d]
1940	67	2	n.a.	48	6,427[d]
1941	91	6	n.a.	52	5,335[d]
1942	94	6	n.a.	71	7,195[d]
1943	83	10	n.a.	120	7,623[d]
1944	130	16	n.a.	141	n.a.
1945	79	1	n.a.	163	3,901[e]
1946–49	9,855	−59	n.a.	639	6,721[f]
1950	6,477	249	n.a.	1,273	5,435[g]
1951	12,835	1,161	n.a.	1,018	5,228
1952	12,930	1,471	n.a.	1,407	5,345
1953	17,494	1,720	n.a.	3,830	5,341
1954	16,887	1,417	n.a.	4,893	5,269
1955	20,735	1,893	n.a.	4,994	5,171
1956	44,168	4,116	n.a.	7,732	5,915
1957	54,464	4.760	n.a.	12,325	5,826
1958	57,913	5,647	n.a.	15,549	6,510
1959	83,991	8,385	n.a.	26,232	8,756
1960	123,868	11,069	n.a.	44,842	11,446
1961	146,645	14,146	n.a.	64,255	12,531
1962	158,652	15,942	n.a.	68,906	15,176
1963	201,732	19,802	10,302	84,472	18,811
1964	234,805	21,908	12,008	100,642	22,643
1965	260,138	21,185	12,785	112,907	24,351
1966	341,090	31,166	17,066	131,026	28,284
1967	529,656	44,238	27,138	138,469	34,078
1968	728,252	60,078	35,778	156,196	36,689
1969	837,561	61,508	38,808	257,302	40,365

TOYOTA MOTOR COMPANY

Table 4.2.   (continued)

Fiscal year[a]	Net sales	Net profit		Fixed assets[b]	Number of employees[b]
		Before tax	After tax		
1970	1,026,075	66,414	37,914	282,789	40,918
1971	1,126,133	97,813	57,013	309,790	41,256
1972	1,325,860	106,626	65,826	387,558	42,892
1973	1,473,852	45,608	21,908	469,160	44,880
1974	1,735,858	125,455	61,512	449,925	44,584
1975	1,995,742	192,659	99,559	468,206	44,474
1976	2,288,069	217,877	116,777	540,317	44,798
1977	2,617,407	206,786	116,286	619,287	45,203
1978	2,802,469	200,658	102,058	680,643	45,233
1979	3,310,181	288,668	143,568	797,709	47,064
1980	3,506,412	231,227	132,727	1,005,658	48,757

Notes: [a]   Fiscal years varied over time.

Fiscal year	Began	Ended
1937	28 August 1937	28 March 1938
1938–50	1 April	31 March
1951	1 April 1951	31 May 1952
1952–73	1 June	31 May
1974	1 June 1974	30 June 1975
1975–80	1 July	30 June

[b]   As of end of fiscal year.
[c]   As of November 1938.
[d]   As of August of the year shown.
[e]   As of January 1946.
[f]   As of December 1947–50.
[g]   As of December 1950.

Sources: Toyota Jidōsha (1958), p. 663 and (1967), pp. 793–96; Tsūshō Sangyō Shō (MITI), *Waga kuni kigyō no keiei bunseki* [Analysis of Financial Statements of Japanese Firms], 1968–81 editions, Tokyo.

(1) Distribution of paid-in capital

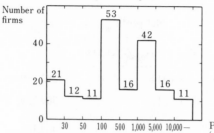

(2) Distribution of number of employees

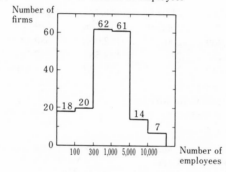

(3) Degree of dependence on Toyota Motor in sales

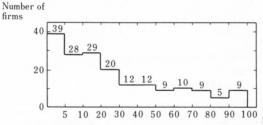

Fig. 4.3.   Profiles of Toyota-Related Ancillary Firms

Sources: Auto Trade Journal (1979), pp. 294–313, 505–756.

110

vehicles in Japan, accounting for approximately one third of total domestic sales, inclusive of mini-cars and three wheelers. Nearly half of output was exported, with vehicles going to almost every part of the world. During the high-growth years of the 1960s and '70s all Toyota vehicles were marketed through Toyota Motor Sales Company, Ltd., which had been the marketing department of Toyota Motor Company, Ltd. until 1950, when it was separated. (They were reunited in 1982.) With these two companies as the core, sixteen (as of 1975) closely associated firms formed the so-called "Toyota Group." Data on the company's growth are given in Table 4.2.

Toyota procured parts, components, and other supplies from more than 200 subcontractors, not counting some large-scale suppliers of basic materials (mainly various iron, steel and non-ferrous metal materials), specific intermediate products (such as glass sheets, tires, batteries, seals and bearings), and various machinery. These 200-plus subcontractors were grouped into three categories according to the type of products or services they supplied.

1. Manufacturers of automobile parts and components (170 firms)
2. Manufacturers of dies, gauges, tools and fixtures (21 firms)
3. Suppliers of other types of products and services such as construction facilities, etc. (36 firms).

Each of the groups formed an association, a kind of informal membership club with the purpose of maintaining cooperation and joint prosperity among the members and Toyota.

Figure 4.3 presents profiles of the parts and components suppliers by the distribution of paid-in capital as well as the number of employees and the percentage of Toyota procurement in their total sales.

4.2.2 Historical Development

Toyota Motor Company was founded in 1937 as a spin-off from Toyoda Automatic Loom Works, Ltd. Prior to the formal establishment of the company, however, there was a long and hard period of preparation for the business.

The company's story may be started in 1910 when Toyoda Sakichi, founder of the automatic loom manufacturing company, visited the United States to study the technology of the American loom manufacturing industry. Although he stayed in the country for only four months, his exposure was not limited to automatic loom manufacturing. It was the first opportunity for the inventor-entrepreneur to experience the highly mechanized American culture. In particular, he was deeply impressed with the extensive use of automobiles. His visit was just two years after the introduction of the Ford Model T. The impression was so strong that Toyoda told the story over and over again to his son, Toyoda Kiichirō, who was then managing director of the loom manufacturing company.

In 1930, Toyoda Sakichi died at the age of 63. Shortly before his death, while lying in his sick bed, Sakichi told Kiichirō, "The automatic loom business was my life's work. ... Just the same, you should have your own life's work. I believe in the future of the automobile; it will become an indispensable tool for human life. Why not challenge the automobile business?" (Toyota Jidōsha 1967, p. 18). Sakichi gave his son one million yen for a research fund. The money was the royalty income Sakichi had received from Pratt Brothers, the leading British loom manufacturer, for the release of the manufacturing patent of his automatic looms to Pratt. The technologies embodied in the patent were actually the joint efforts of the father and son.

Although Sakichi had finished only elementary school, his son was a graduate of the University of Tokyo with a bachelor's degree in mechanical engineering. In 1929 Kiichirō had visited Europe and the United States in connection with drawing up technological agreements with European and U.S. companies, and had also been impressed by the motorcar. Thus, even before receiving the advice of his father, Kiichirō was determined to take up the challenge of automobile manufacturing.

In those days, however, the Japanese automobile market was almost completely dominated by American nameplates (Ford and General Motors), although three local firms were operating on a limited scale. Ford and GM had erected assembly plants in Yokohama and Osaka, respectively, where American-made CKD (completely knocked-down) packs were assembled. A considerable gap existed in cost and quality between the American and the three local makers. Everybody, including Toyoda Risaburō, Kiichirō's brother-in-law and president of the Toyoda Automatic Loom Works, thought Kiichirō's idea unrealistic and even dangerous.

Sometime in 1930, Kiichirō began a series of preparatory actions, while keeping his intentions to himself. In cooperation with the managing director in charge of production and technology, he began introducing a large number of new high-performance loom-making machines, many of which were either American- or German-made and of unsurpassed engineering standards. In addition to various types of high-precision machine tools and a chrome-plating facility, he also procured a modern molding machine and an electric furnace for use in his foundry. Moreover, he completely rearranged the plant layout with the adoption of a conveyor assembly line.

As the engineers and the workers of the company gradually got acquainted with the sophisticated machines, in late 1930 Kiichirō gave special assignments to two young engineers (Shirai Takeaki and Iwaoka Jirō). A set of small, French-made engine parts was given to them; Shirai was to sketch the parts and examine the materials used, while Iwaoka was to study the manufacturing process. Being extra duties added to their usual jobs, the assignments had to be carried out after regular working hours. By the summer of 1931, however, they completed the study of ten small engines (60 cc each), which were then mounted on bicycles for test runs. The experiments ended successfully. Also in 1931, Kiichirō acquired a locally-made passenger car, ordered his engineering staff to practice driving inside the factory site, and encouraged them to get drivers' licenses.

On 1 September 1933, Kiichirō finally confided what he had been doing to a few close associates. With an informal group of about ten people, he established a fenced shop in a corner of a warehouse in the main factory, where the team started experimental operations. A 1933 Chevrolet sedan was disassembled. As the operation was under way, Kiichirō gave a series of lectures on automobile engineering to the group

113

members, as he had by then completed an extensive study of the subject with the help of his friends who worked in various, related engineering fields. As soon as the dismantling was over, all the parts and components were sketched and closely examined. The experimental manufacture of selected parts was also attempted by some members. Later on, Kiichirō successfully enlisted an experienced engineer, Kan Takatoshi, who was then with a competing loom manufacturer, and similarly experimenting on automobile development.

The secret activities were bound to become public before long. At the end of 1933, Toyoda Automatic Loom finally decided, after heated arguments among company officers, to establish an Automobile Division, financing the new venture by tripling capital from one million to three million yen. The operation was now formally recognized and activities expanded in terms of personnel as well as facilities. A test production plant was constructed with a floor space of about 9,000 square meters to replace the tiny shop.

Subsequently, Kan and Ōshima Risaburō, director of the automobile division, were dispatched to Europe and the United States to purchase machinery. They traveled for about six months, visiting many machine tool manufacturers and buying machines from them. They also visited automobile and auto parts manufacturers, where they picked up various production technologies. In this manner, the new division invested most of its money in production machines and equipment for testing and research purposes, whereas the factory building was constructed as cheaply as possible.

Kiichirō's desire to gather experienced engineers was fulfilled with the hiring of several who had worked elsewhere in the trial production of automobiles. Thus staffed, partial operation of the test plant was initiated even before installation of the newly-purchased machinery was completed. The first model followed the engine design principles of the Chevrolet, while the transmission, chassis and axles were based on Ford designs, and the body resembled a DeSoto. Several months later, however, facing serious technical difficulties, the decision was made to base the design of the transmission on the Chevrolet. It was Kiichirō's policy to make all the functional parts and components interchangeable with those of the American models (Toyota Jidōsha 1967, p. 59). Efforts were also made to locate potential domestic suppliers of parts and components, although Toyoda often had to resort to importing items for which they could not find reliable local sources.

In May, 1935, the first prototype model, the Al, was completed, using a mixture of domestic and imported parts, followed in August by the first prototype truck, the Gl. Although Kiichirō's desire was to develop local production of passenger vehicles, reality forced him to give priority to truck manufacturing. Trucks made in the test production plant were immediately marketed and sold at prices that considerably undercut imported models.

To promote sales, Kiichirō recruited, in late 1935, Kamiya Shōtarō, who had been working as marketing manager for GM Japan for some eight years. All marketing functions were placed under Kamiya, who responded by vigorously cultivating dealerships, taking advantage of his experience and personal influence with existing auto dealers. In the meantime, the parent company's paid-in capital was doubled to six million yen in August 1935 and increased to nine million yen in late 1936. Most of the increase went into the automobile division.

Birth of a New Company and Its Wartime Expansion

In 1936, a new assembly plant was added, increasing annual production capacity to 2,000 vehicles, and press and tool manufacturing machines were introduced at the test production plant. When the Automobile Industry Act was put into effect the same year, Toyoda Automatic Loom Works was approved as one of the registered manufacturers.

On 27 August 1937, the automobile division became an independent corporation named the Toyota Motor Company. "Toyota," a slight change from "Toyoda," taken after the company's trade mark, was chosen in a contest that had been held in major newspapers the previous summer. Toyoda Risaburō, president of the mother company, assumed the presidency of the Motor Company, while Toyoda Kiichirō took the position of executive vice president. Toyota started with paid-in capital of nine million yen and 3,123 employees, leaving just 1,000 workers in the mother company.

One of the first tasks for the new company was to construct a plant of its own. Since late 1933 Kiichirō had been looking for a spacious site for future expansion. Finally, in December 1935, he purchased approximately two million square meters in the countryside near Nagoya. Kiichirō chose Kan to draw up a plan for the new factory, since Kan had designed the old test production plant.

Toward the end of 1936, Kiichirō described to Kan the principal features of the new factory. To Kan's great surprise, Kiichirō was aiming at a monthly capacity of 2,000 units, much larger than the Ford and GM plants in Japan. This scale of production seemed utterly unreasonable. After all, Ford and GM together dominated the Japanese market. How much chance would there be to overtake such strong front runners?

To Kiichirō, however, the choice was quite reasonable. He saw there would be no chance to compete successfully unless Toyota could establish sufficient capacity to realize scale economies. In fact, 2,000 units per month were the very least he would ask for. But this was only the first step. The plant would occupy only one-third of the site. Kan was again surprised as Kiichirō disclosed his intention to construct a second factory in the middle of the lot with a monthly capacity for 10,000 commercial vehicles. "By the time the second plant is completed," Kiichirō explained, "the first plant shall be renovated to concentrate on the production of passenger cars with an upgraded capacity of 10,000 units per month (Mainichi Shimbun Sha 1971, p. 145)."

Kan spent nearly a year designing the new plant, which had to satisfy two objectives. First, it had to be able to produce 2,000 units (1,500 trucks and 500 passenger cars) monthly on a one-shift basis. Secondly, it had to have maximum flexibility for future rearrangements and modifications. To meet the second objective, Kan first drew an ideal second-stage plan, and then worked back to a first-stage plan that was feasible under the constraints of a very tight budget. Construction began at the end of September 1937, a month after the founding of the new company.

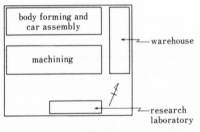

(Total floor space: 8,900m²)

Fig. 4.4.   Toyota's Test Production Plant

Sources: Toyota Jidōsha (1967), p. 54.

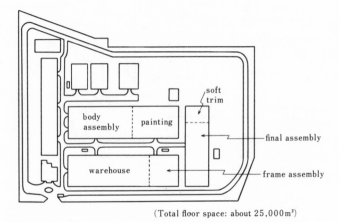

(Total floor space: about 25,000m²)

Fig. 4.5.   Toyota's Pilot Plant for Car Assembly

Sources: Toyota Jidōsha (1967), p. 83.

The factory building was completed in about a year, and all 102 machines were transferred from the old test production plant. In addition, newly purchased machines arrived from the United States.

The new plant started operations on 3 November 1938, and was

117

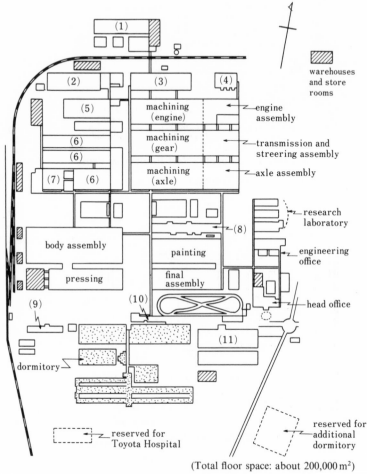

(Total floor space: about 200,000 m²)

Fig. 4.6.   The Layout of Toyota's Koromo Plant

KEY: (1) forging shop   (7) core making shop
      (2) tool and jig shop   (8) enamel painting shop
      (3) heat treatment shop   (9) Toyota Technical School
      (4) plating shop   (10) clinic
      (5) steel casting shop   (11) service/maintenance shop
      (6) foundry shop

Sources: Toyota Jidōsha (1967), p. 125.

named for the town (Koromo) where it was located. Figures 4.4 to 4.6 show how the company expanded its automobile production facilities from the first test production plant to the Koromo plant.

Throughout these years of rapid transformation, extensive efforts were continuously made to attempt the in-house production of essential components, and to identify local suppliers who were capable of producing parts that could substitute for imported parts and components. The domestication of all necessary parts and components was completed by 1940, shortly before the outbreak of the war.

Kiichirō also had aspirations to operate his own steel mill, in order to maintain control over the quality and specifications of the steel materials he used. Accordingly, Toyoda Steel Works was founded in March 1940. Toyota created Toyoda Engineering in May 1941 to take over manufacturing small-sized machine tools for internal use as well as modifying and remodelling purchased machinery.

For several years before and during the Pacific War Toyota devoted all of its manufacturing abilities to the production of military trucks and airplane components. While production capacity was expanded, the company's research and development activities were also reinforced to cover a wide range of automobile engineering fields in order to overcome various technological difficulties and to improve the quality of its products.

Rehabilitation and Growth

At the end of World War II, about 9,600 people were working at Toyota producing military trucks and airplane components. With the war over, about two-thirds of them left the company; many were college students and young women who had worked under orders from the armed forces. But Toyota was left with 3,700 employees.

A few months after the war, when the General Headquarters of the Allied Forces (GHQ) granted the Japanese government permission to resume truck manufacturing with a maximum capacity of 1,500 units per month for the entire industry, Toyota reopened part of its production lines. But it had to continue with miscellaneous side businesses such as

119

the production of metal cookware, chinaware, furniture, and so on, to maintain its employees. These were dismal days for the automobile industry.

But Kiichirō saw a bright side. As peace was restored, he was convinced the day would come when Toyota could concentrate on the production of passenger vehicles for the first time in its history. The dream he had cherished throughout the long years of hardship would be realized. Consequently, in October 1945 he requested that his engineers develop a passenger vehicle with the following specifications:

1. Good fuel economy
2. An engine capacity of between 1,000 and 1,500 cc
3. 4.5 meters or less in length
4. Simple construction and precision performance

While pursuing truck manufacturing on a limited scale and several side businesses, the company and its allied group went through a period of restructuring. First, at the end of August 1945, the company's truck body plant was separated to form Toyota Auto Body. The Spinning and Weaving Department of Toyoda Loom, which had been added during the war, became an independent company again in May 1950 (later renamed Toyoda Spinning and Weaving Company). The manufacturing facilities for airplane production were sold to a group member company, Aichi Kōgyō (later Aisin Seiki) in June 1946. In September 1947, Toyoda Industry Company, the holding company of the Toyoda group, was dissolved and the trading department formed a new company, Nissin Tsūshō Company, in July 1948. Finally, in December 1949, Toyota separated its Electrical Parts Department, which came to be known as Nippondenso Company.

There was also a need for internal rehabilitation. For instance, a number of machines and other equipment, dispersed in rural districts to avoid damage from bombing, were brought back to the plant. As most of the production facilities, including these machines, had been claimed and registered as reparation goods, the company had to maintain them in the best condition possible even when they were not in use.

In 1947 GHQ allowed the company to start production of passenger vehicles, although the volume was not to exceed 300 units per year. Two years later (in October 1949), however, GHQ lifted all restrictions regarding the manufacturing of motorcars. By that time a number of prototype passenger vehicle models had been experimented on and marketed in the guise of small pick-up trucks. While marketing commercial vehicles, the company faced a series of technical problems and user complaints, which were overcome by the engineering staff led by Kiichirō himself. As the government's Economic Reconstruction Plan proceeded, it seemed as if the automobile market would start to recover, although it was still dominated by small- and medium-size trucks.

Beginning in the latter half of 1949, however, Toyota was caught in a financial crisis caused by the shrinkage of the automobile market. In April 1949, GHQ had ordered the Japanese government to follow the so-called Dodge Line. The policies included, among other things, the maintenance of a balanced government budget, the abolition of government subsidies to industries, and the adoption of a uniform foreign exchange rate. While the Dodge plan cooled the postwar inflation that had been a source of instability in civilian life, it also threw the economy into a serious recession. This naturally affected Toyota by reducing sales and access to working capital. The company also experienced a labor dispute that lasted two months. In 1950 the marketing division was incorporated as Toyota Motor Sales Company, with financial backing from a banking syndicate.

Immediately after the strike was over in July 1950, Kiichirō resigned from the presidency, taking responsibility for the company's unfavorable business performance. He was succeeded by Ishida Taizō, then president of Toyoda Automatic Loom. However, Ishida was no stranger to Toyota, as he had been head clerk of the Toyoda family and had long worked under the directorship of Toyoda Risaburō. At the same time, the Teikoku Bank (renamed Mitsui Bank in 1954), the company's lead bank, installed Nakagawa Fukio in the position of managing director.

Shortly afterwards, the Korean War brought sizable special procurement orders from the U.S. military. These could not have come at a better time, for, as a consequence of a dramatic change in market structure, many Japanese automobile manufacturers had just completed a series of drastic measures to modernize their production and upgrade their technological level. A number of modern high performance machines were imported, and many foreign production technologies introduced. Toyota was no exception, although it never had a comprehensive technological agreement with any foreign firm to assemble foreign models, as many of its competitors did.

Under the direction of Ishida, top management formulated a five-year plan for modernization of the company's production facilities, which was to start on 1 April 1951. The plan aimed at doubling monthly production capacity from 1,500 units to 3,000 units with no increase in the number of employees. To achieve this objective, a fund of 5.8 million yen was provided, and the following eight sub-targets were established:

1. The replacement of old, wornout machines with new ones
2. Improvement in production efficiency through the rationalization of production lines and of material handling systems
3. Improvement in product quality by introducing efficient, high precision machines
4. Improvement in working conditions by upgrading safety measures, lighting and sanitation facilities
5. The rationalization of production management systems through the use of various communication devices
6. Reduced utility usage (electricity, etc.) to cut down on manufacturing cost
7. Improvement in the standard of inspection by the introduction of automatic testing devices
8. The rationalization of administrative procedures by the adoption of various business machines

As it happened, the government disposed of a number of machine tools owned and used by the army arsenals at nominal prices. Many of these machines were old, but of high performance standards and had been maintained in excellent condition. About 200 were procured by Toyota in 1953, and consequently contributed enormously to the attainment of these targets. Throughout the process of modernization,

Toyota, like other leading manufacturers in Japan, emphasized special-purpose automatic machines.

Towards the end of the five-year plan (in January 1955), Toyota introduced the Crown (1500 cc) as its first mass-produced passenger vehicle. The introduction of the Crown was not only the realization of Kiichirō's dream, but also the beginning of the company's phenomenal growth. However, Kiichirō had not lived to see the Crown. He died suddenly on 27 March 1952 at the age of 57.

Because of Kiichirō's untimely demise, Ishida, who had planned to step down in the summer of 1952, carried on to direct the company until 1961, when he was succeeded by Nakagawa Fukio. In 1967, Toyoda Eiji, who, in his youth, had received extensive on-the-job training from Kiichirō, his cousin, on every aspect of automobile manufacturing, became president.

With the Crown as a start, a series of new passenger car models was released one after another: the Corona (1000 cc), introduced in 1957, and the Publica (700 cc), which in 1961 opened a new age of public motorization in Japan with the catch phrase "a $1,000 car." Another best-seller, the Corolla (1100 cc) was added to the product line in 1966, followed by the Century (3400 cc; 1967), the Sprinter (1968), the Mark II (1968), the Carina (1970), and the Celica (1970). In a similar fashion, truck and other commercial vehicle product lines were also expanded in the succeeding years.

With a product line gradually diversifying in response to growing domestic demand, the company's production and sales set new records almost every year. At the time of the Korean War, the company surpassed the highest production figures of the war years (2,000 units/month). In 1957 output reached 30,000 units per month, in 1968 it reached 100,000 units, and 200,000 in 1972.

This rapid growth was possible because the company continued to expand production while maintaining efforts at rationalization. In fact, most of the company's profits were reinvested in expansion and modernization. By the end of the five-year plan (1956), for instance, the production capacity of the Koromo plant, renamed the Honsha (head office) plant, was extended to 3,000 units per month. In the following two years, the plant was further enlarged to 10,000 units per month with the addition of new shops for foundry, forging, heat-treatment, pressing, machining and final assembly.

In 1958, the company began the construction of a new plant 2.5 km away from the Honsha plant. The first stage of construction of the Motomachi plant was completed in June 1959. It was the first factory specializing in passenger car production in Japan, and was filled with advanced production facilities such as multi-welding machines, under-drive pressing machines, quick-die-changing systems and 300-meter main conveyor lines equipped with shuttle mechanisms, etc. Successive expansions filled the site by 1964, so a third and fourth plant were erected, starting operation in 1965 and 1966, respectively. (The third plant, Kamigō, manufactured engines and transmissions, and the fourth, at Takaoka, was engaged in body stamping and passenger car assembly.)

Meanwhile, Toyota established business relations with Hino Motors Company (in 1966), and with Daihatsu Motor Company (in 1967), both of which came to share in the production of some Toyota-nameplate vehicles. Then more plants were added: Miyoshi in 1968 (chassis parts manufacturing), Tsutsumi in 1970 (passenger car manufacturing), and Myōchi in 1973 (chassis parts manufacturing). An eighth plant (Shimoyama) was established to specialize in production of emission control devices, which were needed to meet legal restrictions on exhaust emissions.

During this growth process, the automobile industry was strongly supported and protected by the Japanese government by means of economic policy measures such as various bounty systems, high import tariffs, restrictions on foreign investment, etc. Toyota was a major beneficiary of this support. However, one must not discount the importance of the company's own efforts in its successes. Even in a sheltered market, Toyota's remarkable growth after World War II, accompanied by continuous introduction of new models, would have been impossible but for the tremendous efforts made by company

124

personnel at all levels.

According to Toyota management, the quality of its products equalled international standards by 1965, and from then on, greater emphasis was put on cost reduction. Improvements in product quality and in cost economy have been made continuously, culminating in the competitive strength of Toyota cars in the worldwide market.

Equally important, Toyota's success owed much to the ancillary firms that cooperated closely with it in raising the quality of automobile parts and components. Throughout the process of development, the primary firm concentrated on the manufacture of a handful of functional components such as engines, transmissions, axles, and bodies, and a few highly strategic parts, plus the final assembly operations. This meant most of the numerous parts and components came from ancillary firms. Consequently, they were obliged to expand production at the same rate as Toyota. Some of them had to expand even faster, because Toyota discontinued in-house production of some parts and components.

4.2.3   The Domestication of Parts Manufacturing

Toyota's first prototype automobile in the 1930s, the model A1, took design principles from three American models, a Chevrolet, the Ford Model T, and a DeSoto. In the initial stage of experimentation, Kiichirō's policy was to make all the functional parts and components interchangeable with those of the three American cars. As soon as Toyota formally established the automobile division, its engineering team prepared detailed drawings of all the parts and components on the basis of sketches of the relevant items, disassembled from the three models. As the drawing went on, the team started to manufacture selected parts and components, as well as to search for domestic supplies of other parts.

Engines

Kiichirō chose engine production as the first item to be achieved by his team. There were several reasons for this. First and foremost, the engine was one of the most essential components. Second, the company had a relatively strong technological potential for engine manufacturing. As a loom producer, it had its own foundry and machining shops, and had experience with these processes. Moreover, the workers and engineers had already been accustomed to high-performance modern machinery, introduced by Kiichirō, prior to the establishment of the automobile division.

In June 1934, after a final check of the drawings, the team started trial production of cylinder blocks and gears, followed shortly by the production of pistons. When the foundry operation began, however, it produced nothing but piles of defective products. The castings were obviously of poor quality even to untrained eyes. The main reason seemed to be the poor quality of the molds, which resulted from an inappropriate choice of basic materials. Toyoda Automatic Loom had been accustomed to making casting molds using a mixture of river sand, coke powder, and clay. But the inner structure of a cylinder block is far more complicated than the forged parts of automatic looms.

Facing this difficulty, the team tried all the molding techniques they knew, such as plastering the core surface with carbon powder or black lead, inserting thin wires as paths for the cores, and others. Nevertheless, all their efforts produced only minimal improvement.

About two months later, Kan returned from the United States, where he had been buying machines, and suggested a method he had seen practiced at Ford. It consisted of using a mixture of silver sand and certain plant oils. The first trial was a complete failure. Although the mold looked perfect, the molten metal exploded when it was poured into the mold. The team stuck to this method, however, for lack of anything better, constantly changing the formula, while group members traveled to many places searching for better sand. After a month of experimentation, they managed to get good-lookings results. However, when they tooled the castings with boring machines, a number of blow holes were discovered inside the castings.

Autumn had begun, but the team was still at a trial-and-error stage. This time, however, the design of the engine was modified to eliminate several technical difficulties, while maintaining the interchangeability of the parts with the original model. With the design modifications, toward the end of September, the team finally succeeded in producing good castings for all the necessary engine parts. The parts were carefully polished and assembled. The result was the first prototype engine, and it functioned satisfactorily.

There still remained the problem of performance. The prototype produced an output of only 30 HP at 3,000 rpm, compared to Chevrolet's 60 HP at 3,000 rpm. The crew checked to see which parts caused the poor performance by replacing one part at a time with identical items from the Chevrolet model and testing the engine performance. By the process of elimination, they detected a significant difference in engine power when their own intake-manifold was mounted. A further inspection led them to conclude the difference was because of the lack of smoothness in the inner surface of the manifold. The manifold was recast and retooled carefully to achieve a smoother inner surface. With this recast part, performance improved 50 percent, reaching 45 HP at 3,000 rpm.

Similar efforts were continuously made day after day, but the performance of the engine never exceeded 50 HP. The problem was eventually solved in May 1935 whin Kan designed a new cylinder head, introducing a circular-motion effect inside the head to improve exhaust efficiency. With this new cylinder head (named after Kan), the engine easily registered 62 HP at 3,000 rpm—a level slightly better than the Chevrolet engine being copied.

Transmissions and Differential Gears

Shortly after the start of engine manufacturing, another team set out to manufacture various transmissions and differential systems, which were then being obtained from the Japanese branch of Republic Company, a U.S.-based international supplier of replacement gears for Chevrolet and Ford cars.

At the outset, it was decided that the design principles for the gears should follow Ford. After a few months of trials, however, they switched to a Chevrolet model because the Ford gears were too sophisticated. In fact, even with the simpler Chevrolet model, the engineers met insurmountable difficulties in replication.

Eventually, the chief engineer of the team, Iwaoka, was dispatched to Tōhoku Imperial University, where a high school and college classmate of Kiichirō's (Professor Nukiyama Shirō) was in charge of the mechanical engineering department. At the professor's suggestion, Iwaoka spent forty days with Dr. Naruse Masao, a student of the professor and a leading scholar in his field, well-known for his unique analytical approach. Naruse gave Iwaoka personal lessons on the most advanced theory of gear engineering. As the special lectures went on, Iwaoka proceeded with an analysis of the Chevrolet gears that he had brought with him.

The secret of the Chevrolet gear lay in its being based on "involute curve theory," a then new theory in gear manufacturing. The analysis was completed in due course, and when Iwaoka went back to Toyota in mid-December 1934, he found little difficulty in designing all the gears the company needed. However, he still faced a number of manufacturing problems. It took another year before he obtained a sufficient degree of precision and durability in his products, through improved materials and tooling technology. In the manufacturing stage, Naruse often times visited the shop and shared his expertise with Iwaoka and his team. It was an exciting time for the young scholar, since it was his first opportunity to apply his theoretical knowledge to practical matters. (Toyota's involvement with Naruse is also described in Naruse 1976, pp. 213–17.)

Other Parts and Components

Beside engines and transmissions, Toyota manufactured axles and bodies, although hand-made body parts were purchased from outside in the initial stages. Tires, batteries, and window glass were already available in standard specifications from dependable domestic makers.

For other parts and components, Kiichirō had to dispatch some of his team to look for reliable domestic suppliers. The company had little tehnological expertise in fields other than foundry and machining.

In general, there were three possible sources for the domestic supply of automobile parts and components. First, there were the spare-parts manufacturers that had mushroomed around big metropolitan districts, catering to the growing demand of automobile users (the number of automobiles exceeded 100,000 in 1933). Second, Japanese automobile manufacturers shared varying degrees of common interest in locating domestic suppliers of parts and components. In certain cases, therefore, Kiichirō's group chose suppliers already engaged in providing parts for other domestic assemblers. Third, the team members approached selected industrialists, and asked them to undertake trial manufacturing of certain parts and components. In general, it took several years before all the items could be supplied by local companies.

To give a few examples, Toyota entered subcontracting agreements for radiators and bearings with two large-scale manufacturers in Tokyo. It also found a medium-scale forging shop in Tokyo that could supply forged parts such as crankshafts and connecting rods, although the company, especially in the initial stage, relied on imported items as well. Four wheel makers were located in the Nagoya and Osaka districts. Toyota was unsatisfied with the two electric machinery producers supplying various electrical parts and components, and switched to in-house production as soon as its project team succeeded in developing products superior in quality. The department, which engaged in the production of electric parts, was separated after World War II to become an independent corporation, the Nippondenso Company.

Raw Materials and the Means of Production

The domestic source of iron and steel items was Yawata Iron and Steel Works, the largest steel manufacturer in Japan. The poor quality of the materials, however, often created serious problems for Toyota's production lines. Not only was the capacity and technology of Japanese steelmaking backward by international standards, but the automobile industry was not a particularly attractive customer for steelmakers because of the industry's limited consumption. It was only after World War II that steel manufacturers paid serious attention to the specific requirements of automobile manufacturers. Toyota was fortunate, however, because it was able to purchase specifically formulated iron and steel materials from Toyoda Automatic Loom, which had a small iron foundry. Later, when demand surpassed the capacity of the foundry, Toyota established its own steel shop in its Koromo plant. The steel mill spun off in 1940 to form an independent corporation, Aichi Seikō, 21 percent of whose equity was still owned by Toyota in the mid 1980s.

Until well into the 1950s, most of the machinery was imported from the United States and Europe (especially Germany), as the domestic supply of machinery was limited only to general-purpose types. However, Toyota made some of its small-scale machinery, and encouraged domestic producers.

Chapter 5

SELECTED ANCILLARY FIRMS

5.1   Aisan Industry Company, Ltd.[1]

5.1.1   Company Profile

Incorporated	:	December 1938
Origins	:	1924
Stock held by primary firms (1979)	:	33.9% (Toyota)
Sales (1975)	:	¥24.6 billion
Profit before tax (1975)	:	¥988 million
Production lines	:	carburetors, fuel pumps, engine valves, synchronizing rings and others
Number of employees (1975)	:	2,500
Number of factories (1975)	:	2
Number of branch offices (1975)	:	5 (of which 3 were located abroad)

Aisan is one of the largest firms supplying parts and components to Toyota. Founded in 1938 as an arms manufacturer, Aisan grew steadily after the Korean War (see Table 5.1).

Aisan's two factories, each devoted to the production of different product lines, are about one hour's driving time from Toyota's engine plant. Inasmuch as the company emphasized in-house technology development, it had constructed extensive research and development facilities. In addition, it maintained a technical agreement with Carter, a

---

[1]   This section draws on the company-published history, Aisan Kōgyō (1973). Interviews were conducted in 1976.

Table 5.1. Selected Data on Aisan Industry Co.

Year	Paid-in capital (million yen)	Total sales (million yen)	Profit before tax (million yen)	Debt-equity ratio (percent)	Employ-ment	Number of engineers	Value added per employee (thousand yen)	Capital intensity (thousand yen)	Average monthly wage per employee (thousand yen)
1938	0.5	0.1	−0.	95.0	80	9	—	5	—
1945	0.5	1	0.2	41.5	130	14	—	2	—
1950	3	111	5	20.9	381	41	142	31	8
1955	27	222	8	38.9	309	33	353	86	15
1960	100	1,167	99	33.9	648	70	736	515	20
1965	300	2,440	136	31.9	1,180	127	1,009	953	23
1970	600	9,655	245	17.5	2,036	220	1,953	2,376	41
1975	800	24,584	988	19.6	2,494	294	4,794	3,286	103

Sources: Aisan Industry Company.

leading carburetor manufacturer in the United States.

5.1.2 Historical Development

The company may be traced back to 1924, when Fujita Tatsujirō established himself as a subcontractor making ring spindles for a manufacturer of cotton spinning looms. As a young man, Fujita had worked for the Army Arsenal for some years, gaining work experience and expertise in machinery production. These were the principal assets with which he started his own business. Fujita's venture proved to be a success, and his company was duly reorganized as a joint stock company in 1927. Situated in Nagoya, Fujita Company operated as a partly-owned subsidiary of Toyoda Automatic Loom Works.

In 1938 the Army Arsenal found it necessary to increase arms production. Consequently, it placed an order with Fujita for a substantial quantity of hand grenades. Finding itself incapable of fulfilling the demand, Fujita decided to set up a completely independent organization, later named Aisan Industy Company, Ltd. The move to establish the new company was partly underwritten by Toyoda Automatic Loom and by Hirata Cotton Textile Manufacturing, then customers of Fujita.

Aisan Industry was incorporated and began operations in late 1938, with Fujita as president. The company drew heavily from the manpower, machinery and various kinds of technical assistance transferred from Fujita Company. Many of the old machines and equipment were redesigned and modified to suit the manufacturing requirements for munitions.

The new company had approximately 80 employees, its plant had 3,760 square meters of floor space, including three machine shops, a heat treatment shop, forging shop, trial manufacturing shop, offices, dining hall and kitchen (see Figure 5.1). It had a paid-up capital of only half a million yen.

The war against China was already in progress, and demand from the Arsenal was growing. The new company's immediate task was to increase production. Working hours were extended as much as possible for all employees, and the number of employees was gradually increased.

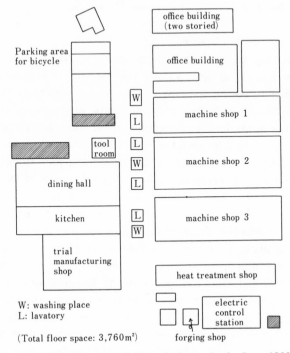

Fig. 5.1. Plant Layout of Aisan Industry in the Late 1930 s

The company also opened its own technical training school. All materials were supplied by the Arsenal, so procurement was not a problem. In 1941, Aisan came under the direct control of the armed forces to manufacture various arms products including some machined parts for military planes.

Meanwhile, Fujita resigned and Ishida Taizō took over the presidency. Ishida was then managing director of Toyoda Automatic Loom, and later became president of Toyota Motor. As World War II neared its end, manufacturing operations declined because of inadequate material supplies from the Arsenal. Finally, the major part of its operations ceased when the main factory was destroyed in a bombing raid in May, 1945.

Search for a New Direction

Military production came to a halt as a consequence of defeat in the war. Aisan was closed down temporarily, but reopened quickly, transformed into a manufacturer of parts and components under special arrangements with Toyota Motor. Two weeks after the war ended, president Ishida announced the company would begin producing automobile carburetors and a few other auto parts that had been manufactured by Toyoda Loom. Aisan received from Toyoda Loom a team of 46 men and a set of production machinery. They arrived about a month after Ishida's announcement, and carburetor production started on 1 October 1945. The team consisted of one senior engineer (Yamamoto Rokujirō, who was to become factory manager), one design engineer, four section managers, four foremen, and thirty-six experienced production workers. The machinery arrived in two batches. The first set consisted of 28 multi-purpose lathes, while the second set had 11 items, including several types of machine tools such as two milling machines, three boring machines, and three machines.

For the first few years, the company experienced various difficulties. Aisan's original personnel were completely unfamiliar with the production processes and technologies for auto parts. At that time the company had 179 machines, but the older machinery and equipment had to be either readjusted or remodeled. In addition, the company had to rebuild its bombed-out factory. The company also suffered a severe shortage of materials. Moreover, in June 1946 all its production facilities were designated as reparation goods to be claimed by the allied forces. The company was, therefore, ordered to keep all the machines clean and in the best working conditions, and was told that they might be taken away at any time on short notice. Fortunately, the designation was withdrawn in May 1948, but it was only in April 1952 that all the production facilities came back under the company's control.

Despite these conditions, production increased in step with growth in automobile production by Toyota. In addition to machinery, Toyota

135

extended technological assistance to the company. Aisan's product quality in carburetors, fuel-pumps and oil-brakes was recognized in mid-1948 by the central government, when it designated the said products as "qualified automobile components."

The company added some loom parts for Toyoda Loom to its product line in June 1948. The postwar years saw an increased demand for textile products, but many textile machines had been converted or cannibalized for production of weapons. As new orders for looms began rolling in, Toyoda Loom received more orders than it could possibly cope with. At about the same time, Aisan also started to manufacture carburetors for the Agricultural Machinery Department of Toyoda Loom.

In 1950, Ishida resigned the presidencies of Aisan and Toyoda Loom and became president of Toyota Motor Company. Nishimura Shōhachirō, managing director of Toyota Motor, joined Aisan, as president. In 1953, the conclusion of the Korean War induced another serious recession, and Ishida resumed the presidency of Aisan concurrently with that of Toyota Motor.

New Age of Growth

In 1957, Aisan entered a new phase of its development as Matsui Isaku joined the company as managing director. Matsui was a managing director of Toyoda Loom and president of its Mexican subsidiary before moving to Aisan. In October 1957, Aisan moved its head office and main factory from its small original site to a new factory, the Kyōwa plant, which had a land space of 17,521 square meters and a floor space of 7,781 square meters (including the office area).

As managing director, Matsui was authorized to supervise the overall management of the company while president Ishida acted as a policy advisor. Having acquainted himself with the operations of the company, Matsui began a series of dramatic reforms. First, he decided to discontinue the subcontracting operation for Toyoda Loom and moved to direct all the company's resources to automobile parts manufacturing. In this regard, Matsui often visited Toyota Motor to seek more orders.

Having narrowed the company's focus, Matsui directed management to undertake modernization and strengthening of production facilities and technologies, with the goal of becoming a high-quality parts manufacturer. The first major step in this endeavor was moving die-casting and plating operations in-house. The company had previously relied on subcontractors. This was prompted by a desire to produce parts in addition to carburetors. However, Toyota's reply to requests for orders for other parts was always the same: "How dare yor ask to produce all those items without even having a die-casting device?"

To help Aisan bring production in-house, Toyota purchased a 250 ton die-casting machine as well as a plating facility and loaned them to Aisan. In addition, Toyota lent testing equipment, provided necessary guidance in the development of engineering designs, and finally offered a training course in production engineering. As a result, the production staff of Aisan found no difficulty in handling the new die-casting machine, although repeated experiments were necessary to master production technology and thus improve product quality.

In addition to die-casting, the company installed several belt coveyor systems to allow mass production of various components. All these innovations took place in about a year (1957–58). The company also actively invested in modern, high performance machinery. Altogether, 149 new machines were acquired and introduced onto the floor of the Kyōwa plant. Toyota helped Aisan finance this transformation, lending about 40 million yen from 1956 to 1958 (see Table 5.2 below).

Modernization and expansion continued in the 1960s. For example, the internalization of the die-casting process was followed by the introduction of a die-making process in 1960. Eight selected production workers were sent to Toyota to receive training. During the training, which lasted an average of 45 days, the trainees became deeply impressed with the high morale of Toyota employees.

As the domestic and foreign automobile markets expanded, procurement orders from Toyota showed a significant increase every year. The company's product line expanded year after year, as Toyota transferred to Aisan its in-house operations for various components, such as rocker-arms, vacuum pumps, and engine governors. The number of carburetors and fuel pump models also increased as Toyota's product line was diversified.

In 1960 a second factory was established, approximately the same size as the first. Lines to make engine valves were set up, taking over production from Toyota. The new factory space had been badly needed to relieve the strained capacity of existing production lines.

Again, trainees, this time two batches, each consisting of two engineers and two production workers, were dispatched to Toyota to practice the actual handling of the lines in a two-shift operation. The training lasted nearly two months, beginning in early June and lasting through July. The machining process was moved to Aisan's new factory, installed in three days, and production began immediately. The forging and heat treatment processes followed. At the time of the transfers, the machines and equipment were loaned by Toyota and were subsequently purchased by Aisan.

These efforts at modernization and expansion continued and even accelerated with the passage of time. For instance, in 1961 the company adopted a chrome plating process. In 1963, an independent factory was built to specialize in aluminum die-casting. In the latter case, technical training took place at Aisin Industry Company, a producer of precision machinery and another member of the Toyota Group. As capital formation progressed, greater emphasis was placed on the use of fully-automated devices to save on skilled manpower as well as to improve product precision. Along with this policy, Matsui, who was promoted to the presidency in 1965, particularly stressed the importance of quality control.

A milestone for the company was the signing in 1962 of a technological agreement with the Carter Carburetor Division of ICF Industries, a leading carburetor manufacturer in the United States. Contact was initially established through Nippondenso Company, which had gotten news of ICF's search for a Japanese partner. ICF and Aisan held a series of meetings in the U.S. and Japan, while exchanging inspectors to check each other's production and research facilities. At ICF's request, a representative of Toyota also attended the meetings. In fact, establishment of the intercompany relationship was no mere coincidence, as Toyota's original carburetor, prior to the transfer of production to Aisan, had been modelled after Carter's. Royalty payments were set at two percent of Aisan's sales of the items concerned; this was reduced to one percent in 1965 and to one-half percent in 1967, provided sales exceeded $350 million per annum.

Another important policy objective set by Matsui in the late 1950s was Aisan's financial independence from Toyota. Although the company owed much to the primary firm's generosity, which had manifested itself in repeated direct and indirect financial aid, Matsui viewed it as essential for Aisan to diversify its sources of financing.

As it happened, the central government began in the 1960s to extend various forms of assistance to the machine-producing industry, with special emphasis on medium- and small-scale firms. Under the Provisional Act for the Promotion of Machinery Industries (*Kishin hō*), the Japan Development Bank occasionally extended sizeable loans to Aisan. Aisan no longer found it necessary to depend on Toyota for financing. Table 5.2 records the historical circumstances regarding the company's reliance on different types of financial resources.

The forms of Toyota's technical assistance underwent subtle changes as Aisan gained strength as an independent corporation. In the 1950s Aisan had to seek considerable guidance from Toyota to improve its statistical quality control system, which had been adopted in 1953 at the insistence of Matsui. Also, the company needed special help from the primary firm in order to develop an industrial engineering plan in 1959. In 1960, however, greater emphasis was placed in production management. For instance, Toyota's unique approach to inventory and production control, commonly called the "*kanban* (just-in-time, or supermarket) method," was introduced in close consultation with Toyota.

Finally, as better production management began to improve product quality and delivery times, emphasis was shifted to cost management, as exemplified by the frequent use of terms such as value analysis (VA) and value engineering (VE). On these occasions, Toyota provided Aisan with

139

Table 5.2.   Loans Extended to Aisan, 1956–75

(In million yen)

Fiscal year	Loans extended by			Total
	Japan Development Bank	Commercial banks	Toyota	
1956	0	0	22.4	22.4
1957	0	70	7.6	77.6
1958	0	0	10	10
1959	0	60	0	60
1960	27	90	0	117
1961	30	150	0	180
1962	30	160	110	300
1963	30	110	0	140
1964	60	350	0	410
1965	50	170	0	220
1966	50	170	0	220
1967	50	560	0	610
1968	150	1,030	0	1,180
1969	200	530	0	730
1970	250	1,160	0	1,410
1971	0	370	0	370
1972	0	0	0	0
1973	450	30	0	480
1974	400	2,500	0	2,900
1975	300	720	0	1,020

Sources: Aisan Industry Company.

a series of introductory training programs, which the majority of Aisan's employees were invited to attend. These programs were naturally supported by many forms of assistance as the company faced problems in implementing its production objectives. In addition, through the association of Toyota's ancillary firms, *Kyōhō Kai*, Aisan picked up much

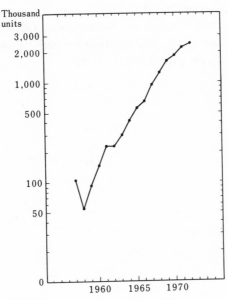

Fig. 5.2.   Growth of Carburetor Production by Aisan: 1957–72

Notes: Semi-log scales.
Sources: Estimated from Aisan Kōgyō (1973), p. 371.

technical information and useful knowledge on production management from the experience of other Toyota-related parts suppliers. As a consequence of such efforts, Aisan Industry achieved rapid sales growth, and remarkable improvement in production facilities and management practices. Figure 5.2 offers some statistical data pertaining to this.

In 1960 Aisan established an association of its own ancillary firms, consisting of 20 member companies selected from a total of 66 that had subcontracting arrangements with Aisan. Selection was primarily on the basis of the length of the business relationship, and the degree of dependence on Aisan, as measured by the proportion of Aisan's procurement in total sales. The association, called *Aikyō Kai*, held periodic meetings to exchange ideas and share experiences. It ran joint training courses, coordinated multi-company endeavors to improve managerial efficiency through the formation of QC (quality control) circles, and encouraged value engineering and so on, all in close collaboration with the primary firm, Aisan.

5.2   Kojima Press Industry Company, Ltd.[2]

5.2.1   Company Profile

Origins	:	May 1917
Stock held by primary firms (1978)	:	1.6% (Toyota)
Product lines	:	various metal pressed auto parts (such as air cleaner cases), plastic auto parts (such as dashboards and front grills) and pressing dies
Number of employees (1976)	:	867
Number of factories (1976)	:	2

In the late 1970s Kojima Press Industry formed the Kojima Group with the following eight sister companies:

Company names	Products (functions)
Kojima General Planning Co. Incorporated: 1967 Sales (1976): ¥36 million	Planning and information center for the members of the group
Kojima Sangyō Co. Incorporated: 1962 Sales (1976): ¥2.1 billion	Processing and trading of steel, plastic and petrochemical materials, and manufacturing of pressing dies
Uchihama Industry Co. Incorporated: 1961 Sales (1976): ¥600 million	Pressing, welding and painting of various metal auto parts, and manufacturing of reinforced plastic auto parts
Wako Plastics Industry Co. Incorporated: 1942 Sales (1976): ¥1.9 billion	Manufacturing of various plastic auto parts (such as bush-knobs, nylon washers, air ducts and plugholes) and shells for plastic moulding
Shinwa Industry Co.	Manufacturing of various small pressed

---

[2]   The company-published history, Kojima Press (1975) is the principal written source for this section. Interviews were conducted in 1976.

Incorporated: 1968
Sales (1976): ¥1.2 billion

Wakayama Industry Co.
Incorporated: 1962
Sales (1976): ¥300 million

Kiso Industry Co.
Incorporated: 1970
Sales (1976): ¥30 million

Kojima Tool and Die Co.
Incorporated: 1966
Sales (1976): $230,000

parts (such as ashtrays, wire harness clamps, core props, washers and others)

Manufacturing of auto parts for special-purpose vehicles (e.g., buses, jeeps, etc.)

Manufacturing of machine tools, gauges, jigs and fixtures, and small pressed auto parts

Design and manufacturing of shells for plastic moulding in the U.S.A.

The members of the Kojima Group were all specialists whose products and services were delivered mostly to the Toyota Motor Company, with the exception of Kojima Tool and Die, which was located in the United States. A small percentage of the products were consumed internally. In 1976 the group supplied more than 6,000 different types of parts and components to Toyota. Job orders for the parts and components came first to Kojima Press and were then distributed among the group members according to their expertise and rates of capacity utilization.

5.2.2 Historical Development

Kojima Press Industry Company and its group were founded and developed by Kojima Hamakichi, who was already 46 years old when he started auto parts manufacturing. Until then he had gone through a long period of hardship, searching for the right line of business for himself.

Kojima Hamakichi was born in Chiba Prefecture in 1891 as the second son of a craftsman, Watanabe Torakichi, who was well known in the region as an expert in oar-making. Hamakichi's original family name was Watanabe, but was changed when he was adopted by the Kojima family at the time of his marriage. At the age of 12, when his mother died, he went to Tokyo to look for work. For a few days he worked for a trading dealer of raw silk and rice, but finally transferred to a small manufacturer of mosquito coils and body warmers (*kairo*).[3]

As a poor boy having completed only elementary school, Hamakichi had to start work from the very bottom as an apprentice (*detchi*). In those days it was still common for an employer to fire or transfer employees (apprentices in particular) as freely as if they were his own property. Hamakichi was quite lucky in this respect, as his new employer, Kondō Ryōjirō, was a warm-hearted and thoughtful merchant. In turn, the boy was not only a very diligent, hard worker but was also ingeniously talented in creative thinking. He learned from his master, step by step, how to run a business, and discovered specific ways to contribute to the shop's management and eventually to its sales promotion. It was no accident therefore that the boy was gradually recognized by his employer as well as by the customers as an important staff member of the small company.

In 1917, at 26, Hamakichi married Kondō's daughter. She had been adopted by the family of a former chief clerk at the Kondō's shop, named Kojima, who had become an independent (though small) distributor of the products of the Kondō shop stationed in the Nagoya district. Hamakichi's father had been dead for eleven years, so he decided to join his wife's adopted family and succeed to their business. As was the custom in such cases, he took the family name Kojima.

After his marrige, Hamakichi moved to Nagoya to take over the business of his father-in-law, who was now also his adoptive father. Excited by his new environment, he worked even harder to run the business, assisted by his wife and the senior Kojimas. The small shop (Kojima Shōkai, or Kojima Trading Company) was well patronized, and its sales went up steadily with the supply of high-quality products from Kondō.

In 1921, Hamakichi set up a new company in Nagoya jointly with Kondō and another businessman named Kanie Matsutarō, the matchmaker for his marriage, to expand the sales of mosquito coils and body

[3] *Kairo* were small, portable heaters (about 6 × 8 × 1.5 cm) designed to keep a portion of the body (usually the abdominal area) warm. They were generally metal containers tightly packed with charcoal sticks or benzene-soaked asbestos.

warmers. The purpose of the joint venture was simply to sustain and improve Kondō's business, which had been on the decline since the departure of Hamakichi, and was facing financial difficulties brought on by the recession immediately after World War I.

The new company, Nōsan Kōgyō Company, began operation on 3 March 1921. Kanie assumed the presidency and Kondō a managing directorship. Hamakichi was also named a managing director, while he continued to run the small Kojima shop.

For a while the new company seemed to be off to a good start. Unfortunately, however, it was seriously damaged by two big typhoons that hit the Nagoya area in late June and September of 1921. The first typhoon blew away the company's mosquito coil shop and ruined most of its product inventory; the second typhoon caused less damage because of improved preventive action. Tragedy struck again in the form of the Kantō Earthquake in 1923, which killed Kondō and his wife.

Having lost his mentor as well as the most important market for his products, Kojima critically reviewed the status of the joint venture (Nōsan Kōgyō Company). He separated the press shop of the company to form a new corporation (Nippon Kairo) with financial support from a local banker, to specialize in press work. However, the serious nation-wide financial panic of 1927 destroyed all his efforts. Kojima was severely criticized by some stockholders. Because of the internal troubles created by the crisis, Kojima finally withdrew from the joint venture as well as from Nippon Kairo. Both went into bankruptcy two years after he left them.

After this series of difficulties, Kojima had only the small shop inherited from the elder Kojimas. He was already 40 years old. But he had learned many lessons and gained much experience in running a business.

In 1932, Kojima rented from the central government the production facilities of the insolvent Nippon Kairo Company, and started to develop new model mosquito coils and body warmers. New products such as five-colored mosquito coils and colored body-warmer sticks pleased his former customers and attracted new clients.

In this manner, Kojima started to prosper, although the adverse circumstances of prior years had made him slightly more conservative and tight fisted than before. In five years he managed to redeem the production facilities he had rented from the government. No sooner had he accomplished this than he set himself to search for new products. The mosquito coil was sold in the summer season, and was produced during the winter. On the other hand, the body warmer was marketable in the winter season, and manufactured in summer. This meant spring and fall were slow seasons. Kojima wanted to increase the utilization of his production facilities, and started looking for other products.

Entry into the Business of Auto Parts Manufacturing

Kojima read a newspaper account of the government's Automobile Industry Act of 1936 (*Jidōsha seizō jigyō hō*). It was clear to him that the government intended to regulate the operations of GM and Ford in Japan and to encourage the development of a local motorcar industry— a measure to reinforce Japan's military strength. In addition, he happened to know that Toyoda Automatic Loom Works had already established an independent automobile department in the Nagoya area. It did not take much time before he concluded that the production of automobile parts and components might be the answer to the problems he faced. The automobile parts business was not only a year-round activity, but seemed something entirely new and challenging.

By a happy coincidence, a friend of his wife was working for Toyoda Loom. One day in November 1936, with the introduction of this gentleman, Kojima visited Toyoda's procurement office and sought agreement that he be allowed to supply auto parts. Although the reply was a flat no, Kojima did not give up easily. Thus began frequent calls on the Toyoda office. During the nine months that followed, despite persistent negative responses, whenever he found the time, he spent two hours in travel (each way) to visit the Toyota office.

One day in July 1937, Iwaoka Jirō, then chief engineer of Toyoda in charge of auto parts, paid a visit to Kojima. Kojima showed Iwaoka his products and the factory, which was equipped with five presses and employed seven workers, and explained how the company operated.

147

About a week later he was summoned to Toyoda's office and received the first order: several units of sand-carrying buckets for the foundry shop. Though a little disappointed by the simplicity of the product, he did his best to make sure the buckets met the requirements.

Shortly after delivery of the buckets, Kojima was given an opportunity to meet Toyoda Kiichirō, then managing director of Toyota Motor Company, which had been formally organized only several days prior to the meeting. Kiichirō was encouraging, and talked softly but with enthusiasm about the future of the industry. On the same day, Kojima was given Toyota's second order, which was to produce washers. Afterwards, orders for radiator grills and core stays followed.

Restructuring and Involvement in the Toyota Group

The next year (1938) Kojima acquired a 677 square meter piece of land in the neighborhood of his residence and moved his tiny old factory to this larger site. All the wooden structures of the old factory were dismantled and utilized in construction of the new building. He also took this opportunity to procure used machine tools (a few press machines and a shearing machine) through second-hand equipment dealers in Osaka. When construction was completed in May 1938, he renamed his company Kojima Press Manufacturing to commemorate "the new beginning." Growing orders rushed to the new company with Toyota's increasing demand for various parts. By April 1939, Toyota had enlarged the scale of its truck production to 1,000 units per month. Accordingly, Kojima had to eventually give up, though reluctantly, the manufacture of his original product lines, mosquito coils and body warmers, because of the shortage of materials and the shrinkage of the market during World War II.

With the war, a new series of ordeals awaited Kojima. In addition to suffering from incessant air raids, the Nagoya district was twice hit by earthquakes, one in late 1944 and the other in early 1945. It is estimated that more than 4,000 people were killed by the quakes. The loss of an employee and a dormitory caused by the second quake, together with the increasingly heavy bombing, led Kojima to think seriously of the long-standing advice of Toyota that he transfer both his factory and his residence to Koromo, a suburb of Nagoya, where Toyota's factory was located.

Upon the final decision by Kojima to move, Toyota quickly arranged housing not only for Kojima and his 16 employees, but also for Kojima's two neighbors, who wanted to accompany the Kojimas to the new area. Acquisition of the new factory site and physical structures was also aided by the primary firm. Furthermore, Toyota lined up trucks and drivers (in extremely short supply in those days) to help Kojima move his production facilities. It took 60 round trips for the four-ton trucks and more than 40 days to complete the transfer, while avoiding the daily bombings. Kojima Press was by then in possession of 26 machine tools, including ten power presses, three foot presses, four hand presses, one lathe, and two boring machines. At midnight of the final day of the move, after the last truck load of goods departed from Nagoya, the old factory was directly hit by a bomb and destroyed. Having thus managed a safe transfer, Kojima told his family and employees that they should never point their feet toward the primary firm when they went to bed. This is a traditional Japanese expression of deep gratitude.

As the local automobile industry grew in the wake of the 1936 law restricting foreign activity, some of the subcontractors supplying automobile parts and components to Toyota thought it worthwhile to meet regularly to exchange ideas and other pertinent information. Their first meeting was held in Tokyo on 8 November 1939, with representatives of 18 participating companies and four persons invited from Toyota's procurement office. At this meeting, the group was formally organized and named the *Toyota Kyōryoku Kai* (Toyota Cooperative Circle).

During World War II the Circle contributed in no small way to sustaining efficient production of trucks in the face of severe shortages of materials and production resources. Meetings were convened periodically at Toyota's Koromo plant, and members cooperated with the primary firm in such matters as materials supply, replacement of drafted skilled manpower, and the evacuation of factories and of production equipment. In December 1943, the Circle was reorganized to become a more integrated organization and to include Toyota as a formal member. It changed its name to *Kyōhō Kai* and elected Akai Hisayoshi, then executive vice president of Toyota, as chairman. Kojima was chosen to serve as vice chairman. Soon, Kojima was devoting more than half of his time and energy to the association, working out better means of coordination between the primary and ancillary firms and among the ancillary firms. The service came naturally to Kojima as he felt deeply obligated to the primary firm.

Postwar Reconstruction and Preparation for Future Growth

When the war ended, automobile production in Japan came to a halt. Consequently, Toyota drastically cut the number of its employees. At that time Kojima employed eleven workers, who lived under the same roof with the Kojima family. Kojima let five of them return to their home provinces. With the remaining six, he began making various metal wares, using the worn-out machines and inventory of materials left over in his factory. All of the products were related to food production in one way or another: agricultural equipment such as hoes and spades, many kinds of kitchen utensils such as pans, ladles, baking grills, etc. He even invented a simple weeder.

Kojima kept himself busy visiting Toyota almost every day to discuss with the latter's procurement staff how to reestablish the network of parts suppliers. In January 1948, when *Kyōhō Kai* was split into three geographical divisions, Tōkai, Tokyo and Kansai, he assumed the chairmanship of the *Tōkai Kyōhō Kai*, which coincided with the Nagoya division of the old *Kyōhō Kai*.

Hamakichi had two sons-in-law, who, like him, had taken the name Kojima at the time of their marriages. The elder, Hideshi, had been Hamakichi's right-hand man since joining the family in 1941. The second, Gorō, had worked in Toyota's procurement office before being drafted into the army. On returning from the war in December 1945, he married and resumed work at Toyota. Gorō advised Hamakichi that the government would release used press machines of superior quality from the Army Arsenal, and Hamakichi jumped at the opportunity. In addition, the company purchased some second-hand, high-quality machine tools from Toyota at nominal prices. The acquisition of those machines renovated the company's worn-out production system. Thanks to them, Kojima Press was able to match the phenomenal rate of growth of the primary firm.

Gorō transferred to Kojima Press at the end of 1946, when Hamakichi's eldest natural son, Ryōjirō, reached 18. With these three young men as partners, Hamakichi (then 55) was ready to expand his company. However, a few years later, Hamakichi faced a serious health problem for the first time in the 57 years of his life: he suffered a cerebral hemorrhage in 1948 while walking to the railway station on his way to Toyota. Fortunately, he recovered from this within a month, and went back to his busy schedule, although from then on he had to carry a walking stick to support himself. In January 1950, Hamakichi incorporated as a stock company, appointing himself chairman, Ryōjirō, president, Hideshi, executive director, and Gorō, managing director. The starting capital of the new company was 500,000 yen.

Hamakichi began other new ventures as well. He established a new company for Toyota in 1948, shortly after recovering from his illness. The main functions of the company (named Kyōhō Shearing) were to recover the usable portions of scrapped steel sheets piled up in Toyota's body-stamping shop, and to supply them to ancillary firms engaged in the production of small-sized pressed auto parts. In 1953, he assigned Hideshi to begin a study on the development of plastic auto parts. The study led to the establishment of a plastics division in 1957, producing such things as ashtrays and front-grill components. In 1957 the company established its own research and testing laboratory, albeit of modest size—just 26.4 square meters of floor space. This was remarkable progress for the company, for it had previously relied on the primary firm for all its testing procedures which were necessary for product improvement and development.

Kojima's efforts were recognized by the Ministry of International Trade and Industry (MITI) in 1954 when it awarded the company a prize for its high standard of technological efficiency, which was judged commendable for a company of its size.

With a three million yen capital increase in 1955 and an additional loan from a bank, Kojima Press opened a new plant in Shimoichiba in 1956 in order to cope with the ever increasing car and truck production of Toyota. Both the new and old plants were expanded in 1958, whereupon the older specialized in the manufacturing of plastic auto parts. The new plant became corporate headquarters in 1959. The company built its own die-making shop in 1960 at the Honsha (main) plant, formerly called the Shimoichiba plant.

In 1958, the company was awarded a prize by the Labor Standards Bureau for its excellent performance in industrial safety. Also in this year, the Ohju Medal (Medal of Merit) was conferred on Hamakichi by the Emperor in appreciation of his contributions to the development of the auto parts manufacturing industry. By this time, his two youngest sons had graduated from school and joined their one natural and two adoptive brothers at the company. The number of employees had exceeded 200 and was growing rapidly. In the same year, he retired from the chairmanship of *Tōkai Kyōhō Kai* and was designated honorary chairman of the organization.

Growing as a Business Group

In 1961, Kojima Press Manufacturing started to form a group of affiliated companies by separating portions of its product lines and other managerial functions. The first was Uchihama Industry (1961), followed by Wakayama Industry (1962), Kyōei Shearing Company (1962; later renamed Kojima Industry), Kojima Tool and Die Company in the United States (1966), Kojima General Planning Company (1967), Shinwa Industry (1968) and Kiso Industry (1970). In 1970, the group added another member, Wakō Plastics Manufacturing Company, through the acquisition of the latter's stock. Each of these member companies was headed by a member of the Kojima family and specialized in certain product lines or some specific functions, which continuously expanded and diversified.

Parallel to the growth in sales, the group jointly attempted rationalization in management practices. For instance, in 1961, Kojima Press introduced a system of statistical quality control with the guidance and help of Toyota. The concepts and techniques of quality control (QC) permeated among the employees under the direction of Kojima Gorō, leading to the awarding of a Deming Prize to the company for its accomplishments in QC activities. Similarly, Kojima Press started a "zero-defects (ZD)" movement to improve the quality of its products by upgrading managerial controls. As a result, it received a PM (productive maintenance) Prize in 1972 from the Japan Institute of Plant Engineers. Starting in 1973, however, the main focus of improvement shifted to cost aspects, whereupon an annual target for cost economy was determined and successfully achieved during the 1970s.

Along with these campaigns for the rationalization of management, the company also initiated internal production of some machine tools. To achieve this, Kojima Press set up the Machine Tool Division in 1973 by renovating its former Die-making Section (established in 1963) and initially employing a staff of 100.

Kojima Hamakichi died on 20 April 1974 at 82. The funeral service was headed by Saitō Shōichi, then chairman of Toyota, and was attended by more than 2,000 people.

5.3 Nippondenso Company, Ltd.[4]

5.3.1 Company Profile

Incorporated	:	December 1949
Origins	:	1933
Stock held by primary firms (1978)	:	22.0% (Toyota Motor), 9.1% (Toyoda Automatic Loom)
Sales (1975)	:	¥226.7 billion
Profit net of tax (1975)	:	¥7.7 billion
Product lines	:	various electrical components (such as starters, dynamos, distributors, ignition coils, spark plugs and others), meters, car air conditioning units and heaters, and other automobile parts and components
Number of employees (1976)	:	approximately 20,000
Number of factories (1976)	:	7
Number of overseas subsidiaries	:	10

By 1970 Nippondenso (officially spelt in capital letters) Company was an internationally-recognized manufacturer of electrical parts and components for automobiles. Although well known as a member of the Toyota Group, it supplies a considerable portion of its output to other customers including such automobile manufacturers as Mitsubishi Motors, Isuzu, Hino, Tōyō Kōgyō (Mazda), Fuji Heavy Industries (Subaru), Honda, Suzuki and Daihatsu. In turn, the company obtains raw materials, parts, equipment and services from more than 300 firms,

[4] There are three company-published histories (Nippondenso 1964, 1974 and 1984), as well as memoirs by former employees (Nippondenso 1959–60) and autobiography by Suzuki Ryūichi (1959), who was with the company in key roles from its beginnings. Interviews were conducted in 1976.

of which some 50 selected subcontractors belonged to an industry association called *Densō Kyōryoku Kai* (Densō Cooperative Association), which is aimed at upgrading the managerial and technical capabilities of its members.

5.3.2 Historical Development

Nippondenso was, until 1949, a department of Toyota Motor Company. When Toyoda Automatic Loom Works decided to establish its automobile division in late 1933, Toyoda Kiichirō wanted to explore the possible domestication of the production of electric parts and components. The task was assigned to a group of three electrical engineers who had been involved in an ongoing project to develop a new spinning machine. The group was later increased to five, but concentrated effort on the new task had to wait until late 1935, when the spinning project was completed.

Subsequently, in early 1936, four engineers from the original group were joined by another engineer and a female production worker to form a specialized task force. A tiny experimental shop, with a floor space of ten square meters, was set up in a corner of the spinning and weaving laboratory. Before the end of the year, the task force had expanded to nine people, and moved into a larger experimental shop (with a floor space of 33 square meters) in a corner of the tool manufacturing shop.

Of all the electrical parts and components, only batteries were readily available in the local open market at that time. In addition, wire harnesses were supplied directly by Yazaki's factory (described in Section 5.5 below). It seemed, therefore, that essentially all the key electrical components (e.g., starter, distributor and dynamo) had to be supplied by the primary firm itself. The task force thus began by disassembling and sketching major European and American car components, followed by drawing original designs based on studies of the imported components. These designs were taken to the adjacent tool shop, where experimental production took place when workers had time to spare.

In October 1936, shortly after the approval of Toyoda Loom as a registered automobile manufacturer under the Automobile Industry Act of 1936, Kichirō decided to erect a pilot plant for electrical components. The plant, with a floor space of 660 square meters, was constructed by the end of the following month, and the task force was enlarged by some 30 new members. Eighteen new machines were housed in the plant, including a variety of lathes, presses, and milling machines. As the task force had its own manufacturing facilities for the first time, it agreed to impose on itself a production target: 250 sets of starters, distributors, dynamos and ignition coils.

The pilot plant faced a number of difficulties, including the in-appropriate choice of materials and the lack of suitable machinery. Even in cases where the exact specifications were known, certain materials such as carbon brushes, condenser paper and high-temperature paraffin were simply unavailable locally. Some materials were poor in quality. Moreover, heavy dependence on manual operations resulted in lack of precision in the final products.

Faced with such obstacles, Suzuki Ryūichi, later managing director and a core member of the task force from the very beginning, sought counsel from a college classmate, Dr. Okamoto Shōzō, a staff member of the Ministry of Communications' Electrical Laboratory (*Teishin Shō Denki Shikenjo*). Okamoto was able to provide technical advice, and helped them overcome their difficulties. For example, substitutes were either suggested or developed for materials not available in the country. Furthermore, Okamoto made arrangements for the group to have access to some equipment at his laboratory. With this help and the group's own effort, the target output was attained in April 1937, although the quality and performance of the products were not quite comparable to the imported items.

In the meantime, the Automobile Division of Toyoda Loom decided to procure electrical components from an outside source. Accordingly, the company management identified six candidate firms judged capable of supplying such items: Mitsubishi Electric, Kokusan Electric, Shinkō Electric, Tōshiba Electric, Fuji Electric, and Hitachi. Tōshiba and

Hitachi were supplying electrical parts and components to Ford Motor Japan and Nissan Motor, respectively, while Kokusan and Shinkō had had previous experience in the manufacture of similar items for airplanes, and Fuji was known to be a good manufacturer of various types of direct-current equipment. Toyoda management finally chose Hitachi as the major subcontractor primarily because Hitachi had basically followed the same Delco Remy design as Toyota.

Having secured a local source of supplies, Toyoda proceeded to substitute domestic electrical parts and components for imported items, one after another, with Hitachi accounting for the largest share, especially in the beginning. In later years, however, in-company production came to play an increasingly dominant role, especially after a series of complaints (in 1973) from users who were disturbed by defective starters supplied by Hitachi.

In September 1938, a month after the incorporation of Toyota Motor Company, most of the production facilities for motor cars were transferred from the old Kariya plant to the newly constructed Koromo plant. The Kariya plant was turned over to the electrical components group and the body-forming group (which became Toyota Auto Body in 1945). Each of the two groups occupied half of the plant (which had a total floor space of 250,000 square meters). At the same time, the electrical parts group absorbed a small task force that had been engaged in the experimental manufacture of radiators in Tokyo. In the opinion of Toyoda Kiichirō, radiators and electrical components shared common characteristics in their material requirements and production processes; for example, both relied heavily on copper as the basic material and were dominated by pressing and soldering operations.

The electrical components group was given as a new assignment the production of 1,200 sets of starters, distributors, ignition coils and dynamos. Of the 1,200 sets, 1,000 were designated as original equipment while the remaining 200 were to be spare parts. To increase production capacity, the group was allowed to purchase a number of new machines including a turret lathe, an automatic lathe, a milling machine, two milling cutters and a grinding machine, all of which were high-performance brands imported either from Europe or from the United States.

At the same time, the group started to design production tools for its own use, beginning with a one-ton air press followed by a 15-ton power press, a small turret lathe and milling cutters. Also developed were an automatic press feeder and a semi-automatic machine for the production of starter-conductors. Production of radiators was initiated when a unique automatic tube manufacturing machine was developed by Murase Jun, a foreman, who, as a skilled textile machinist had been responsible for a number of innovations. On all these occasions, manufacturing was entrusted to the Machine Tool Department of Toyota Motor.

In August 1943, when wartime demand reached its peak, the electrical component group moved to the Kariya-kita plant of the Chūō Spinning Company, a sister company of Toyota Motor that had lost its markets because of the war and was scheduled to merge with Toyota Motor in a few months. With the increased plant space and additional production facilities, the group began to produce electrical components and radiators for fighter planes in addition to those for automobiles. However, as the war turned increasingly unfavorable for Japan, the group dispersed to several plants, and many of its facilities were appropriated for military uses totally unrelated to the manufacture of electrical components.

When the war ended in August 1945, the first thing the group did was to get the dispersed machines back to the Kariya-minami plant (called the Kariya parts plant at the time) and recondition them. Production of electrical components resumed as soon as the General Headquarters of the Allied Forces (GHQ) permitted automobile assemblers to produce a limited number of trucks, which was in late 1945. In order to maintain a reasonably high rate of utilization of production facilities, however, the group also produced such miscellaneous items as small direct-current motors, radio sets, electric heaters, hot plates, electric irons and even cooking pans. Table 5.3 summarizes the group's production records through this period by major product categories.

Table 5.3. Nippondenso's Production, 1935–47

(In physical units)

Year	Electrical auto parts					Direct current motors	Radio sets	Home appliances		
	Dynamos	Starters	Distri-butors	Spark plugs	Alarm systems			Heaters	Hot plates	Electric irons
1935	----experimental stage----				—	—	—	—	—	—
1936	494	410	500	500	—	—	—	—	—	—
1937	1,038	1,046	1,073	1,280	—	—	—	—	—	—
1938	3,881	5,947	5,101	7,200	—	—	—	—	—	—
1939	14,332	13,779	1,427	14,079	—	—	—	—	—	—
1940	13,442	15,957	16,602	16,315	—	—	—	—	—	—
1941	15,904	12,195	24,764	18,402	—	—	—	—	—	—
1942	13,226	12,599	7,485	5,290	—	—	—	—	—	—
1943	7,990	7,079	6,738	3,940	—	—	—	—	—	—
1944	21,399	20,783	22,660	3,940	—	—	—	—	—	—
1945	12,344	11,940	12,940	14,251	—	—	—	—	2,404	—
1946	11,077	10,985	10,131	16,173	4,864	1,476	330	4,845	36,442	16,316
1947	10,465	10,863	13,827	21,259	11,798	2,096	3,007	5,809	—	16,245
Total	125,592	123,583	123,248	140,299	16,662	3,572	3,337	10,654	38,846	32,561

Sources: Nippondenso (1964), p. 96.

Period of Independence and Technological Progress

The electrical parts group was separated from Toyota Motor and came to be known as Nippondenso Company on 16 December 1949 when the mother company faced serious financial difficulty. The new company started with a work force of 1,445. Hayashi Torao, former managing director of Toyota, became president of the new company. Besides the Kariya plant, the company had sales offices in Osaka and Tokyo. Other directors of the new company included Suzuki Ryūichi, chief engineer of the 1936 task force, Iwatsuki Tatsuo, who became president in 1967, and Shirai Takeaki, a key engineer at Toyota from its initial stage of development and president of Nippondenso after 1973.

The early days of the new company were not particularly happy ones, for it faced a grave financial crisis. For one thing, it was in the middle of a serious recession brought on by the attempt to break inflation. It inherited from the mother company (Toyota) an accumulated deficit amounting to about ten times the size of its capital. Under the circumstances, management deemed it an absolute necessity to overhaul the entire corporate structure. Accordingly, management announced a restructuring plan including a wage-cut of ten percent and the discharge of 473 employees—almost one-third of the total. The plan was immediately turned down by the labor union, which called a strike that lasted 29 days. The dispute was finally settled on 28 April 1950 when management promised the union to do its best to reconstruct the company and to give laid-off personnel first priority in rehiring. At about the same time, Toyota was going through an even longer strike.

The outbreak of the Korean War on 15 June 1950 drastically changed the situation. It is estimated that Japanese industries received special orders from the United Nations' armed forces totalling as much as $315 million during 1950. Of this, $22.7 million was for 10,280 trucks. The newly formed National Police Reserve (later renamed the Self Defence Force) brought the industry some additional procurement orders. The war boom helped the general economy recover, and this led to a drastic expansion of the automobile market.

The company seized this opportunity to accumulate further strength.

President Hayashi made it the policy of the company to place maximum emphasis on the rationalization of production. At the time, the company estimated the technical level of Japanese industries was at least ten years behind that of the United States and Western Europe (Nippondenso 1974, p.32). For this reason, management looked eagerly for ways to fill the gap at the earliest chance possible. In 1951, when the government released machinery formerly owned by the Army and the Navy Arsenals, the company immediately rented a large number of precision machines, most of which were high performance, imported models from Europe and the United States. More than 80 truck loads were necessary to transport all of the machines. They were purchased for about 40 million yen when the Peace Treaty went into effect in September 1951. In December 1951 Nippondenso was listed on the Nagoya Stock Exchange.

In May 1952 Hayashi dispatched two executive directors (Suzuki and Shirai) to the United States to observe and learn the latest production technology in that country. They visited many American auto parts manufacturers including Delco Remy, American Bosch, Autolite, Borg Warner and MacCord. In August of the same year, shortly after their return, management decided to invest in a large-scale expansion and modernization. The investment amounted to about 160 million yen, more than three times the company's paid-up capital. Under the project, the company purchased 21 pieces of large equipment and many smaller machines from both foreign and domestic machinery manufacturers.

In addition, Hayashi asked the Production Engineering Section of the company to promote the in-house manufacture of production equipment. Most of the equipment was special-purpose variants, which included boring, tapping and grinding machines. The precision machine tools acquired from the former arsenals played a great role in manufacturing the mass-producing machinery.

It also happened that the Robert Bosch Company of West Germany was looking for an opportunity to expand its network of international operations. In the autumn of 1951 Bosch had dispatched Karl Zehender, a managing director, to Japan. Realizing this might be a good opportunity for Nippondenso, Toyoda Kiichirō, acting as an advisor to

Toyota Motor, requested that the branch manager of Nippondenso's Tokyo office prepare materials to be transmitted to Zehender, including descriptions of the company's production lines and other pertinent information. Obviously interested, Bosch sent a production engineer named Gundert in November 1952 to check Nippondenso's technological standards and production system. Subsequently, in May 1953, a contract was signed in Tokyo. The terms of agreement were as follows:

1. Bosch granted Nippondenso exclusive right to manufacture and sell certain Bosch products in Japan, and would provide all the patents and utility models to facilitate manufacturing activities. The products were dynamos, starters, distributors, ignition coils, high-voltage magnetos, auto lamps, switchboards, turn signals, electric alarms, heating plugs for diesel engines, car heaters, and tools and equipment for inspection and/or repairing of electrical auto parts.

2. Nippondenso was permitted to export these parts if they were either assembled on Japanese cars as original equipment or supplied as spare parts, or if Bosch's patents and licences were not in effect in the destination countries.

3. Nippondenso became sole agent for Bosch products imported into Japan.

4. Nippondenso was granted the right to utilize all kinds of Bosch technologies and know-how (including product designs, manufacturing methods, factory construction, facility planning and inspection).

5. Two Bosch engineers acted as advisors during the initial stage of the agreement, and three Nippondenso engineers were trained at Bosch for six months.

6. Nippondenso was permitted to use "Nippondenso" as the brand name of its products, provided "Licensee of Bosch" also appeared.

7. Bosch acquired a ten percent equity interest in Nippondenso, a ¥40 million lump sum payment, and an annual royalty of three percent of sales of the Bosch-licensed products. Bosch still owned

about seven percent of Nippondenso in the late 1970s.

The period of agreement was for ten years, renewable automatically unless either party requested the contrary.

As soon as the initial signing was complete, Hayashi visited Bosch in West Germany, accompanied by Aoki Katsuo. Hayashi was deeply impressed by Bosch's high technological standards and appealed to his employees afterwards with the slogan, "We shall catch up with Bosch in ten years!" As part of his program to realize this objective, Hayashi announced in his New Year message to employees in 1954 the adoption of the following ten policies:

1. Upgrading product quality to international standards
2. Expansion of sales and service networks
3. Improvement of precision standards of materials and parts procured from outside suppliers
4. Active modernization, expansion and rationalization of the company's production facilities
5. Rationalization of clerical and administrative procedures
6. Improvement of working conditions and welfare facilities
7. Development of production skills through investment in human resources and the enforcement of the right-man-in-the-right-place principle
8. Introduction of a two-shift system
9. Establishment of standard rules for the most efficient staffing of personnel
10. Retrenchment of expenditures in general

Rapid Growth and Internationalization

Under the first five-year plan implemented under and supported by the technical agreement with Bosch, Nippondenso began expanding its product lines and business activities. Luckily, the timing coincided with the opening phase of motorization in Japan.

In 1954, the company's old-fashioned car heaters were switched to the Bosch-type, a move warmly welcomed by the Japanese market. In the same year, new windshield wipers were also introduced. The product line

163

was expanded or improved every year. Some of the new products were Bosch designs introduced under the agreement, but the majority were Nippondenso's original items, developed partly as a result of intensive study of Bosch technology. As an example, Nippondenso developed an air conditioning unit, which was the first marketed in Japan.

It was not merely the introduction of Bosch products and its manufacturing technologies that benefited Nippondenso. In fact, only a limited number of Bosch products were actually introduced. According to management, more valuable was the flow of various technical and managerial information, ranging from plant layout, the choice of machinery, ideas on jigs and fixtures, to tips on the management of research and development.

Management revised and extended the first five-year plan in August 1956 in response to the enactment of the Provisional Act for the Promotion of Machinery Industries (*Kishin hō*) in June 1956, by calling for an even faster rate of expansion and rationalization of the production system. Table 5.4 below illustrates the annual targets of the new

Table 5.4. Revised First Five-Year Plan and Actual Performance of Nippondenso

Year	Sales (in million yen)		Investment in fixed assets (in million yen)		Number of employees	
	Planned	Actual	Planned	Actual	Planned	Actual
1956	3,003	3,364	335	144	1,820	1,745
1957	4,009	4,680	741	656	2,099	2,422
1958	4,718	4,757	454	419	2,367	2,389
1959	5,505	6,779	296	685	2,503	2,823
1960	5,876	11,039	253	1,606	2,649	3,875
Total	23,111	30,619	2,579	3,510	—	—

Sources: Nippondenso (1974), p. 48.

plan as compared with actual performance. In this period, 1956–60, the company's investment program was partly financed by a series of long-term, low-interest loans from the Japan Development Bank in accordance with the provisions of the Act.

A big typhoon hit the Nagoya area in September 1959, seriously damaging all the machinery in the newly-acquired Nagoya plant. The plant had been specializing in the production of Bosch spark plugs, and all its production functions had to be temporarily transferred to the main plant. In addition, the typhoon killed eight family members of company employees, destroyed the homes of many employees, and damaged machinery at the main plant in Kariya, in the countryside south east of Nagoya. These serious losses notwithstanding, the projected goals of the five-year plan were successfully attained in the fourth year.

In the second five-year plan announced in January 1961, president Hayashi suggested the following corporate objectives and corresponding policy measures:

1. Objectives
   A. Attain internationally competitive standards both in product quality and in output prices
   B. Export of ten percent (by value) of total production by 1965
   C. Achieve predominance in the domestic market by increasing the company's market share by 20 percent
   D. Expand production three-fold in physical units and two-fold in value
   E. Realize the principle of "high productivity and high salaries"

2. Policy measures
   A. Extensive practice of scientific management especially in the area of quality and cost controls
   B. Reinforcement of research and development activities
   C. Advanced rationalization of production facilities
   D. Upgrading of the production capabilities and management capabilities of the subcontractors

E. Further expansion of the company's sales and service network

F. An increase in human assets through extensive educational and training activities and the improvement of welfare facilities

Of all the policy recommendations, special emphasis was placed on quality control activities. The company had introduced statistical quality control (SQC) techniques in 1950 when it supplied rifle parts to the United States Army. This practice was reinforced when the company signed the agreement with Bosch, which entailed the standardization of its production operation and facilities. After 1957, the company expanded its QC activities, leading to the adoption of the so-called system of total quality control (TQC), which put greater emphasis on the cost aspects and advocated full involvement of all employees. Within a year after introduction of the system, in November 1961, the company was awarded the Deming Prize, certifying the high standard of the company's QC activities.

Encouraged by the success of its QC activities, the company proceeded to set up various management systems such as cost control, productive maintenance, industrial safety, pollution control, and so on. Toyota extended valuable support and guidance in implementing these innovations.

All of the major objectives of the second five-year plan were fully accomplished. The production system of the company was expanded at an impressive speed: every year a few new shops were added and old ones enlarged, while the factory sites were expanded to allow more space for the new plants. To equip the production shops, the company purchased a large number of highly efficient precision machines, more than half of which were brought to the Machine Tool Department and were employed in manufacturing mass-production equipment such as transfer machines, which gained popularity in the country during the middle of the second five-year plan period. Also established were lines for alternators, plug-assemblies, starters, distributors and wipers, with the maximum use of machinery produced by the Machine

Tool Department. In addition, a number of new product models were developed and brought to market. Most of them were improvements of older Nippondenso or Bosch models but some were of completely novel design, newly developed by Nippondenso.

In 1962, the technological agreement with Bosch was modified and extended six years, with the following changes:

1. VM distributor-type fuel injectors (V standing for Verteiler Pump) were included as licensed products
2. Licensed products were divided into two groups, to which different royalty rates were applicable (both being lower than the original rates)
3. Nippondenso was allowed to export licensed products not only as part of completely built-up models and as spare parts, but also as part of completely knocked-down packages
4. The stipulation that the exports be channelled through the Bosch distribution system was removed, allowing Nippondenso to export directly, except in some specified regions

As production increased, the company expanded its facilities and personnel devoted to marketing activities. All of the company's seven branches moved into new, larger office buildings during this period, and a number of service stations and sub-stations was established. In December 1962, the Export Section was established, and within a year was expanded to a department. Its export objectives were achieved with no difficulty.

Table 5.5 summarizes the process of growth of Nippondenso during the second five-year plan. In 1963 Denso introduced the "divisional control system" whereby each division was made functionally independent, and was expected to realize as high a rate of return as possible. The seven divisions established were: electrical parts I, electrical parts II, chemical products, air conditioners, fuel injectors, spark plugs, and filters.

In early 1967, just after the company launched into its third five-year plan, the presidency passed to Iwatsuki. Hayashi became chairman of the board of directors, a position he held until his death in 1970 at age

Table 5.5.   Growth of Nippondenso, 1961–65

Fiscal Year	Total sales (in million yen)	Net profit before tax (in million yen)	Number of employees	Investment in fixed assets (in million yen)
1961	14,066	1,412	4,968	3,464
1962	15,104	1,614	5,260	1,544
1963	19,761	2,434	5,569	1,988
1964	25,429	2,682	6,697	3,804
1965	27,919	2,441	7,182	2,835

Sources: Nippondenso (1984), p. 58 and Ōkura Shō (Ministry of Finance), *Yūka shōken hōkoku sho sōran* [Report on Corporate Securities], variable issues.

77. Under its new president, Nippondenso recorded even faster growth in every aspect of its business. During this period, three new divisions (exhaust systems, meters, and electronics) were added.

There was no more room for expansion at existing factory sites by the end of the second five-year plan, so two factories were built at new sites in 1965: the Hiroshima plant to manufacture radiators for Tōyō Kōgyō (Mazda) and Mitsubishi, and the Ikeda plant to produce car heaters and coolers. In 1967, the company built still another factory (the Anjō plant) to produce regulators, alternators, starters, and magnetos. Each of these grew, in terms of floor space, to be equal to, or even larger than the main factory. The introduction of new machinery was also actively undertaken to keep the factories continuously expanding in capacity and improving in performance. As before, many of the mass-production machines were developed and manufactured by the company's own Machine Tool Department.

The expansion and modernization of the production system continued in the succeeding period. In addition to improvements in the existing production facilities, the construction of a huge new factory (Nishio plant) was started in 1969 to house mass production lines for car heaters, air conditioners, motors, fuel injectors and new elements for emission control. By the time three-fourths of the factory was completed (1973), the total floor space of the company's seven shops exceeded 870,000 square meters. In 1974, still another new factory (the Takadana plant) was added, where large-scale mass production lines were installed for the manufacture of autometers and filters.

A new feature in the history of the company emerged during the third five-year plan: internationalization. In May 1966, Nippondenso opened its first overseas branch in Chicago and liaison offices in Los Angeles and Detroit, in the United States. The New York Office was inaugurated in 1968. In 1971, the Los Angeles branch was incorporated to become Nippondenso of Los Angeles, Inc. Following this, the company established a number of other overseas subsidiaries to market Nippondenso products:

1972: Nippondenso (Australia) Pty, Ltd.
1972: Nippondenso Thailand Company, Ltd.
1972: Nippondenso Canada, Ltd.
1973: Nippondenso (Europe) B.V.
1973: Nippondenso Thailand Sales Company, Ltd.
1976: Nippondenso Philippines Company, Ltd.

In addition to sales activities, the subsidiaries in Thailand and the Philippines were equipped with production facilities. The company also established licensing agreements with many auto parts producers in developing countries. With these setups, demand for Denso products expanded both for original equipment and spare parts. Consequently, the company's exports started to show a marked growth in every part of the world.

5.4 Maruyasu Industries Company, Ltd.[5]

5.4.1 Company Profile

Founded	:	August 1956
Origins	:	1895
Stock held by primary firms (1979)	:	none
Sales (1976)	:	¥26.1 billion
Profit net of tax (1976)	:	¥471.1 million
Product lines	:	double-shielded tubes (e.g., brake tubes, fuel tubes and injection pipes), functional auto parts using vibration-proof rubber (e.g., front and rear suspensions, engine mounts, and couplings) and various dies and gauges
Number of employees (1976)	:	877
Number of factories (1977)	:	3

Maruyasu Industries is relatively small among first-tier ancillary firms dealing directly with Toyota Motor Company. Nonetheless, it is well known for its unique products (especially its double-shielded tubes) and its highly automated modern production system. At the time of the survey (1976), more than 90 percent of the company's products were delivered to Toyota Motor and members of the Toyota Group. The proportion was expected to change in the future, however, as Maruyasu was in the process of expansion by adding new product lines for the manufacture of parts and components for electrical applications.

5.4.2 Historical Development

Although it was 1956 before Maruyasu Industries was formally

---

[5] No history of the company has been published. Interviews were conducted in 1976.

organized as an independent firm, the origin of the company goes back to the end of the previous century. In 1895 a man named Andō established Maruyasu Steel Works in Okaya, a major silk-producing town in Nagano Prefecture (west of Tokyo), to engage in the manufacturing of silk spinning machines. Okaya imported most of its spinning machines from Italy. Similarly, two other major silk producing towns, Maebashi and Tomioka (both in Gumma Prefecture, direcly to the east of Nagano), relied mostly on machines imported from France and Italy. Being a well-known inventor full of novel ideas, Andō saw a good chance for success in the domestic production of spinning machines. (Andō's personal history cannot be traced prior to his making this decision. It is said that he had manufactured a reed organ and other novel instruments.)

Andō managed to keep his new business running, and in 1930 received capital participation from Katakura Spinning Company, a leading spinning concern at the time. (Katakura spinning was later transformed into Katakura Industry, a leading producer of silk products in Japan, and later also of women's apparel.) Eight years later (in 1938) Andō's company was incorporated as Maruyasu Machinery Manufacturing.

During World War II, Maruyasu Machinery added metal parts and components for airplanes to its product lines by taking advantage of its expertise in foundry and machining operations. Before long, the company began processing vibration-proof (VP) rubber, originally developed in Germany for use in aircraft components and later adopted by the Japanese Navy for use as a component for submarines and airplanes. Subsequently, Sumitomo Electric arranged for one of its affiliates, Tōkai Rubber Company, to produce VP rubber for the Navy.

When the war ended, Tōkai Rubber approached Toyota Motor and received orders for fan belts. At around the same time, Tōkai Rubber and Maruyasu Machinery jointly undertook a study to develop automobile shock absorbers. The study resulted in the regular production of shock absorbers by the two firms for Toyota, beginning in 1950. In this joint venture, Tōkai was to produce rubber parts, while Maruyasu handled the manufacturing of metal parts, assembly, finishing operations, and final delivery to Toyota. In this manner, the wartime cooperative tie between Tōkai and Maruyasu was fully revitalized.

Foundation of a New Company

Several years later, the management of Maruyasu decided to spin off the manufacturing of auto parts into a new company. Among the major reasons given for the decision were:

1. The highly promising prospect for growth of the automobile market in Japan
2. The close geographical location of Maruyasu to the primary firm (Toyota) and to the partner (Tōkai Rubber)—an obvious advantage for the company to act as an ancillary firm
3. The significant difference in precision requirements and in cost structure between the manufacturing processes of mass-production oriented auto parts and the relatively more labor intensive textile machinery

The new corporation, named Maruyasu Industries, came into being in August 1956 with a paid-up capital of three million yen. Yamada Iwao, a former executive of Maruyasu Machinery became president. Maruyasu Industries and Tōkai Rubber reinforced their partnership by each acquiring 15 percent of the other's stocks.[6]

In addition to capital financing, Maruyasu Machinery, as the parent company, continued to support Maruyasu Industries in other aspects. During the initial years, for example, the salaries of the latter's top executives were subsidized by the parent. Moreover, the new company depended heavily on the parent for product design and experimentation for new products.

Toyota proved to be another source of extensive support. First, Toyota dispatched four of its own personnel, who joined Maruyasu Industries to reinforce its production expertise. One of them, Ikeda

---

[6] The two companies were quite dissimilar in size: in 1956, the paid-in capital of Tōkai Rubber was more than thirty times that of Maruyasu Industries. As of 1977, financial ties were still maintained, with each company holding about an eighth of the other. Maruyasu had grown more than Tōkai, so in 1977 the latter had not quite six times the capitalization of Maruyasu.

Sasuke, was immediately appointed engineering director. The others were a shop foreman and two specialists, one in tools and jigs and the other in routing. The four played an essential role building up Maruyasu's engineering foundation for auto parts manufacturing. Second, Toyota offered continuous technological support; it made its own testing facilities available whenever Maruyasu Industries wished to check on new materials or to experiment on new products. Moreover, Toyota would send its engineering staff to give technical instructions and advice.

With the help and support from both the parent company and the primary firm, Maruyasu Industries experienced steady growth. In fact, it was commended in 1960 by the government of Aichi Prefecture as a model factory, only four years after its founding.

Marketing of the double-shielded tube supplied the real break-through for the company. Ever since the start of the company, management had wanted to produce some functional parts of more consequence than shock absorbers in the production of motor vehicles. Appreciating this, Toyota suggested Maruyasu develop a new brake tube.

In the 1950s, Japanese auto makers used simple tubes for piping fluid to the brake system, whereas American manufacturers had already adopted seamless steel tubes with copper plating inside. Of all such tubes, the American "Bandy Tube" was the best-known in the world, and Bandy had already chosen a licensee in Japan. A simple copper tube is weak in mechanical strength and durability, and the cost of copper was unstable.

The engineers at Maruyasu Industries set themselves to developing their own process for manufacturing Bandy-type tubes, while continuously receiving technical assistance from Toyota. It took three years but by 1958 they had established a new production process. However, management was not fully satisfied with its productivity and cost performance.

It then learned there was a patented new technology that would produce the steel tube to the desired specifications. The inventor was a

173

Japanese engineer named Takanashi Satoshi. Management further discovered Tōkyō Sanyō, a Japanese electrical manufacturing firm, had already been experimenting with the patent without much success. Maruyasu Industry managed to acquire the right to use Takanashi's patent, while simultaneously organizing a special task force of selected engineers, who started a process development project in 1959.

During the experimental process, the company had access to custom-made steel sheets, supplied by a major specialty steel manufacturer (Nisshin Seikō) backed by the primary firm and the parent company. Takanashi, the patent holder, subsequently joined the special task force and led the development project. Other assistance continued to be extended by Toyota, including technical advice and the free use of experimental facilities. The group also acquired valuable advice and aid from a researcher at the Industrial Promotion Center of Osaka Prefecture named Dr. Takase Takao.

In 1961, about two years after the establishment of the special task force, mass production of the double-shielded brake tubes was achieved. Accordingly, the old style brake tubes on Toyota vehicles were changed and the newly-developed variants used. Four years later (1965), double-shielded fuel tubes were introduced. With the introduction of the new products, the growth of the company was considerably accelerated. Moreover, this coincided with the beginning of motorization in Japan.

In 1964, when the headquarters (Honsha) plant reached the limit of physical expansion, the company decided to construct its second plant in Okazaki about 40 km away. The new plant site was spacious (48,200 square meters), more than ten times that of the Honsha plant. The first stage of construction was completed in February 1965, but because of continuous expansion, by 1976 even this huge site was fully occupied with modern production facilities (covering 23,500 square meters), necessitating the erection of a third plant.

A notable feature was the emphasis placed on research and development. In 1966 the "Laboratory for Quality Assurance and New Product Development" was set up within the Okazaki plant. The laboratory eventually grew to become the Research and Technology Center with three sections: research and development, product design, and chemical testing.

In the middle of its rapid growth, the management of Maruyasu was faced with a supply shortage of experienced managers. Accordingly, the company implored the primary firm to spare some of the latter's experts and indicated the exact qualifications of the needed personnel. Toyota gladly obliged and during 1967 and 1968 transferred several people: an ex-manager of Toyota's Procurement Department, two engineers of middle-management rank, and a few skilled workers who were qualified as shop foremen.[7]

With these two changes implemented, the company was now ready for continued expansion. New product lines were added annually, existing

Table 5.6.   Growth of Maruyasu Industries, 1967–76

Year	Total sales (in million yen)	Profit after tax (in million yen)	Number of employees	Average monthly wages, excluding bonuses (in thousand yen)
1967	2,983	17	476	28
1968	4,606	29	528	31
1969	6,491	78	559	36
1970	7,846	133	590	44
1971	9,239	90	675	51
1972	11,615	122	740	60
1973	15,589	322	823	72
1974	19,483	191	845	95
1975	22,700	192	852	104
1976	26,104	471	877	114

Sources: Maruyasu Industries.

[7]   The former manager of Toyota's procurement department, Muraoka Seiichi, was later promoted to executive director of Maruyasu; the two engineers, Kiyooka Toshiji and Sakai Takeichi, became managing directors of the company. At the time of the survey, the three were still active on the executive board, which consisted of 16 members.

lines were expanded, and sales records rose yearly. Moreover, top management made it a major policy to encourage production engineers to develop and manufacture the company's necessary production equipment internally. The policy also emphasized the importance of acquiring "machinery that manufacture machines." It was no accident, therefore, that Maruyasu Industries started to manufacture and sell various dies and gauges. Later, it even manufactured several automatic welding machines for the primary firm. It also started to produce various metal and rubber parts for electric appliances. In other words, the company was no longer totally dependent on the automobile parts and components market.

Table 5.6 illustrates some of the characteristic features of the growth of Maruyasu Industries.

5.5   The Yazaki Group[8]

5.5.1   Company Profile

Founded	: October 1941
Origins	: 1929
Sales (1976)	: ¥104,020 million
Affiliated corporations	: see below

Member Companies of the Group (as of 1976)*

Company Names	Product Lines	Number of employees**
Yazaki Corporation 　Founded　　　: 1963 　Paid-in capital　: ¥600 million 　Stock held by primary firms 　　(1979)　　　: none	Central administration of the Group	1,891 (1,291)
Yazaki Electric Wire Co. 　Founded　　　: 1941 　Paid-in capital　: ¥50 million 　Number of factories: 2	Copper wires, alumi- num alloy wires, aluminum electric wires	968 (802)
Yazaki Meter Company 　Founded　　　: 1950 　Paid-in capital　: ¥100 million 　Number of factories: 3	Meters for auto- mobiles, airometers (for household gas consumption)	2,243 (1,143)
Yazaki Parts Company 　Founded　　　: 1959 　Paid-in capital　: ¥50 million 　Number of factories: 2	Wire harnesses, gas- operated air con- ditioners	2,223 (1,424)
Yazaki Engineering Works 　Founded　　　: 1965 　Paid-in capital　: ¥10 million 　Number of factories: 3	Metal dies, special- purpose machine tools, industrial robots	502

[8]   A biographical sketch of the corporation's founder, Yazaki Sadami, is found in Satō (1975). Interviews were conducted in 1977.

Yazaki Resources Co.
  Founded   : 1965
  Paid-in capital : ¥10 million
  Number of factories : 1

Transportation
services of merchan-
dise, automobile
maintenance, etc.

198

Yazaki South Wire Co.
  Founded   : 1974
  Paid-in capital : ¥330 million

Importation, manu-
facturing and sales
of aluminum alloy
products

n.a.

Notes: * Excluding nine joint-venture companies located overseas.
         ** Number of male employees in parentheses.

Yazaki is in a rare position in the world of automobile parts and components manufacturers in Japan because it has successfully maintained ties with several primary firms, including an American one. This was possible because Yazaki originated as the sole producer of wire harnesses in Japan and, as such, at one time dominated the market. By the mid-1970s its activities had expanded to include a variety of merchandise such as gauge meters for gas consumption, for use either by motor cars or by households, solar energy collectors for domestic use, etc. Still, automobile parts and components accounted for approximately half of the company's annual sales in 1977.

As Table 5.7 indicates, the number of Yazaki emloyees increased at an average annual rate of 15 percent, reaching a maximum of about 10,000 in 1973, at which time management began conscious efforts to check the rising trend. The number declined rapidly after that, as the company stopped filling posts vacated by employees (mostly women) who left the company. As of 1977, employment totalled about 7,300, of which approximately 5,500 were directly involved in production, inclusive of R&D staff. About 30 percent of the total were women.

At the time of the survey (1977), the company took advantage of centrally administered personnel management in adjusting manpower overloads or shortages among group companies. Correspondingly, Yazaki employees were organized into a single enterprise union, which was directly affiliated with *Dōmei* (the Japanese Confederation of

Labor). The average age of employees was about 27, which was at the low end of the range for companies in the industry. Wages were basically determined by length of service.

Newly-recruited workers underwent brief introductory training, after which the men were rotated among various sections before being assigned to jobs according to individual aptitude. (The women were mostly put into dead-end assembly jobs.) Normally it took the men about six months to become familiar with their assignments, and a few years to learn them thoroughly. Several male production workers have moved up to become top executives.

Aside from on-the-job training, the company did not practice formal vocational training, because manufacturing wire harnesses does not require sophisticated labor skills. Although the company used to run correspondence courses, one for junior-high school graduates and the other for young female employees, these were discontinued when the country's rising education level made it unnecessary to provide such services. To promote morale, however, the company established a scholarship fund, which enabled up to ten male blue-collar workers at a time to enroll at a private university for four years. (The company emphasized those receiving the scholarship would not necessarily receive management jobs on completion of their studies.)

A notable feature of the company, from the point of view of personnel management, was that it operated a plant designed exclusively for the physically handicapped. The factory, in Tenryū (half way between Tokyo and Nagoya) and administered with production subsidies from the Shizuoka prefectural government, manufactured gas meters and related products. For its wage system, the factory adopted a variant of the piece-rate system.

5.5.2 *Historical Development*

Yazaki Sadami (1911–74), a native of Matsumoto in Nagano Prefecture, worked for about six years at Morita and Sons Company, a wholesaler of clothes and other miscellaneous merchandise in downtown Tokyo. In the late 1920s, Yazaki was in charge of promoting sales of

Table 5.7. The Growth of the Yazaki Group

Fiscal year[a]	Total sales (in million yen)						Total number of employees
	Automobile components (wire harnesses and gauge meters)	Electric wire	Airometers	Air-conditioners	Exports	Grand Total	
1941	0.8	—	—	—	—	0.8	200[b]
1942	0.7	—	—	—	—	0.7	200[b]
1943	1.3	—	—	—	—	1.3	400[b]
1944	1.8	—	—	—	—	1.8	502
1945	4.3	—	—	—	—	4.3	413
1946	12	—	—	—	—	12	397
1947	50	—	—	—	—	50	351
1948	183	—	—	—	—	183	430
1949	207	—	—	—	—	207	523
1950	422	—	—	—	—	722	602
1951	654	—	—	—	—	654	639
1952	645	—	—	—	—	645	662
1953	1,296	—	—	—	—	1,296	748
1954	1,093	138	—	—	17	1,248	728
1955	1,570	535	—	—	10	2,115	858
1956	1,882	1,681	—	—	13	3,576	1,138
1957	2,061	1,269	—	—	10	3,340	1,210
1958	2,541	1,432	—	—	64	4,037	1,947
1959	3,540	3,047	—	—	98	6,685	3,649
1960	4,966	4,658	—	—	78	9,702	4,211
1961	5,180	4,659	—	—	67	9,906	4,639
1962	5,042	3,478	288	—	266	9,074	5,894
1963	5,928	4,616	376	—	338	11,258	5,207
1964	6,750	5,163	149	—	846	12,908	5,021

Table 5.7. (continued)

Fiscal year[a]	Total sales (in million yen)						Total number of employees
	Automobile components (wire harnesses and gauge meters)	Electric wire	Airometers	Air-conditioners	Exports	Grand Total	
1965	8,053	5,738	199	—	1,109	15,099	5,006
1966	11,114	6,881	513	—	2,996	21,504	6,007
1967	14,797	8,759	1,231	—	3,468	28,255	6,827
1968	18,362	10,435	1,656	—	2,673	33,126	7,141
1969	24,804	13,536	2,494	—	2,173	43,007	7.498
1970	26,560	16,402	4,127	60	2,107	49,256	7,971
1971	28,818	18,819	5,162	590	2,454	55,843	7,962
1972	33,518	28,856	7,566	2,255	3,640	75,835	9,012
1973	46,128	49,631	13,785	6,528	3,984	120,056	10,088
1974	51,225	32,298	11,335	5,575	4,269	104,884	8,514
1975	51,439	34,895	7,293	6,124	4,269	104,020	7,373

Notes: [a] Fiscal years begin on 21 June.
[b] Estimates.
Sources: Yazaki Corporation.

electric wires, and this paved the way for his personal acquaintance with Toyoda Sakichi, the inventor and the founder of Toyoda Automatic Loom Works.

When Yazaki paid his first visit to Toyoda Loom in February 1929, Toyoda was examining a newly-arrived Ford. Toyoda wished to learn about the electric distribution system of the automobile, and eager to help, Yazaki hurriedly crawled under the car. The dirt and grease stained his white shirt as well as his hands and face. Minutes later, he was describing the vehicle's wiring system to the old man. Yazaki's responsiveness as well as his outgoing character made a very favorable impression on the great inventor.

Shortly after the encounter, Yazaki decided to become an independent dealer of wire harnesses. Toyoda Sakichi encouraged him when he learned of the young man's determination. In fact, he assured Yazaki that the automobile industry had a promising future. At the same time, the inventor suggested the young man call on Ishikawajima Company and Datsun Motor, two other major corporations experimenting with domestic production of motor cars.

Having no capital, Yazaki started his business by acting as a middleman. After establishing the product design, he went around to collect the necessary materials. Then he contracted with small shops to undertake the manufacturing. This he could easily do because of the personal connections he had cultivated through association with Morita and Sons. At that time most of his wire harnesses were marketed as replacement goods, used mostly on imported cars. Since not much was known in those days about automobile mechanics and less about wire harness manufacturing, Yazaki had to learn the various technologies involved as he went along. He was only 23.

In 1931, minimum monthly gross sales of ¥1,000 were necessary to support Yazaki (he was a bachelor until 1934) and his younger brother, Yoshimi, who had agreed to be a partner in the new venture, in addition to three regular employees. By the end of 1933, prospects had brightened for the domestic production of automobiles: both Toyota and Nissan formally announced plans to launch commercial manufacturing. Faithful to the advice offered by Toyoda, Yazaki saw to it that he had business dealings with both companies.

By 1934 he was running a small manufacturing shop with a dozen or so employees producing wire harnesses, while subcontracting part of the production out. As he needed a growing number of skilled workers for the expansion of his business, he recruited from among his subcontractors, being careful, however, not to damage his commercial relationships with them.

From Take-off to Accelerated Growth

The business outlook improved appreciably in 1937, when Toyota Motor became an independent corporation. The growing prospects also lured new entries into the wire harness market. However, the volume of total sales remained relatively small, at least not large enough to attract the attention of big business circles.

In 1938 Yazaki bought a factory site in the Ogu area, northeast of Tokyo. In July of the same year Yazaki's shop was incorporated with a paid-up capital of 100 thousand yen, which was increased to 280 thousand two years later. In October 1941, the company integrated with Mitsuya Electric Wire Manufacturing and became a stock corporation. The number of employees had by then increased to about 60. In November 1942, the company took over an old factory site from Toyoda Textile Company at Washizu in Shizuoka Prefecture (about 260 km southwest of Tokyo). Construction of a new factory building was undertaken with materials supplied by Toyoda. Operation began in December 1944.

During the early 1940s Yazaki consciously built up his top management staff. Monna Yoshihei was section chief at a local police station, in charge of the area where the Ogu factory was located, and well versed in wartime factory regulations such as the Factory Law, wage-price controls, restrictions on the purchase of producers durable equipment, and so on. Wartime "mutual help" activities brought him together with the Yazaki brothers. Yazaki Yoshimi frequently cooperated with Monna in organizing young managers in the community in response to the government's plea to establish an industrial council for managers and workers called *Sangyō Hōkoku Kai*. After Yoshimi joined the army in 1943, Yazaki Sadami approached Monna and offered him an administrative post in the company. In addition, Higuchi Shigeji joined the company in 1945. Despite rapid growth, Yazaki had not even adopted double-entry bookkeeping, and the company desperately needed someone who could take the lead in this endeavor.

At the end of World War II the company operated two factories (Ogu and Washizu) with about 200 workers. The company resumed production about 70 days after the war, and was incessantly plagued by lack of raw materials such as copper and lead. In addition, it could not rely on orders for automobile components to sustain the company. Consequently, Yazaki began the production of electric wire. By 1949, however, replacement demand for auto parts was gradually coming back. Fuji Motor, for instance, became the sole contractor for the repair of military jeeps, whose wire harnesses were to be supplied by Yazaki. The years 1950 and 1951 were already exceedingly profitable for the company.

With these seemingly bright prospects in mind Yazaki made four important decisions. First, in 1950 the company took over a meter-production plant. Early meter production was facilitated greatly by licensing agreements between primary firms (excepting Toyota) and Western companies. These provided a constant source of new ideas. An especially notable innovation was the introduction of plastic. Second, the company purchased, in 1951, an old ammunition factory which had belonged to the Army Arsenal. The factory, located in Numazu in Shizuoka Prefecture, later formed the central base for Yazaki's production activities; smelting facilities for copper and aluminum, for example, were all located in this factory.

To everyone's surprise, the company president declared a pull back from production of electric wire. This market had traditionally been dominated by major corporations, and he defended his decision by saying it would be best for the company to concentrate in the area where its comparative advantage lay. The decision proved to be a good one, for the major corporations quickly recovered their strength and dominated the wire market as soon as the postwar recovery was in motion.

Sadami wanted very much to secure his own supply of copper ingot. For one thing, the company's output was more and more restricted by availability of ingot, the supply of which was largely controlled by major corporations. However, the company's lead bank was reluctant to finance the necessary expenditure. The amount of copper production from the proposed furnace (50 tons per month) far exceeded the company's daily requirements, and the unit cost would be much higher than the copper supplied by existing producers, as the furnace would not benefit from economies of scale. But Sadami carried through with his initial decision even at the cost of terminating commercial relations with the bank that declined to support the venture (1951). Construction as well as operation of the reverberatory furnace for copper smelting was accomplished with no outside help. Other copper smelters would not provide assistance to the potential intruder into their market. All the technical know-how for production, therefore, was acquired through trial and error.

When Sadami learned of the German-made Thomas furnace in 1956, he quickly decided to introduce it while simultaneously demolishing the old one. The new furnace had an output capacity of 300 tons per month, which was eventually increased to 1,000 tons per month. In order to consume all the copper produced, the company had to exert special effort to persuade influential users of copper (such as electric companies and the national railway system) to place new orders. Afterwards, in 1969, a continuous copper smelting and refining operation was introduced from the United States, replacing the Thomas furnace. The new system (the dip forming process) was superior in that it generated less pollution.

It is characteristic of Yazaki Sadami's personality that on both occasions he shut down the old furnace *prior to* the completion of the new one. This was his way of demonstrating to his colleagues the extent of his determination and thus stirring up employees' morale. For many years, copper smelting remained the only section in the entire company that failed to yield a profit.

Engineering Development in Wire Harness Production

It was only after the Korean War that modern wire harness production was initiated. At that time Nissan was engaged in repair work on GM jeeps, while Mitsubishi Motor was operating under a licensing agreement with Willis for production of Jeeps. For three years in succession, beginning in 1950, Yazaki underbid its competitors (including well-known, large corporations) and received wire harness orders from Nissan.

It was only then that Yazaki engineers learned of a product design known as a "wire harness" and saw electric wires coated with vinyl. Until that time the product had been visualized only in terms of prewar concepts. Prior to the 1950s, in fact, the product had no specific name and was simply called *jidōsha-yō kumi densen* (electric wire system for motor vehicles).

In the prewar days, handicraft-type methods of production were sufficient, mainly because the rate of car production was only two or three units per day. The process involved bringing ordinary electric wires into the plant where cars were being assembled, connecting pertinent terminals to the wires, and bundling them together with simple covering materials. The product was simplicity itself; it consisted of a group of rubber-covered, thin electric wires, several of which were joined together, first by cotton thread, then by several coatings of lacquer. In essence, it was a service-oriented operation rather than the manufacturing of a specific automobile component. This also meant that the wiring system could be repaired easily by owner-drivers using simple tools.

After a year's experience with GM jeeps, Yazaki came to realize that it would be difficult to earn a profit with the prevailing level of production runs. The minimum required rate of production was judged to be about 34 thousand units per month using the old production system. This led the company to renovate its production system.

The old-style production system consisted largely of piece work: insulated electric wire was first marked for the required length, cut, stripped at both ends, oxidized, and tipped with terminals. The new system, in contrast, attempted to realize the merits of mass production as much as possible: several wires could be cut simultaneously, the shearing operation was greatly improved, terminal ends would simply be pressed onto the wires, and natural gas replaced the use of charcoal in the manufacturing process. Company officials say these new methods resulted in improvements in production efficiency ranging from 10 to 20 times those of the old system.

By the same token, Yazaki had to work carefully to improve the quality of the raw materials used. Adjustments were necessary, for instance, in any material that was affected not only by heat but also by humidity. Vinyl coating for electric wires was originally imported, but the company cooperated with a leading chemical company to develop a domestic source.

The Automobile Comes of Age: Two Decades of Expansion

By 1953 the automobile industry had fully recovered. At Yazaki, the Ogu factory began to specialize in the production of meters while the Numazu factory produced wire harnesses.

Beginning in the late 1950s, Yazaki made special efforts to diversify its activities by setting up separate corporations, each engaging in the manufacture of specialized goods and services. Yazaki Parts Company was established in 1959, Thai Yazaki Electric Wire in 1961, Yazaki Engineering Works in 1965, Thai Kōyō (a joint venture) and U.S. Yazaki in 1966. All the production companies were to operate under the general management of Yazaki Corporation (Yazaki Sōgyō), which was newly set up in 1963. At the same time, new products were actively sought and introduced. To give a few illustrations, the production of tachographs was started in 1961, airometers for propane and regular household gases in 1963, aeroizers (compressors for use by air conditioners) in 1965, and gas-operated air conditioners in 1974.

Yazaki also began in-house manufacturing of machine tools. In 1977, all the metal dies as well as machine tools produced by Yazaki Engineering were used by various Yazaki factories. Jigs, tools, and newly developed machinery were supplied mostly to sister companies. In addition, the company manufactured connecting rods for electric wires. On the average, approximately 10 percent (in value) of Engineering's output was sold outside the group.

Yazaki Engineering originated as a section of Yazaki Electric Wire Manufacturing, specializing in the supply of dies for internal use. The division became an independent corporation in 1965. The company

187

wanted to keep as much of this work in-house as possible, for two reasons. First, Yazaki wanted to retain the technology it had painfully accumulated, and management feared its technical secrets would be lost if the production of machine tools, etc., was subcontracted. According to company executives, the technologies embodied in the machinery could be easily copied by purchasing the machine. Moreover, some basic capital goods had to be designed and manufactured according to the company's own specifications. The making of a metal die, for instance, required sophisticated technology, particularly in the selection of the basic materials and in processing operations such as heat treatment. Second, Yazaki felt the introduction of a new company would be justified not only in meeting the growing demand for dies but also in resolving the shortage of skilled labor.

Another interesting feature of the Yazaki group was that it utilized a system of branch factories (BFs) in its manufacturing of wire harnesses. Making harnesses was extremely labor intensive: labor costs accounted for 35 to 40 percent of costs, and material about 30 percent. In the 1950s, Yazaki had produced all the wire harnesses internally. However, this became increasingly difficult, due to a shortage of young women workers. Yazaki hit on the idea of moving some plants to densely-inhabited areas and hiring housewives for three or four hours each day on a semi-flexible time basis on three overlapping shifts under the leadership of a few male supervisors. These plants were named the "branch factories." The plan was implemented in the early 1960s.

The female workers employed at the BFs were temporary employees, engaged on an hourly basis (¥300 to ¥500 per hour as of 1977). They could be discharged on short notice. Yazaki kept a roster of all the available workers, numbering about 1.5 times the number on the payroll. As of 1977 Yazaki operated twelve such BFs in the Gotemba area at the foot of the Mount Fuji. In addition, Yazaki had about 20 subcontracting firms for subassembly operations.

The cost-saving efforts of the Yazaki group, as exemplified by the improvement in the production technology of wire harnesses, eventually helped Yazaki win a contract with Mitsubishi Motors, replacing imports from Amps in the United States. Moreover, the cost-reduction campaign impressed Toyota, leading to its growing reliance on Yazaki's products. Similarly, the Yazaki group received an order from Ford in 1968.

In part, improved production efficiency was a result of standardization of the product. In the early 1960s the primary firms were seriously concerned with measures to strengthen their price competitiveness in the world market. As a result, they stressed the importance of standardization of parts and components. Toyota, for example, adopted such a policy before it marketed the Corolla. Accordingly, Yazaki introduced as many belt conveyors as possible; in some cases it made use of revolving tables instead of the conventional production line.

It should be noted, however, that standardization contributed to production economy only insofar as mass production was the suitable method of manufacturing. In the making of luxury cars, by contrast, it proved to be more expensive, because such models did not justify high production runs. Furthermore, the belt-conveyor system failed to save on cost unless temporary employees were excluded from line. In any event, the primary firms modified their policy on standardization in the early 1970s as proliferation of models made it less practical. In addition, the primary firms began designing longer wires in order to save on assembly costs. All in all, the number of different types of existing wire harnesses rapidly increased by 1977. Many of them were essentially custom creations.

Development of Subcontracting Network

In its effort to achieve cost economy, the company decided, about 1953, to go to in-house production of vinyl-coated electric wires. Its ensuing success, at a substantially reduced cost, took the major producers of electric wires by surprise. By way of retaliation, beginning in 1955, new entries into the wire harness market followed one after another (Table 5.8). As of 1977 Yazaki still enjoyed an approximately 65 percent market share in wire harness production. In the middle of the same year, Yazaki's average monthly sales of original equipment,

Table 5.8. Marketing of Wire Harnesses

A. Wire Harness Manufacturers (1977)

Rank, by market share	Company	Is wire harness production subcontracted out?	Ties with major primary firms
1	Yazaki	No	See panel B.
2	Sumitomo Electric	Yes	Daihatsu, Honda, Nissan and Toyota
3	Shinagawa Electric Wires	No	Mitsubishi and Nissan
4	Furukawa Electric	Yes	Fuji, Toyo Kogyo and Toyota
5	Fujikura Electric Wires	Yes	Fuji and Toyo Kogyo

B. Approximate Share of Yazaki Brands in Total Wire Harness Purchases by Primary Firms (1977)

Primary Firm	Yazaki Share (% of value)	Approximate monthly purchase from Yazaki (in billion yen)
Isuzu	95	?
Mitsubishi	80	0.6
Toyota	70	1.5[a]
Nissan	50	0.8[b]
Toyo Kogyo	50	0.35
Daihatsu	?	?
Fuji	?	?
Hino	?	?
Nissan Diesel	?	?
Yamaha[c]	?	?

Notes: [a] All Toyota-related firms.
         [b] All Nissan-related firms.
         [c] For motor cycles.
Sources: Personal interview with a company official.

inclusive of both wire harnesses and meters, totalled approximately 4.5 billion yen and for spare parts an additional 1.3 billion yen; 70 percent of the total sales were accounted for by wire harnesses while the remainder was meters and other products.

Yazaki had kept in close contact with Nissan from 1933 when Nissan was organized as an integrated corporate entity. Yazaki dealt with Honda and Suzuki until about 1960, when capacity limits forced the company to decline some of their purchase orders. Subsequently both companies stopped all purchases from Yazaki.

Yazaki has maintained by far the closest ties with Toyota. During and after the war, when there was acute shortage of raw materials, Toyota often assisted Yazaki in procurement of materials such as rubber and copper, through special arrangements with the Japan Auto Parts Industries Association. Sometimes even the supply of additional labor was arranged via this route. Tools and instruments (e.g., crucibles) were also purchased from Toyota on occasion. Moreover, when the Washizu factory was destroyed by an earthquake in December 1944, the materials needed for reconstruction were supplied by Toyota. These events were indicative of Toyota's concern for Yazaki's growth as an ancillary firm. At the same time, however, Toyota proved to be the toughest negotiator of all the primary firms in its constant demand for reduced unit cost as well as for improved quality of the components.

Yazaki exerted great effort to respond to the demands of the primary firms. For instance, Yazaki Sadami's motto was to care about his customers. In practical terms this meant he took delivery schedules seriously. When a fire turned the Ogu factory to ashes, he rushed to the plant to make sure nobody had been injured. On discovering no one was, he at once took measures to meet the original delivery commitments. The fire had hardly been extinguished when he sent for a carpenter to draw up plans for reconstruction. Before the evening was over, a canteen was converted into a temporary factory building and operations resumed two days later.

Assistance from the primary firms was very important in developing Yazaki's technological capabilities. In the 1940s and early 1950s, the sales staff used to take a morning train to make product deliveries to a primary firm, and they inevitably carried back rejected goods in the evening. There were many discouraging moments, but the primary firms' sustained interest in upgrading the company, especially the QC (quality control) movement which began in 1955, helped Yazaki gradually improve its system of production. Unlike most ancillary firms, Yazaki did not import personnel from primary firms. Moreover, the company did not borrow equipment or rely on its customers for engineering help or designing its products.

The basic contracts between Yazaki and the primary firms contained no terminal dates as such. As the quantities of required components were determined according to the expected production volumes of the respective automobile models, unit prices underwent renegotiation every six months.

Yazaki did not anticipate relying on its overseas plants (such as those in Taiwan) to produce wire harnesses for use by the Japanese primary firms during the 1970s. There was a high frequency of design changes to Japanese vehicles and a desire on the part of Yazaki to keep to exact delivery schedules. But the most compelling reason was probably the fact there was little cost advantage after the inclusion of import duties, which were designed to protect domestic producers such as Yazaki from meaningful foreign competition.

The frequent revisions in product design necessitated by model changes made it extremely difficult for Yazaki to standardize its production processes. (Ford was an exception, as it stuck to simple, standardized components as long as possible.) Furthermore, the primary firms' efforts to economize their production costs sometimes necessitated a change in wire harness design even for the same model, and this often added complications to Yazaki's production procedures. The primary firms also had a tendency to eliminate, though gradually, the sub-assembly steps. This shifted work to the ancillary firms (e.g., the integration of fuse boxes with wire harnesses). Such work shifting would be a way to effectively lower price, especially if the same price was paid for a more complex assembly.

192

Yazaki has been active in coordinating and promoting the activities of industry associations organized by the first-tier ancillary firms, particularly the one related to the Toyota group (*Kyōhō Kai*). Yazaki's ancillary firms formed their own association called *Yazaki Kyōryoku Kai* (the Association of Yazaki Cooperators). Yazaki had consistently managed to upgrade the engineering and managerial abilities of the member companies through assistance in the purchase of new equipment, the practice of quality control, and in other ways. From the early days of its existence, Yazaki had made it a point to pay its subcontractors in cash at the earliest possible date. Moreover, the company always extended various other forms of assistance as well. For example, when one subcontractor lost his factory in a fire in 1958, he was surprised to find Yazaki Sadami right on the spot, offering him an unused factory building in Yazaki's Ogu plant. The building was duly dismantled, moved, and rebuilt within a month, and production activities resumed a month later. Such forms of spontaneous assistance were perfectly in line with the personality of the company president. At the same time, however, he was perhaps, in part, following the example previously set for him by the Toyota group.

5.6 Topy Industries, Ltd.[9]

5.6.1 Company Profile

Founded : December 1934

Origins : 1920s

Stock held by primary firms (1979) : 3.4% (Nissan), 1.8% (Toyota)

Sales (1978–1979) : ¥119,334 million

Profit net of tax (1978–1979) : ¥1,022 million

Product lines : wheels for motor vehicles; steel (section steel, H-steel, I-steel, UM plate, etc.) and sheared steel (plate, sheet, stainless); parts and components for construction machines; and structural steel for buildings and bridges

Number of employees (1979) : 3,332

Number of plants (1979) : 8

Number of ancillary firms (1979) : 14

Number of domestic branch office and service stations (1979) : 8

Topy (officially spelt in capital letters) Industries was the largest manufacturer of automobile wheels in Japan in 1979, a position it had enjoyed for some time. With monthly production capacity of over a million units, its market share was 50 percent for passenger vehicles and 70 percent for trucks and buses. As a result of a policy to grow as a comprehensive manufacturer of transportation equipment, the company had diversified its product lines, so automobile wheels accounted for only a quarter of total sales.

A member of the Nippon Steel group (that company is the largest

9 Company-published histories include Sharin Kōgyō (1964) and Topy Kōgyō (1971). Interviews were conducted in 1979.

shareholder), Topy supplied wheels to almost all the major assemblers, while maintaining a relatively independent position from all of them. At the request of primary firms that were starting assembly of knocked down packs outside Japan during the 1970s, the company concluded several technical aid contracts with manufacturers of automobile wheels in Asian countries.

The company had 14 ancillary firms of its own. Among them, Topy Jitsugyō and Topy Kaiun were the most tightly afffiliated, specializing in sales and transportation, respectively, of the materials and finished products of Topy. The other ancillary firms engaged in such businesses as marketing wheels abroad, processing subcontracted parts, producing items marketed by Topy Jitsugyō, and so forth.

5.6.2   Historical Development

The origin of Topy Industries can be traced back to three companies, two dating from the 1920s (Figure 5.3).

Miya Steelworks was founded by Kōzuma Toshihide, who was born in 1882 in Miyazaki Prefecture to a local Shintō priest. His father always told his children, "As long as you live and work, do something good for

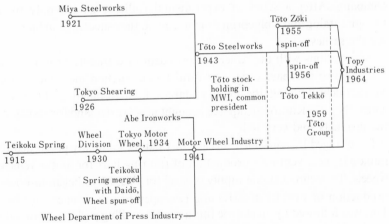

Fig. 5.3.   Topy Industries' Family Tree

others." Kōzuma graduated from the Tokyo College of Commerce (now Hitotsubashi University), served as chief of Asano Iron & Steel's business department, and then brokered scrap steel disposed of by Asano.

One day, Hamano Nagamatsu, chief engineer of the mill he sold scrap to, suggested Kōzuma establish a rerolled steel mill. Rerolling is a rather simple process, and at the time, Kōzuma was bored and felt harrassed by criticism of his sale of scrap steel. Somebody had said to him, "how dare you sell steel bars with such flaw holes!" So, he decided to act on the suggestion, establishing Miya Steelworks in 1921 in an eastern suburban area of Tokyo, by purchasing machinery and other equipment on deferred payment.

With about twenty employees and two rolling machines powered by a 300-horsepower motor, the factory began to produce rerolled steel from bars rejected by Asano. Huge quantities of the mill's output were purchased by Nippon Steel Tube Company to construct a new plant.

One day in 1922 a stranger from Osaka came to the factory and asked whether Miya could produce steel sashes similar to those made by a well-known British company. Kōzuma and Hamano became interested in the new venture, as it would strengthen the technological capability of the company. After a series of experimental rollings, guided only by a foreign catalog and a blueprint drawn from it, they succeeded in fabricating the sashes.

Negotiations with the American president of a trading firm won the first massive purchase order—to furnish construction material for the Marunouchi Building, the country's largest modern building of the day. Then, the 1923 Kantō earthquake brought massive demand for sashes, so the products sold very well.

Encouraged by continued success, in 1930 the company proceeded to initiate its next venture—production of rim ring bars for motor vehicle wheels. To secure a stable supply of steel for this, Miya began in-house production of steel by constructing two open-hearth furnaces in 1935. This was followed by an electric furnace and a rolling mill, to coordinate production capacity between the materials supply and the processing operations. Thus, by the early 1940s, the company had turned into a full-fledged steel producer.

Tokyo Shearing was established in 1926 as a subsidiary of Asano Shipbuilding. As this suggests, its major activity was shearing steel plates for shipbuilding and the utilization of scrap steel. Located across from Miya, its plant, with four shearing machines and three electric cranes, had been purchased from Osaka Shearing. The company's business involved both manufacturing and wholesale trade, so it could profit by buying the material cheaply and selling its product at the highest price possible. With the same objective in mind, the company built its rolling mill to enhance efficient use of scrap steel. An open hearth furnace was built in 1938.

Tokyo Motor Wheel Manufacturing, the key company in the history of Topy, was established in 1930 as a division of Teikoku Spring. Tokyo Wheel was spun off when Teikoku merged with Daidō Electric Steel in 1934. Teikoku Spring had been established by Nonagase Tadao in 1915 and initially engaged in manufacturing various types of spring for ships, railway cars, and machines. Daidō was one of its steel suppliers.

Nonagase was born in Wakayama Prefecture in 1878. Like many youth of his day, he aspired to become a military officer. Because of his myopia, however, he had to give up that ambition. Deeply disappointed, he dropped out of junior high school and in 1903 went to the United States. He attended a technical school in Ohio, studying heat treatment of steel, and acquired other professional techniques used in the manufacture of steel products, while working as a dishwasher and at other part-time jobs. Nonagase's ten-year stay in the United States coincided with the advent of the age of motorization, brought on by the appearance of the Model T in 1908.

On his return to Japan, Nonagase worked for two years at Tokyo Steel as an engineer before founding Teikoku Spring in 1915, the pioneer of the spring industry in Japan. After the company had established its spring business, in the late 1920s Nonagase turned his attention to the production of motor vehicle wheels.

Nonagase insisted on the need for the domestic production of wheels at the earliest date possible. Teikoku was already producing springs for the Japanese plants of both Ford and Chevrolet, and bumpers and spare wheel carriers for Ford trucks.

At first Nonagase and his team attempted to produce spare wheel rims for Ford and Chevrolet but failed to meet the required standard. The major difficulty lay in their inability to perform taper rolling. Then they developed a special disc wheel for adapting imported passenger vehicles to Japanese road conditions; this was the forerunner of wheel production. After the government's announcement, in 1931, of the Standard Model (*hyōjun jidōsha*) by the Ministry of Commerce and Industry, the company supplied wheels for domestically produced trucks and buses. In the end, the company's wheels were accepted by Ford (in 1935) and by Chevrolet (in 1937).

In 1935, after the spin off from Teikoku Spring, Tokyo Wheel imported an advanced, though second-hand, wheel manufacturing plant from the United States. With this plant, the company developed wheels acceptable as original equipment to both Ford and Chevrolet. In 1937, sales to Ford and Chevrolet accounted for about half of total sales, and the company had become the largest manufacturer of automobile wheels in Japan. Following the restrictions imposed by the Automobile Industry Act of 1936, Ford and Chevrolet were forced out of Japan in 1940. This was, fortunately for Tokyo Wheel, accompanied by the rapid growth of domestic car production.

The War Years

With the ongoing militarization of the economy, all three companies exprienced reorganization, while shifting production to munitions.

Tokyo Wheel was amalgamated with Abe Ironworks and the wheel department of Press Industry to form Motor Wheel Industry in 1941, making it the monopoly supplier of wheels for motor vehicles. In connection with this, the company was granted exemption from income and corporate profit taxes, although this was of little benefit to the company, as the government also controlled most prices. Motor Wheel was the only parts maker registered under the Automobile Industry Act, joining the three major assemblers: Nissan, Toyota, and Diesel (now Isuzu). As the war progressed, wheel production stagnated as greater emphasis was placed on munitions, and the company was put under even tighter control by the military.

Miya Steelworks and Tokyo Shearing also merged, forming Tōto Steelworks in 1943. Even before the merger the two companies had been under government control, as steel was a strategic commodity. A major purpose of the merger was to attain a more favorable allocation of raw materials from the government.

Postwar Recovery

At the end of the war, both Motor Wheel and Tōto dismissed all their employees and restarted operations by re-employing a minimum number of workers.

Tōto Steelworks resumed operations with 300 employees, a drastic reduction from mid-war figure of 1,300. Those remaining turned out pans, pots, spades, hoes, hatchets, etc. The agricultural implements won a nationwide reputation for their excellent quality. The layoffs and the Occupation's encouragement of the labor movement contributed to significant labor-management friction. Fortunately for Tōto, the iron and steel industry enjoyed priority status (together with coal) in the economic reconstruction plans of the government. Thus, Tōto's mills had resumed steady operation within a few years after the war, and this allowed rehiring workers and otherwise making peace with their new union.

In October 1948, the number of employees passed 1,400. The major product lines, by plant and number of employees are listed below.

Miya   Rim ring bars, sectional steel, steel bars; 520
Sunamachi   Steel bars, spring steel, cutlery, sheet bars; 640
Chigasaki   Cast steel and iron, steel ingots, shaft materials for shipbuilding; 168
Shinagawa   Spades, hoes, hatchets, cutlery; parts for railway tracks; 47

Motor Wheel dismissed 300 employees and resumed production with only 47. There was little choice but to make household utensils such as frying pans, tempura pots, and ashtrays, using leftover wheel disc materials. These gloomy days did not last long, however. Having been the monopoly producer of wheels during the war, the company had a leg up when demand recovered. In December 1945, Toyota began purchasing 7,000 wheel units per month. In addition, Toyota dispatched 20 workers from its plant to assist Motor Wheel in bolstering its production capabilities.

Toyota's order served as an impetus for the postwar recovery of the company. From 1947 onward, increasingly large quantities of wheels were sold in an expanding market. This culminated in massive procurement orders from the United States military and the newly established National Police Reserve in 1950. The Korean War boom was succeeded by a gradual expansion of the domestic passenger car market. In 1951, for the first time, production of wheels for small cars exceeded that for large vehicles. Sales went from ¥52 million in 1947 to over ¥1,000 million in 1953, and profits increased thirty-six fold.

The growing market naturally attracted the interest of foreign automobile makers. It became evident to the Japanese manufacturers that the only way to survive foreign competition was to rationalize production, while keeping foreigners out of Japan with various trade barriers. Thus, rationalization became a key issue for both assemblers and parts makers.

Motor Wheel sent three members of the company, including president Ishii Takichi, to the United States in 1952 to observe both assemblers and wheel manufacturers. They brought back a great deal of valuable information concerning ways to improve efficiency and precision in production.

From 1953 through 1959, the company undertook a three-stage, full-scale revamping. As shown in Table 5.9, emphasis shifted from large to small wheels, reflecting the shift of Japanese motorcar production from trucks and commercial vehicles to passenger cars. The rapid expansion of Toyota and other assemblers in the Tōkai region necessitated building plants in that area—Toyota City and Toyokawa being the towns chosen.

Table 5.9.   Rationalization of Motor Wheel Industry Co.

Period	First stage (1953–54)	Second stage (1955–56)	Third stage (1957–59)
Purpose	efficiency improvement	quality improvement and cost reduction	extension and modernization of production facilities
Facilities	1. rim line for large wheels 2. painting conveyor	1. taper roll machine 2. R&D laboratory	1. rim line for small wheels 2. assembly line 3. painting line
Capital requirement (in million yen)	140	68	620

In 1964, production facilities at the Shinagawa and Rokugō plants in central Tokyo were relocated to a new plant at Ayase, on the periphery of the metropolitan area. This enabled the company to better cater to assemblers in the region. The company received a tax exemption for profits from the sale of the old plant sites under the Provisional Act for the Promotion of the Machinery Industries (*Kishin hō*).

Formation of the Tōto Group

Propelled by the Korean War boom, Tōto began diversifying to mitigate effects of business fluctuations. The company took its first step in this direction by becoming Motor Wheel's largest shareholder in 1951. Fujikawa Kazuaki, president of Tōto, simultaneously took on the presidency of Motor Wheel. Thereafter, exchanges of engineers and other staff members took place frequently.

In accordance with the managerial strategy of Tōto to increase the share of processed products relative to steel materials, the company undertook development and marketing of bulldozers and cutting blades

201

for earth moving equipment. The technology for this endeavor had originally been acquired during the war. In 1943, the company's president had been summoned to the Navy's Construction Department and shown a bulldozer captured from the Americans. Tōto's plant engineers succeeded in experimental production just as the war was ending.

Tōto absorbed a subcontractor, Takahama Manufacturing (formerly, Taiyō Kōki), in 1955. Subsequently, Takahama and Tōto's Shinagawa plant were spun off as Tōto Zōki, specializing in tie plates and connecting plates for railway tracks. In 1956, Tōto Tekkō was established as a manufacturer of structural steel for buildings and bridges. Both firms purchased steel from Tōto Steelworks, and Fujikawa served as their board chairman.

Collectively these three companies plus Motor Wheel were known as the Tōto Group. In 1959, the group established a management council, which took charge of administering the companies' rationalization programs. This meant the four interdependent firms operated under a unified management policy. An early major decision was to expand capacity, by building a new mill at the former Navy air base in

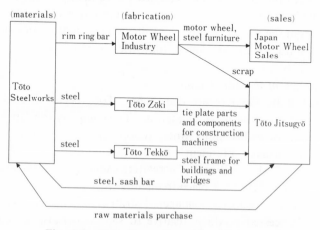

Fig. 5.4. Tōto Group Inter-Firm Linkages

Toyohashi. The plant commenced operation in 1960, equipped with two electric furnace of the largest capacity of the day, and a high efficiency rolling mill. Inter-firm linkages are illustrated in Figure 5.4.

The group also decided to become a member of the Yawata group, led by Japan's largest manufacturer of iron and steel, Yawata Iron and Steel Works (now Nippon Steel), in order to receive assistance in procurement and marketing activities.

The Birth of Topy Industries

The need to rationalize production had been a major reason for the formation of the Tōto Group's management council in 1959, and by 1960 the possibility of merging the companies was being considered as another step in making the companies internationally competitive.

After consultation with Yawata, Fuji Bank, and Nikkō Securities, the four merged to form Topy Industries in 1964. In addition, two companies, Japan Motor Wheel Sales and Tōto Jitsugyō, hitherto engaged in trading activities for the other four, also merged, forming Topy Jitsugyō. The mergers had seven objectives.

1. Stabilization of business: the diversification of products, encompassing steel material as well as fabricated products, would enable the merged company to mitigate the effects of business fluctuations.

2. Concentration and specialization of products: the production of a few specialized products by each plant would make it easier to reap the benefits of economies of scale.

3. More efficient research and development activities: integration of research staffs would lead to more enterprising and cost-effective R&D activities; for one thing, enhanced R&D would improve the quality of the products, leading to the promotion of sales.

4. Reduction of administrative costs: unification of the main and branch offices would reduce the number of employees and, consequently, administrative costs in general.

5. Strengthening of business capabilities: a centralized system of materials procurement would reduce cost, thereby enhancing the

Table 5.10.   Growth of Topy Industries, 1964–79

(in million yen)

Fiscal Year (1 April to 31 March)	Sales	Net profit before tax	Fixed assets	Number of employees
1964	18,481	449	17,635	4,938
1965	21,232	−1,804	18,420	4,326
1966	27,081	22	19,162	4,171
1967	31,671	110	19,113	4,222
1968	34,820	357	19,586	4,228
1969	24,576	752	20,309	3,846
1970	48,135	975	27,651	3,932
1971	45,081	357	28,949	3,746
1972	55,096	956	34,262	3,530
1973	75,810	1,800	34,530	3,396
1974	95,873	1,427	38,002	3,213
1975	83,102	1,214	33,387	3,658
1976	94,507	1,231	33,757	3,425
1977	103,039	1,029	38,401	3,375
1978	119,334	2,185	39,900	3,332
1979	133,817	2,884	41,251	3,395

Sources: Topy Kōgyō (1971), pp. 386–87 and Ōkura Shō (Ministry of Finance), *Yūka shōken hōkoku sho sōran* [Report on Corporate Securities], various issues.

price competitiveness of the final products of the company.

6. Centralization of investment planning: through a unified investment plan, effective deployment of funds would become possible,
e.g., the more efficient utilization of idle assets, avoidance of
duplicate investment, etc.

7. Upgrading of financial strength: on the basis of reinforced, as
well as stabilized management, the financial position of the
merged firm would be improved.

The expected merits of the amalgamation notwithstanding, the merged firm stagnated its first few years, due to a generally depressed economic environment. In 1965, Yawata strengthened its ties with the company by sending in an adviser. It was not until 1968, when recovery became evident, that Topy realized its new vision of being a comprehensive manufacturer of transportation equipment. Table 5.10 presents some relevant data on Topy's growth.

5.7. Tokyo Radiator Manufacturing Company, Ltd.[10]

5.7.1 Company Profile

Founded : October 1938

Origins : 1905

Stock held by primary firms
(1979) : 25.1%(Isuzu)

Sales (1977–78) : ¥3,050 million

Profit net of tax (1977–78) : ¥142 million

Product lines : automobile radiators, industrial equipment, construction machinery, power machines and agricultural machinery; oil coolers for automobiles, inter coolers, after coolers and air coolers; fuel tanks, sub-fuel tanks, home tanks for central heating; power units: cooling fans and oil pans; and other sheet-metal products

Number of employees (1978) : 753

Number of plants (1978) : 3

Tokyo Radiator (Tokyo Rajietā Seizō, or TRS) has been one of the major first-tier ancillary firms supplying parts and components to Isuzu, which in the 1970s produced a wide range of commercial vehicles and a few passenger car models. TRS supplied Isuzu with all its original equipment (OE) requirements for radiators and fuel tanks in 1979. This constituted about 70 percent of the company's sales, while the remainder went to a number of producers of construction machinery, farm

---

[10] Daiyamondo Sha has published two short books on radiator manufacturers, including the company (1969a and 1969b). Some relevant information can be found in Isuzu Jidōsha (1957, 1977). Interviews were conducted in 1979.

equipment, and others.

TRS' sales volume grew at an average annual rate of 35 percent over the quarter century from the end of World War II. Its fixed assets increased at a comparable rate (33 percent) while the number of employees grew at a much slower pace, reaching a maximum of 957 in 1970, when management began to introduce relatively more labor-saving modern machines and equipment (see Table 5.11).

Among the major radiator manufacturers in Japan, TRS held fourth position after Nippondenso (producing for Toyota), Nippon Radiator (Nissan), and Tōyō Radiator (Toyota and Mitsubishi) in terms of number of radiators produced. The company's stock has been publicly traded on the second section of the Tokyo Stock Exchange since 1953.

TRS was one of the core members of *Kyōwa Kai*, the parts manufacturers association of Isuzu. The company had its own subcontrators' association, *Tōraji Kyōryoku Kai*, established in 1969, comprising 30 firms subcontracting such operations as pressing, metal-sheet forming and welding for TRS. In 1950, there had been only one subcontractor for TRS; by 1961 there were five. The management of TRS considered the benefits of subcontracting to lie in the utilization of cheaper labor and the maintenance of intra-group competition. Although by the late 1970s subcontractors paid more or less the same money wages as TRS, TRS had more extensive fringe benefits and incurred more administrative costs than the subcontractors.

5.7.2 Historical Development

TRS was established in Tokyo in 1938 by the integration of two firms, Nishimura Radiator Manufacturing Company and Nihon Bankin Kōgyō Company.

Nishimura Radiator Manufacturing Company

In 1938, Nishimura Radiator was well into its second quarter century, having been started in Azabu, Tokyo, in 1905 by Nishimura Tsunetarō as a small, privately-owned sheet metal shop (Nishimura Bankin Kōjō) for installing and repairing tin roofs. After some time, Nishimura

Table 5.11. Growth of Tokyo Radiator Manufacturing Company

(In thousand yen, except the last column)

Fiscal Year (1 May to 30 April)	Sales	Net profit before tax	Fixed assets	Number of employees
1938	600	96	499	150
1939	1,860	236	772	329
1940	1,961	382	986	449
1941	2,411	470	1,244	n.a.
1942	2,363	535	1,274	n.a.
1943	2,729	501	1,163	n.a.
1944	3,255	720	1,093	n.a.
1945	2,142	265	845	90
1946 & 1947[a]	21,092	623	888	n.a.
1948	51,933	860	799	n.a.
1949	48,935	2,286	1,184	n.a.
1950	103,275	6,932	8,371	163
1951	193,811	17,200	12,069	n.a.
1952	217,136	23,635	13,121	n.a.
1953	313,947	36,689	41,716	187
1954	273,585	26,548	40,367	181
1955	300,554	25,014	42,499	194
1956	482,656	50,696	76,237	221
1957	623,652	62,946	89,455	243
1958	610,176	62,773	79,138	241
1959	749,319	58,321	112,153	259
1960	1,055,200	76,546	265,359	332
1961	1,481,088	124,125	396,955	407
1962	1,487,045	137,224	384,879	412
1963	1,811,317	91,863	412,066	518
1964	1,867,095	79,039	623	
1965	2,044,803	73,454	766,745	507
1966	2,937,513	135,242	851,617	611
1967	3,860,548	171,927	1,145,442	653

Table 5.11. (continued)

Fiscal Year (1 May to 30 April)	Sales	Net profit before tax	Fixed assets	Number of employees
1968	4,893,517	164,213	1,315,665	833
1969	5,920,726	144,178	1,412,670	925
1970	6,191,331	72,521	1,501,043	957
1971	5,207,184	71,325	1,713,358	841
1972	6,626,774	57,406	2,108,556	883
1973	8,758,576	29,147	2,557,416	899

Notes: [a] TRS had only one fiscal term over these two years.
Sources: Tokyo Radiator Manufacturing Company.

expanded to include replacement parts for machine tools and for automobiles. There is no evidence he possessed any expertise in the production of radiators or any other auto parts when he started the business.

However, around the same time, Japan began to import automobiles. Nishimura, quickly recognizing the potential of the new development, approached a British engineer in 1910, and learned from him how to produce a radiator. Furthermore, he undertook the fabrication of some auto replacement parts such as fenders, hoods, and radiator-shells, although orders for such items were very limited in those days. After a while, the shop came to produce complete radiator units for the replacement market. By then he had succeeded in becoming a subcontractor for Ikegai Iron Works, supplying some steel sheet items (such as oil pans for lathes) as original equipment. Ikegai was a pioneer in Japanese machine tool making, having begun production in 1890. By 1925, the company was exporting to England.

As the number of vehicles in use grew, orders for replacement radiators increased steadily, accelerating in the 1920s after Ford and GM began assembly operations in Japan. Gradually, Nishimura's shop came to be recognized as a good repairer and manufacturer of radiators in the Tokyo area. He manufactured replacement radiators for two major models, Wooseley (British) and Chevrolet (American). In 1929, when Nishimura noted orders for replacement radiators would exceed his production capacity, he decided to open another shop in Gotanda, Tokyo, specializing in radiator production.

Some time after the establishment of the second shop, Nishimura was approached by Usui (later Ōse) Yoshizō, who was in charge of radiator production at the Ishikawajima Automobile Works. Usui sounded out Nishimura on the possibility of supplying radiator masks for Ishikawajima's truck production. The company had just been incorporated as a subsidiary of Ishikawajima Shipbuilding, which had been manufacturing Wooseley's A9 passenger car and a $1^1/_2$-ton truck since 1922 and 1924, respectively, under license. The shipbuilder spun off its automobile department in 1929.

Nishimura accepted the offer and started to supply radiator masks to Ishikawajima. In this manner, Nishimura came to have a subcontracting relationship with an automobile manufacturer for the first time, although the supplied item was only a portion of a complete component and the volume modest (seven or eight units a month).

The demand for replacement radiators continued to increase. In addition to radiators for automobiles, Nishimura's shop began to accept orders for radiators for various other kinds of engines, including military use and gasoline engines installed in locomotives. Recognizing the growing demand, Nishimura decided to concentrate on radiator manufacturing and thus began taking steps to expand his production facilities. In May 1934, he renamed his factory Nishimura Radiator Manufacturing, and in December of the same year, transformed it into a stock company. At about this time, he established a third plant, in Shinagawa, Tokyo, larger than the existing ones. Most of the twenty-plus workers at the time were technicians from northern districts (Hokkaidō and Tōhoku). These areas were good sources of sheet-metal forming technicians because most of the houses had tin roofs—snow slides off tin and the region has heavy snow falls.

Nishimura invited Hirose Taijirō, in 1933, and Umemura Rokunosuke, in 1934, to assume directorships of the company. Both were design engineers from Ikegai Iron Works, which for many years had been one of Nishimura's most important customers.

Nihon Bankin Kōgyō Company

Nihon Bankin, which was to constitute the other half of TRS, was established in July 1937 as a subsidiary of Ikegai Iron Works.

Its establishment as a radiator and other sheet metal item supplier for Ikegai was reportedly a last-minute decision. In May 1937, encouraged by the Automobile Industry Act of 1936, Ikegai decided to diversify into automobile production, and established Ikegai Automobile Manufacturing. Umemura, who had been with Nishimura Radiator, returned to Ikegai and became a core member in the plan to set up Nihon Bankin.

Nihon Bankin started operations in late 1937 (paid-in capital, 200,000 yen) with its head office and factory in Kawasaki, an industrial city adjacent to Tokyo.

Formation of a New Company: TRS

In October 1938, Nihon Bankin integrated with Nishimura Radiator Company to form TRS. Ikegai Hideo, who had been president of both Nihon Bankin and Ikegai Iron, headed the new company. With a capital of 625,000 yen it started with two major factories: the Shinagawa plant producing radiators and the Kawasaki plant producing radiator masks, oil coolers and other sheet metal products.

Shinagawa Plant

Land site:	1,980 square meters
Floor space:	1,530 square meters (including office, warehouse and dining facilities)
Machinery:	lathe (1), shapers (2), boring machines (6), presses (24), pipe drawing machines (5), rollers (4), shearing machines (5), and others (40)

Kawasaki Plant

Land site: 20,000 square meters

Floor space: 1,270 square meters (including office, warehouse and dining facilities)

Machinery: lathes (7), milling machine (1), shapers (2), boring machines (8), grinding machines (4), presses (11), shearing machines (2), and others (18)

TRS had a good start, supported by increasing demand from three sources: Ikegai Iron, Ikegai Automobile, and Automobile Industries (Jidōsha Kōgyō), all of which had immediate access to the military market. (Automobile Industries was the result of the government-encouraged 1933 merger of Ishikawajima Auto with DAT. In 1937 the automobile department of Tokyo Gas & Electric was added. It was renamed Diesel Motor Industries when four other companies were added in 1941. After the war the company became Isuzu. See Figure 4.2, p. 97.)

Because of the war, TRS became part of the munitions industry. In 1940, more than 95 percent of the company's production was for military use, initially for the Army, later primarily for the Navy. TRS had a chance to expand its production capacity during the early stages of the war, but suffered considerable loss during the latter part because of shortages of material, manpower and utilities.

The following were the production facilities owned by TRS in 1941, showing how much the firm had expanded in just four years.

Shinagawa Plant

Land site: 1,980 square meters

Floor space: 1,700 square meters

Machinery: lathes (3), milling machine (1), shapers (2), presses (24), pipe drawing machines (5), and others (40)

Work force: 217

Kawasaki Plant

Land site: 20,000 square meters

Floor space: 4,800 square meters

Machinery: lathes (12), milling machines (5), boring machines

212

(10), grinding machines (2), shapers (3), presses
(22), roller (1), shearing machines (3), bending
machine (1), and others (38)

Work force: 198

In June 1945 TRS experienced an important structural change. While the majority of TRS stock had been held by Ikegai Iron Works, a major portion of its products were supplied to the military forces through Diesel Motor Company. At the suggestion of the Munitions Administration Office, which wanted to keep TRS under complete control of Diesel Motor, all of Ikegai's share of TRS was sold to Diesel Motor. At the same time, all of the TRS directors, with the exception of Hirose Taijirō, were replaced by management dispatched from Diesel Motor. Tsumura Tōkichi then assumed the presidency of TRS.

Postwar Reconstruction: 1945–53

The war left TRS with no market, exhausted production facilities, and no president—Tsumura died in October. For a while its employees reconditioned the machinery and manufactured cooking pans and weeding instruments for their own use with leftover materials. This situation lasted until February 1946. The Occupation Army had issued, in September 1945, the "Memorandum on the Manufacturing Industry," which advised former munitions-manufacturing firms to restart operations to meet civilian demand, within prescribed guidelines. The production of trucks was given a high priority, so TRS could resume production of radiators. Hotta Sei became president in June 1946.

Although the Japanese economy experienced a serious recession from 1949 to 1950 under an anti-inflation retrenchment policy, TRS did not get into serious financial difficulty because it continued to receive steady orders from Isuzu, which had Occupation Army procurement orders.

The outbreak of the Korean War produced sizable demand for special procurement of various commodities. The war boom stimulated the overall economy and brought the country foreign currency, which made possible the importation of badly needed modern machinery.

Trucks and other vehicles constituted a large portion of this demand. The total of the special procurement orders obtained by the three major automobile manufacturers (Toyota, Nissan and Isuzu) from July 1950 to March 1951 amounted to about ten billion yen. Isuzu sold 1,256 vehicles to the U.S. forces. Taking advantage of this opportunity, many industries started modernization and expansion of their production facilities. Encouraged by the overall growth of the economy, the automobile industry entered a new stage of growth, concentrating in the production of commercial vehicles. Isuzu was no exception to this, and it meant that TRS also entered a new stage in its development.

New Age of Growth: 1953–65

TRS had a good opportunity to prepare for expansion just before the start of the high-growth period. In February 1953, Isuzu signed a technological agreement with Rootes Motors to assemble and market the Hilman Minx in Japan. This was TRS' and Isuzu's first experience in producing passenger cars. Isuzu achieved full domestic production of the Hilman in October of 1957. The technological agreement ended in May 1965, by which time Isuzu had assembled or manufactured 51,876 cars.

TRS began to produce radiators, fuel tanks and other components for Hilman models according to the design specifications prepared by the British company. The specifications prepared by Rootes required a much higher level of product quality than TRS could produce with the then existing facilities of the company. Consequently, TRS undertook what it called its "first modernization program" to upgrade its facilities to meet the requirement for product quality as well as the need for larger production capacity. The new machines included an infrared paint drying machine, a set of trolley conveyors, high precision tube drawing machines, and an automatic core cleaning machine. Most of this equipment was imported from either Europe or the United States. This active investment, made mainly in 1953, more than doubled the book value of the company's fixed assets.

The "second modernization program" was carried out in 1957.

Automation was the major focus. A new assembly shop (with a floor space of 1,400 square meters) was erected at the Kawasaki site and filled with either fully- or semi-automatic machines, many imported from the United States and Europe. The major innovations introduced were: an automatic fin-pressing machine, an electric-resistance type core heating furnace, an automatic plating machine, a high frequency induction superheater, a movable infrared paint drying machine, and portable spot-welding machines.

The third modernization period lasted from 1960 to 1962. It was aimed primarily at equipping the company with production facilities to supply radiators for Isuzu's first original passenger car model, the Bellel, which was marketed starting in 1962. The introduction of advanced modern mass production machines contributed to the further improvement of the company's technological capability. A series of large-scale mass production machines were introduced, including a 250-ton double-crank press, two 100-ton power presses, a 300-ton oil-pressure type double-action press, etc. Aside from these large machines, a wide range of production processes were renovated in order to expand production capacity or improve product quality.

In 1960, when Isuzu established a plant in Fujisawa specializing in production of small vehicles, TRS acquired a nearby site (86,383 square meters). By gradually transferring the production of fuel tanks and other products to the new plant, TRS's Kawasaki plant could now concentrate on the production of radiators.

On 24 December 1962, Hotta Hitoshi became chairman of the board and Hirose Taijirō succeeded him as president. In his first address to the employees as president, Hirose emphasized the importance of cost reduction in coping with international competition. In April 1961 importation of commercial vehicles was slightly liberalized. In March and April 1926, Hirose joined the first observation tour arranged by *Isuzu Jussha Kenkyū Kai* (A Joint Study Group of Ten Isuzu-related Companies) to visit vehicle and component manufacturers in the United States and Europe. What struck him during the tour was the considerable gap between production systems there and in Japan. Although TRS had made extensive efforts to modernize its production facilities, Hirose found them still far behind American and European firms especially in the degree of mass production. A typical European or American radiator maker was producing 20 to 25 thousand units per line per shift monthly within regular working hours, while TRS was producing about 10 thousand smaller units with extensive overtime.

A similar tour was organized every year until 1970, and the top management of TRS regularly joined it. The observation tours enabled TRS to select machinery relevant to its facilities modernization programs, including the design of the new Fujisawa plant in 1965. The tours were discontinued when American and European manufacturers belatedly realized how much Japan had learned.

During this period of rapid growth, TRS's sales increased almost seven-fold, from 300 million yen in 1955 to 2,045 million yen in 1965. Its net fixed assets grew 18 times, from 42 million yen in April 1956 to 767 million yen in April 1966.

The rapid growth of fixed assets was financed both by an increase in equity capital and in loans from banks. Paid-in capital increased 18-fold berween April 1956 (30 million yen) and April 1966 (540 million yen). A major portion of the loans came from TRS' main bank, Nihon Kangyō Ginkō. Isuzu facilitated the borrowing by guaranteeing repayment, especially when TRS needed to raise a substantial sum to establish its Fujisawa Plant. According to TRS management, the company made use of *Kishin-hō* financing (government-subsidized, low interest loans from the Japan Development Banks and Smaller Enterprise Loan Corporation) a few times but only for rather nominal amounts.

Product Diversification and International Commitment: 1966–79

TRS had restarted operations after World War II by producing radiators for trucks. A few years later it began to accept orders for other auto parts such as coolers and grill ornaments, although their share of the company's sales were nominal until 1954, when TRS began to produce components for Hilman models. TRS was assigned by Isuzu to produce not only radiators but also fuel tanks and fan guides for the

Hilmans. However, radiator sales still accounted for about 70 percent of total sales in 1965.

Diversification received further impetus in 1966, when establishment of the Fujisawa plant gave the company excess capacity. TRS started to sell shadow masks for color TV sets to Nippon Electric Company, established a mass assembly line for oil coolers at the Kawasaki plant, and a mass line for oil pans in the Fujisawa plant. In 1967, a specialized line for TV mask-frames was built at the Fujisawa plant, and in 1968, a mass production line for fuel subtanks was started. This was followed by a stream of new products and new models. In 1973, TRS established yet another plant, in Kanuma, Tochigi Prefecture, which concentrated on production of oil coolers and inter coolers. This plant was about 40 km from Isuzu's new Tochigi plant. Consequently, the share of radiators in the company's total sales gradually decreased to about 60 percent in 1968 and to about 50 percent in 1977. The share of automobile radiators decreased at an even faster pace, from about 65 percent in 1965 to 51 percent in 1968, and to 36 percent in 1977.

A notable move by the company during this period was its involvement in international economic activities. In November 1969, TRS concluded a technological agreement with Thai Radiator Company, the largest radiator manufacturer in Thailand, which had been in the business for more than a quarter of a century. Thai Radiator had for some years supplied radiators as original equipment (OE) to Isuzu and several European brands assembled in Thailand. In May 1978, another technological agreement was made between TRS and Auto Diesel Radiator Company of Indonesia. In this case, the initiative came from Auto Diesel, as Isuzu had no previous business operations in Indonesia.

Although TRS did not itself engage in export operations, its products spread around the world as Isuzu exported more and more of its vehicles. Isuzu's exports accelerated after 1970, when GM contributed capital and Isuzu became an important base for GM's worldwide production network. In the late 1970s Isuzu exported about a third of its output. All Isuzu vehicles were equipped with radiators and fuel tanks made by TRS.

5.7.3 *Motive Power of Growth*

Basically, TRS' growth has been heavily dependent on the growth of its primary firm, Isuzu. Since 1938, when TRS was formally established, up to the time of the survey in 1979, sales to Isuzu almost always made up more than two-thirds of the company's total sales. All of the

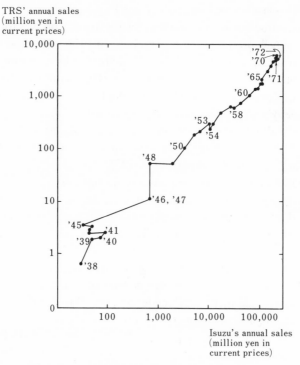

Fig. 5.5. Growth of Sales of Isuzu and TRS

Notes: Log scales.

Sales data refer to May-to-April period.

Sources: TRS: Table 5.11; Isuzu: 1957–72 figures have been taken from Ōkura Shō (Ministry of Finance), *Yūka shōken hōkoku sho* [Report on Corporate Securities], various issues, and 1938–56 figures have been estimated from Isuzu Jidōsha (1957), p. 189.

radiators and fuel tanks used by Isuzu had been continuously, as well as exclusively, supplied by TRS since the end of World War II. Figure 5.5 demonstrates the close correlation between the sales trends of TRS and Isuzu.

This close business relationship was initiated by the establishment, several years before the outbreak of World War II, of a subcontracting relation between Nishimura Radiator and Ishikawajima Automobile Manufacturing. Note, however, that the establishment of this relationship might not have taken place had the Wolseley not been the principal model for which Nishimura Radiator supplied replacement radiators.

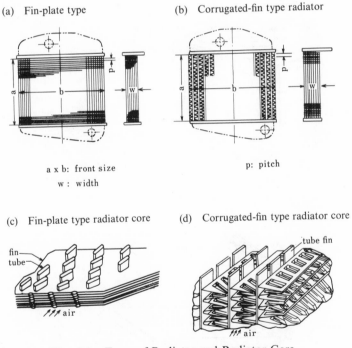

(a) Fin-plate type

(b) Corrugated-fin type radiator

a x b: front size
w : width

p: pitch

(c) Fin-plate type radiator core

(d) Corrugated-fin type radiator core

Fig. 5.6.   Types of Radiator and Radiator Core
Sources: Product catalogue, Tokyo Radiator Company.

5.7.4 *Highlights of Technological Progress*

In the 1970s radiators were classified into two basic types: fin-plate and corrugated-fin (see Figure 5.6). The first was the traditional design, while the second was a postwar innovation. TRS began to produce corrugated-fin radiators in 1963, although the fin-plate type still made up a considerable share of the company's production in 1979.

The basic structure of a fin-plate type radiator-core is illustrated in (c), Figure 5.6. Although the specification differed from model to model, a typical fin-plate type radiator core had about 200 tubes, which passed through about 170 fin-sheets.

In the 1930s the tubes were made solely by hand as illustrated in (a) of

(a) Tube making

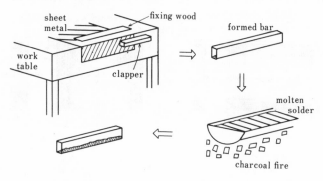

(b) Assembly

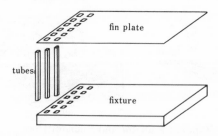

Fig. 5.7. The Early Manufacturing Method of Radiator Cores

Figure 5.7. A brass or copper sheet was bent manually by topping it with a wooden clapper, the formed portion was cut off with snips, then dipped in molten solder to form a tube, and lastly, the excess solder was removed to achieve the prescribed dimensions. With this method, an average worker could produce several tubes (each 50 cm long) per hour. Then the finished tubes were inserted into the holes of the fixure plate, and the fin sheets were slipped over them one by one. A skilled worker assembled about 10 sets of radiator cores per 12-hour day.

By 1938, Hirose had converted two old lathes into drawing benches, each of which could draw a tube of five to six meters in length every minute with one operator. The long, semi-finished tube was then cut into small pieces before going through the soldering and finishing processes.

In late 1945 TRS imported an automatic tube forming machine from K and Rosch Company of the United States under an arrangement made through Isuzu. This machine could process (draw, solder and cut) tubes at a speed of about 32 meters per minute. Although the production speed equalled other contemporary tube-forming machines, TRS found that the quality of the products was rather inferior to those made by the Hirose machine.[11] The speed of manufacturing another key part, the fin plate, was also increased with the introduction, in 1951, of an automatic fin-stamping machine, which produced ready-to-be assembled fin plate from copper coil.

Raw material for the tubes and fins was changed from brass or copper to zinc-plated steel during the war and then to various alloys after the war. The sheet became thinner and thinner over time. The metal sheet for making tubes, for instance, was 0.23 mm thick in the very early days. It was reduced to 0.20 mm when the Hirose machine was introduced and then to 0.18 mm when the automatic tube-forming machine was installed. In the late 1970s TRS used 0.13 to 0.15 mm thick sheets depending on the product models. According to the management of TRS, locally supplied raw materials caused minimal quality problems even in the prewar days.

[11] The most modern soldering-type tube-forming machine in the 1970s could produce 50 meters per minute. Welding-type machines produced 100 meters per minute.

Production of Components for Hilman Models

An important event in the technological progress of TRS was the production of OE components for Hilman models from 1954 to 1964. Shortly after the signing of the technological agreement with Rootes, Isuzu decided to close down its own sheet metal forming shop, which had been producing fuel tanks, and to transfer the operations to TRS. However, a press machine was the only production facility transferred from Isuzu to TRS. In other words, TRS introduced a completely new production process to take over the operation. This was necessary to meet the high quality standards required for Hilman components. For example, the specifications defined by Rootes Motors for Hilman's fuel tanks required seam-welding rather than soldering for assembly operation. Accordingly, TRS imported several seam-welding machines from the United States.

In the case of the radiator, the Hilman design had some features that

(A)　Traditional model

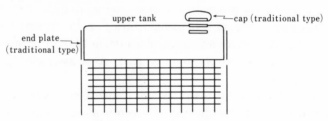

(B)　Hilman model

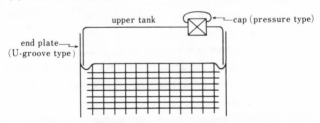

Fig. 5.8.　A Design Change Brought by Hilman Models

were different from TRS models. The most significant was the design of the top part of the radiator. As shown in Figure 5.8, the traditional TRS radiator had an end-plate with right-angled corners and an ordinary screw type cap in the upper tank. By contrast, Hilman's had a base with a U-shaped groove and a pressure-type, special cap, which made it possible for the upper tank to maintain a much higher inner pressure than the TRS type. The capacity for higher internal pressure contributed to the improvement of radiator efficiency and to the miniaturization of radiators by allowing faster circulation of water and reduction in the number of air bubbles in the tubes.

Another important example of technological progress of TRS was the introduction of an infrared paint drying machine. Until that time, painted products had been dried naturally, a process that took five days to assure good appearance of the final product and, occasionally, additional polishing operations were required to take off blurs generated by surface moisture. When one of the top managers of TRS saw an infrared unit in Isuzu's Fujisawa Plant, he was very much impressed with its performance and decided to introduce it at TRS.

TRS absorbed other techological designs and know-how by engaging in the production of Hilman components. In most cases, TRS did this by thoroughly inspecting the sample products sent from Rootes or through new machines introduced by Isuzu. There was no direct contact between the TRS staff and Rootes engineers, although Isuzu received some technological guidance from Rootes. (One engineer from Rootes spent a year in Japan, while engineers and management people from Isuzu visited Rootes from time to time.)

As to product design, TRS prepared its own drawings, in most cases based on measurements of sample products. This process, however, caused one technical problem for TRS engineers: most of the dimensions resulted in metric fractions, because the original designs were in inches.

Isuzu-General Motors Tie-up

According to the management of TRS, there was no specific tech-nological transfer directly from this relationship. However, management recognized it did result in some indirect, favorable benefits for TRS. First, the tie-up brought TRS a larger volume of orders for a greater variety of product designs. Thus, TRS was able to accumulate more technological and manufacturing experience. Second, exporting to GM gave all TRS personnel (management, engineers and workers) an informal yet strong stimulus to be conscious of product quality, especially in the earlier stage.

Commitment to Production Management

Because company management placed priority on the improvement of product quality, significant effort and resources were directed toward attainment of this objective until some time in 1960, when the company started to put more emphasis on cost reduction. To integrate these two objectives, TRS started a TQC (total quality control) movement in 1964 involving all employees. The company also actively participated in the VA (value analysis) activities of *Kyōwa Kai*, the association of Isuzu-related ancillary firms, beginning in 1965.

According to management, Isuzu seldom guided the production-management activities of its ancillary firms and never imposed its own methods on TRS. However, the ancillary firms were expected to make continuous progress in this area if only to meet trade conditions requested by Isuzu. For example, suppliers had to follow an inspection system prescribed by Isuzu for their shipments and had to be prepared to show their control charts on request. Management was proud that TRS met Isuzu's requests for cost reduction, which averaged two percent annually over the 25 years between 1953 and 1978.

Thus, TRS made remarkable progress not only in terms of the growth of its production volume but also in quality improvement and cost reduction. According to the judgment of the company management, TRS attained international standards in product quality in the early 1970s. Management conceded, however, that in the late 1970s the production cost of TRS radiators (and other Japanese manufacturers) was still higher than some American and European manufacturers, mainly because of the comparatively higher costs of various nonferrous metals. Tariff barriers, sheer size of the product, which made its transportation cumbersome, and the close relationship of primary firms to their suppliers kept the foreign components out of Japanese cars.

5.8. NGK Spark Plug Company, Ltd.[12]

5.8.1 Company Profile

Founded	:	October 1936
Origins	:	1921
Stock held by primary firms (1979)	:	2.7% (Toyota)
Sales (1975–1976)	:	¥22,785 million
Profit net of tax (1975–1976)	:	¥1,036 million
Product lines	:	spark plugs for motor vehicles, racing cars, aircraft, agricultural machinery, chain saws, fishing and other boats; glow plugs for diesel engines; and industrial ceramics (ceramic parts for electronic machinery, industrial machinery including ceramic bits, and telecommunication devices)
Number of employees (1976)	:	3,357
Number of plants (1976)	:	3
Number of ancillary firms	:	5
Number of domestic plants (1976)	:	23 including service centers
Number of overseas plants (1976):		4 (Brazil, Malaysia, Thailand and the U.S.A.)
Overseas distributors (1976)	:	4 (England, Singapore, the U.S.A. and West Germany)

5.8.2 Historical Development

Ezoe Magoemon: Entrepreneurial Engineer

The NGK Spark Plug (Nippon Tokushu Tōgyō) Company was

[12] There are three company-published histories (Nihon Tokushu Tōgyō 1957, 1967, 1977), a book in the Daiyamondo-sha series (1966), and a study by Koide (1961). Interviews were conducted in 1979.

formally established in October 1936 when it was spun off from its mother corporation, Nippon Insulator (Nippon Gaishi Company or NG for short). NG had been engaged for quite some time prior to this in the development and domestic manufacture of spark plugs for motor vehicles.

The idea of going into spark-plug production was conceived in 1920 when Ezoe Magoemon, the first president of NGK, visited a Champion Spark Plugs plant in Detroit. Having observed American society, where automobile demand was rapidly developing, Ezoe was convinced a similar phenomenon would repeat itself in his own land. Spark plugs were a logical product for his company, as he could take advantage of its unique technology for ceramic ware manufacturing.

Ezoe was born in 1885, eldest son of a ceramic wares manufacturer in Arita, Saga Prefecture, a town with a long tradition for ceramic wares, called *Arita-yaki*. His father was not a particularly well-to-do businessman and could not even offer his son a higher education. Nonetheless, Ezoe made his own way through specialized training in ceramic engineering, graduating in 1909 from the Tokyo Technical High School (now known as the Tokyo Institute of Technology).

Upon graduation, he was immediately employed by the Noritake plant of Nippon Ceramic Wares (Nippon Tōki), which was then trying to discover proper glazing techniques for production of western dinner sets using domestically available clay. At 26 (in 1910) Ezoe was appointed head of the engineering section, and slowly managed to improve product quality. In late 1911 he succeeded not only in raising the average rate of kiln utilization to 80 percent and maintaining it at this level, but also in reducing the rejection rate and increasing the proportion of better quality (and higher-priced) merchandise. In 1911 the company registered net profits for the first time in many years.

In 1912 Ezoe was offered an opportunity to visit the Victoria factory in Austria, where he observed technology necessary to improve ceramic quality. Subsequently, he met an expert in Berlin who suggested to him an improvement in the use of glazes. Drawing on this experience, Ezoe had, by the end of 1913, finally succeeded in the production of refined ceramic ware. Largely as a consequence, Ezoe was put in charge of NG's production management when it was spun off from Nippon Ceramic Wares (Noritake) in 1919. The major product of the new company was porcelain insulators.

Ezoe surprised his colleagues by abolishing the tradition of the two-grade system, which classified products into two classes, A and B, in terms of quality. At the same time, he emphasized production efficiency and initiated the first standard motion study of insulator production, which led to significant reductions in the rate of defects.

In 1921, Ezoe argued that an electric-engineering company should base its purchasing order solely on the quality of insulators. He insisted that experiments be undertaken whereby his company's insulators would be tested against American and other domestic brands. The experiment disclosed that the NG insulators were superior in average strength to the other brands with the exception of a few inferior NG products that had been impaired by the irregularity of the ceramic bodies: The discovery of these defects seriously upset Ezoe, who then intensified his efforts to improve the consisteny of the quality of his company products.

Also in 1921, NG began experimentation with spark plugs. Noritake's long years of research and experiments on ceramic wares, together with accumulated production know-how, had built a solid foundation on which NG could initiate domestic manufacture of spark plugs. It was obvious where the company's comparative advantage lay.

In 1930, NG began marketing its new product under the NG brand. As demand was meager, the company allotted only a tiny corner of the plant, with a floor space of approximately 100 square meters. Production was only 300–400 units per week, which of course did not justify the installation of a specialized kiln. Metal parts and carton boxes were all subcontracted, but were assembled by NG. Since welding technique was still relatively undeveloped, it was often necessary for the company to readjust the size of the end hole of the insulator through which the electric terminal was inserted. Breakage of the ceramic parts occurred fairly frequently, too. Above all, sales promotion encountered seemingly unsurmountable difficulties.

By 1932, however, 50 production workers were devoted to the production of spark plugs. In the following year, the company built a new kiln exclusively for the manufacturing of spark plug insulators. As the sales volume gradually increased, the company changed its brand name from NG to NGK, heeding a suggestion, made by Ford Japan, that NG could jokingly be associated with "no good."

Formation of the NGK Spark Plug Company

In 1936 Nippon Tokushu Tōgyō, or the NGK Spark Plug Company was spun off by NG with 259 employees, including 227 production workers and an administrative staff of 32. It was headed by Ezoe and had paid-up capital of one million yen. At the beginning, the company could not realistically expect to sell more than 25,000 spark plugs a month. This meant the new company could not possibly meet all its expenses by specializing in the production of spark plugs, so NG (the mother company) persuaded NGK to manufacture other products in the hope of realizing monthly total sales of about 50,000 yen, which was broken down as follows:

spark plugs (25,000 units)	¥15,000
radio shields	20,000
ceramic filters	13,000
acid-resistant cement	2,000.

The new company made a modest start in April 1937. Despite the small size of the operation, management allocated ten percent of its initial endowment to research and development. The initial phase of the war economy was soon to bring a rising demand for motor vehicles and thus for NGK parts and components. The company added a new factory building in 1938 and in 1939 successfully developed a new ceramic body (called P3) for use in spark plug insulators. However, the military administration constantly asked for accelerated levels of production, especially from about 1944. Ezoe was forced to withdraw as company president in the spring of 1944, as he had stubbornly resisted the military's demand. Ezoe's argument was that output could be increased only at the expense of product quality.

New Age

It was only after 1948, that the company entered a phase of sustained rapid growth. Price controls on spark plugs were abolished in October 1948, and the company's stock was listed in May 1949. The business outlook was particularly depressed because of deflation—causing the company to dismiss 336 of its 782 employees. But the Allied Occupation forces lifted all restrictions on automobile production in October of the same year.

Meanwhile, NGK went through a period of critical self-examination as it anticipated the advent of the automobile age in Japan. It realized the need to reassess and strengthen its technological foundation in preparation for the expected subsequent growth. This effort included development of the P5 body, which was completed in May 1951. In 1952, the company organized a management training (MT) course as well as a training-within-the-industry (TWI) program.

In the decade 1948–57 the volume of production tripled. In 1961, when the monthly production of spark plugs exceeded two million units, the company introduced a cold-former which manufactured metallic parts solely by pressing, eliminating the need for shearing operations. In

Table 5.12. Index of Labor Requirements (kōsū)[a] in Spark Plug Production (1948 = 100)

1948	100
1953	42
1958	16
1963	11
1968	5
1973	3
1978	2

Notes: [a] Total labor units directly utilized in the production of a unit of spark plug.

Sources: NGK Spark Plug Company.

1964 the kiln operation was automated. As a result, the level of production tripled again between 1958 and 1964. The work force increased just 50 percent during those sixteen years (1948–64), implying a tremendous improvement in production efficiency. In order to illustrate this, Table 5.12 presents data on historical changes in the company's labor productivity. It is evident that 1949 marked the beginning of a long upward movement, with the rate of growth accelerating after the mid-1960s.

While the domestic market expanded, NGK began to form an overseas network; it received its first orders in 1957 from Saudi Arabia and Taiwan. In the succeeding decades exports became an indispensable part of the company's sales. In the period 1951–55 only 4 out of 100 spark plugs were sent overseas; the ratio went up to an average of 43 out of 100 in the 1971–75 period. Indeed, by 1975 NGK spark plugs attained fourth place in the world market in terms of production volume.

5.8.3 Market Factors
OE vs. SP

Because the spark plug is a relatively short-lived component, manu-facturers could count on an extensive after market even in the early phase of development of the motor car industry. At the very beginning, NGK sold almost 90 percent of its products as replacement goods. The spare-parts to original equipment ratio (SP/OE) declined to four to one during the period 1957–67, eventually reaching the level of two to one in the late 1970s. The ratio may be compared with the corresponding figure in the United States in the 1970s which was said to be about eight to one, or slightly lower.

Sales promotion proved difficult in the early days of the company's development. Aside from replacement demand, NGK constantly sought new OE orders. The approval of the Army's Automobile Training School (in 1931) was thus most welcome. At one time, the company's president, Ezoe, personally approached a Navy official for the possible adoption of NGK plugs. Although the campaign yielded an order of only 300 units, it also led to the registration of the company's name on the Navy's procurement list in 1934.

NGK naturally got in touch with automobile assemblers. Whereas GM Japan never dealt with NGK, Ford Japan agreed to adopt NGK (then named NG) spark plugs as genuine parts on the condition that the contracted price be kept at 0.40 yen per unit as compared with the prevailing market price of 0.70 yen. While the company was willing to go along with this offer, the military administration intervened and prevented a realization of the agreement. The company, however, was in a sense compensated when domestic automobile assemblers such as Toyota and Nissan adopted its spark plugs as original equipment from the very beginning. Domestically manufactured motor cars have seldom made use of imported spark plugs as OE parts.

Sales promotion was no longer necessary after 1937 when war with China led to stepped-up production, mainly for use in military trucks. This event netted the company a profit 2.5 times higher than in preceding years.

During the post-World War II period, a standard spark plug for four-wheel vehicles (with four-cycle engines) normally lasted about a year. The average interval between replacement did not change much over the years.

Market Share

The huge demand for automobile parts during the war explains why the spark plug market in 1946 was shared by at least 15 producers, the most important being (with monthly production capacity in thousands):

> NGK (200),
> Aichi Kagaku (100),
> Morita Nainenki (60),
> Taihei Kōgyō (30),
> Hitachi (10),
> Oki Kōgyō (10),
> Nihon Tokki (10),
> Kunihana Denki (5)

(Nihon Tokushu Tōgyō 1967, p. 46).

When automobile production resumed after World War II, the spark plug market experienced a period of sharp increase in demand. As a result, the market was flooded with rebuilt NGK plugs. This caused some confusion in the market because their external appearance was not readily distinguishable from a genuine new plug. At a time when new plugs sold for 120 yen each, a manufacturer of rebuilt plugs could purchase a used plug for around 10 yen, add fabricating value of about 40 yen, and sell it for 60 yen.

Although spark plugs enjoyed a relatively large (and growing) market, there were factors that discouraged participation. First and foremost, production of the ceramic bodies not only requires very specialized engineering technology, but also is a highly capital-intensive operation. In 1979, for instance, investment in a tunnel kiln would not be economically justifiable unless the scale of monthly production exceeded one million units. It was no coincidence, therefore, that the manufacture of spark plugs in less developed countries was largely confined to assembly operations as well as to machine fabrication of metallic parts. Even in Japan, several companies chose to drop out rather than make the necessary investment. Primarily for this reason, NGK's market share in spark plugs was over 70 percent in the 1960s. However, in 1975, its share was about 65 percent, and in 1980 was just over 60 percent.

As evident from Table 5.13, the role of overseas markets became tremendously important in the postwar years. The earliest export opportunity presented itself with the outbreak of the Korean War, which brought NGK a special procurement order of 600,000 spark plugs, roughly equivalent to four months' of capacity at that time.

It was not until the middle of the 1950s, however, that the company consciously began to cultivate the overseas market. For instance, NGK took advantage of an International Exposition held in Brazil in May 1954, subsequently opening a subsidiary there and in Ecuador. In February of the following year, a top executive visited selected Asian countries for sales promotion. Despite these efforts, however, export demand grew very slowly. Fortunately, around that time, a Honda vehicle won first prize in an international motorcar rally held in

Table 5.13.   NGK Sales, Employment, and Wages, 1937–75

Fiscal Year[a]	Gross sales (in million yen)		Spark plug production (in 10,000)		Total number of employees[c]	Average monthly wages (in thousand yen)[d]		
	Total	Spark plugs[b]	Total	Exported		Male	Female	Total
1937	1.3	n.a.	42	—	439	n.a.	n.a.	n.a.
1938	2.3	n.a.	159	—	870	n.a.	n.a.	n.a.
1939	3.7	n.a.	243	—	1,014	n.a.	n.a.	n.a.
1940	4.1	n.a.	299	—	1,182	n.a.	n.a.	n.a.
1941	4.5	n.a.	314	—	1,333	n.a.	n.a.	n.a.
1942	6.7	n.a.	306	—	1,813	n.a.	n.a.	n.a.
1943	7.4	n.a.	252	—	2,038	n.a.	n.a.	n.a.
1944	13.1	n.a.	98	—	2,276	n.a.	n.a.	n.a.
1945	7.3	n.a.	68	—	579	n.a.	n.a.	n.a.
1946	11.1	n.a.	150	—	775	n.a.	n.a.	n.a.
1947	115	n.a.	248	—	906	n.a.	n.a.	n.a.
1948	142	n.a.	258	60	823	n.a.	n.a.	n.a.
1949	138	n.a.	117	4	422	n.a.	n.a.	n.a.
1950	205	n.a.	203	—	509	n.a.	n.a.	n.a.
1951	397	n.a.	330	36	540	n.a.	n.a.	n.a.
1952	480	n.a.	342	12	649	n.a.	n.a.	n.a.
1953	814	n.a.	593	14	809	n.a.	n.a.	n.a.
1954	738	n.a.	566	31	796	n.a.	n.a.	n.a.
1955	805	n.a.	605	10	769	n.a.	n.a.	n.a.
1956	1,117	929	790	37	800	n.a.	n.a.	n.a.
1957	1,086	874	861	67	746	n.a.	n.a.	n.a.
1958	977	825	764	43	746	n.a.	n.a.	n.a.
1959	1,439	1,145	1,195	88	1,111	n.a.	n.a.	n.a.
1960	2,031	1,599	1,745	131	1,462	35	14	27
1961	2,383	1,896	2,014	190	1,642	33	14	24
1962	2,683	2,212	2,454	284	1,659	29	14	13
1963	3,309	2,635	3,068	378	1,903	34	16	27
1964	3,571	2,839	3,475	546	1,610	33	17	27

Table 5.13. (continued)

Fiscal Year[a]	Gross sales (in million yen)		Spark plug production (in 10,000)		Total number of em-ployees[c]	Average monthly wages (in thousand yen)[d]		
	Total	Spark plugs[b]	Total	Ex-ported		Male	Female	Total
1965	3,804	3,097	3,626	667	1,647	35	18	29
1966	5,175	3,772	4,704	1,149	2,161	45	23	37
1967	6,810	4,530	5,661	1,432	2,582	50	27	41
1968	7,946	5,080	6,291	2,000	2,810	47	28	40
1969	10,455	6,231	7,968	2,554	3,203	59	35	49
1970	13,049	7,874	9,498	3,550	3,648	69	43	59
1971	13,505	9,050	10,909	4,248	3,291	71	46	62
1972	15,194	10,151	11,975	4,618	3,366	87	56	77
1973	19,985	12,066	13,603	5,707	3,636	106	69	95
1974	41,972	14,645	15,417	7,320	3,429	136	88	121
1975	22,785	15,280	13,510	6,297	3,357	152	98	137

Notes: [a] Fiscal year 1937 began on 1 April 1937 and ended on 31 March 1938; similarly for other years.
[b] No data before 1956.
[c] As of end of fiscal year; inclusive of temporary workers.
[d] Inclusive of overtime payment but exclusive of bonuses. Data for years before 1960 are not avaialble.

Sources: NGK Spark Plug Company.

England. Since the vehicle was equipped with NGK spark plugs, the company's product suddenly attracted worldwide attention. The first overseas order of 30,000 spark plugs was received in 1956. Subsequently, the records of export volume were constantly broken until the early 1970s.

Price Behavior

Although not adjusted for quality differences, the data suggest NGK plugs were price competitive with imported products (such as Bosch and

Table 5.14. Distribution of Production Costs of NGK Spark Plugs

(In percent)

Items	1950	1960	1970
Labor	47	33	39
Raw materials	29	36	29
Purchased parts	2	5	7
Others	22	26	25

Sources: NGK Spark Plug Company.

Champion) even in the mid-1930s when the volume of production was physically limited. In 1970, the NGK product was definitely competitive (Nihon Tokushu Tōgyō 1967, pp. 26 and 50).

The behavior of unit prices was significantly affected by the trend in investment in capital equipment. As can be seen from Table 5.14, expenditures for labor accounted for 40 percent of total production cost. The high rate of capital investment in the 1960s resulted in a phenomenal improvement in production efficiency, offsetting the increased costs of labor and raw materials. Consequently, the estimated average ex-factory price showed a clear declining tendency throughout the 1960s.

Intercompany Linkages

The company received little help from outsiders, including primary firms (assemblers), in the course of its development. About the only exception to this was that NGK often counted on the willingness of the military and assemblers such as Ford Japan and Tokyo Gas & Electric (now Isuzu) to provide engines for experimentation and product development in the late 1920s. In like manner, the company leased testing engines from Toyota and Nissan immediately after World War II.

As is the case with the manufacturers of springs, NGK's relatively independent stance is a special characteristic of the relationship between NGK and its primary firms. This is largely due to NGK's well-established technology, especially in ceramic production, and also to the timing of its development, which preceded the full-fledged growth of the automobile industry.

Despite such independence, NGK always faced extremely difficult contractual negotiations with the automobile assemblers. While there were standing orders from the assemblers, the price was subject to annual renegotiation. The primary firms continuously demanded annual price reductions (by two to three percent) on original equipment. In the 1945–79 period, the oil crisis of 1973 was the only occasion when a price increase (in absolute terms) was granted by the primary firms. NGK management complained that the contractual price was often so low that it hardly covered its average unit production cost.

Just as NGK had little managerial linkage with the primary firms, it established only a minimum ancillary network. Metallic components (electric terminals) were originally subcontracted. However, the ancillary firm went bankrupt, so in 1932 NGK switched to in-house supply of these components. Metallic accessories were transferred to in-plant production in 1934 for a similar reason.

Table 5.15. Proportions of Subcontracted Parts: NGK (by value)

(In percent)

1966	3.9
1967	4.3
1968	3.8
1969	3.1
1970	4.8
1971	4.5
1972	4.3
1973	5.6
1974	5.9
1975	6.1

Sources: Nihon Tokushu Tōgyō (1977), p. 88.

In 1961 NGK established an ancillary firm called Nittoku Manufacturing, which specialized in the production of metallic parts for use in spark plugs. Later, four other ancillary firms were added. There were two major reasons for this change of policy: the physical limit to further expansion and the need to create employment opportunities for those who had reached retirement age but still wished to continue working. In any event, the proportion of NGK's components contracted outside of the company gradually increased over the years 1966–75 as shown in Table 5.15.

5.8.4 Technological Factors

Engineering specifications important to the design of spark plugs are the degree of resistance of the insulator to electric current, heat and physical pressures, and the resistance of the metallic terminal to heat and chemical corrosion. When combustion engines operated under relatively low pressures, any ceramic material (even mica) would perform satisfactorily, but as the design of engines improved, internal air pressure increased, necessitating corresponding changes in engine components to assure optimum performance. In addition, the adoption of gasoline containing tetraethyl lead as an antidetonator and iron carbonyl called for the development of an insulator that could withstand new chemical compounds. It was precisely for this reason the use of sinterred alumina was initiated in later years.

NG began exploring the commercial possibility of spark plugs for motor cars as early as April 1921. Following his own visit to the Champion plant, Ezoe dispatched two engineers, Katō Kaoru and Nakamura Takashi to the United States in 1923 to study the manufacture of spark plugs. In the wake of this trip, decisions were prompt and experimentation swift, and by 1926 the company was ready to send samples to the Army's Aviation Training School for testing. The test yielded favorable results. Consequently, the company officially announced its intention to enter the spark plug market later in that year.

This relatively early success was undoubtedly due to the company's previous experience in ceramic production. But Ezoe was also renowned among his colleagues for his zeal in continually improving product quality as well as in maintaining high standards. In August 1926, as the company was about to close its first sale, a few defects were spotted. Ezoe immediately ordered an indefinite postponement of the plan and recalled all the plugs that had already been delivered.

The trouble was ascribed to irregularity of the temperature inside the kiln, which led Ezoe to visit Europe and the United States for the second time in 1927 to look for a more suitable kiln. The choice was a Harrop's tunnel kiln. An American engineer was invited to direct construction, which was completed by the end of August 1928 and put into full-scale operation in February 1929. However, the spark plug division had to share the kiln with other divisions until 1933 when a new kiln was constructed for the exclusive use of the spark plug division. The adoption of the tunnel kiln resulted in a high degree of uniformity in the company's ceramic products, thus enhancing the reputation of the NG brands.[13]

This also led to improvement of the ceramic bodies by combining low-loss cordierite with imported zircon, so that the spark plug insulators could resist rapid and frequent changes in temperature. This was called the P1 body. The company further continued its research efforts, especially to find measures to reduce the rate of ceramic breakage. In particular, the Bosch spark plug exemplified the type of merchandise the company engineers desired to manufacture. Bosch had a major share of the market and high-quality products.

In 1928 the rate of spark plug production was a few hundred per week. Even when the plugs were formally adopted by the Army's Automobile Training School (October 1931), monthly production was only 1,000 units. NG could not afford to purchase automobile engines for experimentation purposes. Consequently, the company secured assistance from Tokyo Motor (Tokyo Jidōsha, now known as Isuzu)

---

[13] For instance, the average annual deterioration rate of the NG insulators used for long-distance high-voltage distribution lines declined from 5.0 percent in 1921 to 1.5 percent in 1929–30. By comparison, the American rate was as low as 1.0 percent in 1921 and other domestic producers had rates around 7.6 percent in 1928.

whenever the former developed a new model.

In 1932 the subcontractor for metallic parts went bankrupt. As a consequence, NG decided to internally manufacture electric terminals. In the meantime, research on ceramic quality resulted in the adoption of a new ceramic body called P3 in 1939.

The demand for spark plugs reached an unprecedented peak with the approach of the war economy; NGK was obliged to concentrate on spark plugs alone, and to give up the production of filters and acid-resistant cement in 1943. At the same time, NGK established a training institute for production workers in a renewed effort to prevent the deterioration of product quality.

The quality of NGK spark plugs in the late 1930s and the 1940s was in all likelihood inferior to that of its western counterparts, particularly with regard to the uniformity and durability. However, this was irrelevant: domestic manufacturers of motor vehicles, particularly the military, were committed to using domestic spark plugs, and tariffs helped price superior foreign products out of the market.

Age of Technological Spurts

The decades of phenomenal technological advance came at the end of World War II. In this regard we can cite two major developments. First, ceramic bodies underwent a series of new developments. To eliminate difficulties in the calcination procedure, cordierite was replaced in November 1947 by a mixture of alumina and mullite to form P4 bodies. In May 1951 the company, in close cooperation with Nippon Keikinzoku (Japan Light Metal Manufacturing), succeeded in developing new bodies, called P5, to match the requirements of passenger vehicles whose engines had higher compression ratios and faster engine speeds than commercial vehicles. In addition, P5 was superior to P4 in physical strength and in resistance to sudden temperature increase.

In 1948 NGK spark plugs were recognized by the Ministry of Commerce and Industry (Shōkō Shō) as high-quality products. Similarly they were awarded JIS (Japan Industrial Standard) marks by MITI (the Ministry of International Trade and Industry) in November

1952.

Second, utmost effort was exerted to manufacture a product of high quality in great quantities at reduced cost. To achieve this, the company marshalled all its technical abilities and responded to the demands of automobile engine manufacturers. Also, domestic air service was resumed in June 1950, and NGK again started production of spark plugs for airplane engines.

With the increase in the average horsepower of automobile engines, not only were the revolutions (speed) of the engines increased, but the size of the spark plugs became increasingly small: the diameter went from 18 mm to 14 mm and then to 10 mm. These changes necessitated corresponding transformations in spark plugs: higher resistance to heat and pressure and better performance in calcination. Accordingly, a new P6 body (high alumina) was developed in 1954. Simultaneously, the company replaced the old machining operation for the production of metallic parts with a press forming process.

An inspection tour by NGK president Matsuo Yoshito to Europe and the United States in 1955 resulted in new ideas to improve the managerial system. It is for this reason that after 1956 the company became increasingly conscious of improving production efficiency. It was by no means a coincidence, therefore, that productivity growth increased around this time. Also, orders began flowing in from various places, e.g., 20,000 units from Japan's Self Defence Agency and 190,000 units from the Japan Auto Parts Industries Association (JAPIA), leading to the realization of scale economies.

Representative measures to improve production efficiency in the decades after 1956 are listed in Table 5.16. The results are clearly reflected in Table 5.12. Particularly after the late 1960s the company record indicates management attempted, and was moderately successful in slowing the increase in the size of its work force while improving its productive capacity.

Some cost calculations may be informative at this point. If one takes the decade of the 1960s, the data suggest workers' wage earnings increased at an annual rate of about 8 percent, while the physical

Table 5.16.   A Chronology of Major Technological Changes in
Spark Plug Production by NGK

1928	Introduction of Harrop's tunnel kiln
1932	In-house manufacturing of metallic parts
1933	Establishment of tunnel kiln for exclusive use for spark plugs
1939	Adoption of P3 body
1947	Adoption of alumina-dominated P4 body
1951	Adoption of P5 body
1954	Introduction of press forming method
1955	Adoption of P6 body
1962	Introduction of vibrating crushing mill
1962	Introduction of spray drier
1962	Introduction of rubber press forming devices
1962	Introduction of cold former
1962	Replacement of metallic shearing by chucking machine
1962	Adoption of rotating glazer
1964	Introduction of fully-automated tunnel kiln
1967	Adoption of high-temperature, small tunnel kiln for P8 body
1967	Introduction of automated binder and automated rubber press
1967	Development of spark plugs for rotary engines
1969	Development of super-wide range plugs
1971	Development of V-plug (good for fuel economy)
1971/72	Development of monolink-type plugs
1975	Development of A-series plugs (good for non-lead fuel)

productivity of labor increased at about 11 percent. At the same time, the wholesale price index of ceramic wares and metal materials went up by at least 2 percent per annum (*Japan Statistical Yearbook*, 1978 edition, p.363). Improved efficiency made it possible to keep the overall level of unit cost almost constant. Indeed, it seems the average cost of spark plug production declined at the rate of one percent per annum during this period.

242

Although engineering problems have emerged from time to time in developing new products, not much difficulty has been encountered since the war in finding qualified production workers. In the late 1970s it took about one year for a male high school graduate to learn a key job, and approximately three years to master the cluster of jobs that constituted a unit of the production line; it would perhaps take him a total of ten years to become a leader in the entire process of spark plug production. Female workers were seldom assigned to key positions because they were expected to quit within a few years and thus required much shorter periods (about three months) to learn their jobs.

No formal training was attempted by the company in the 1945–79 period aside from a short introductory briefing at the time of entry. Essentially all the skill development took place by way of on-the-job training. After 1960, courses on value analysis (VA) as well as value engineering (VE) were held to help increase labor productivity. In April 1979 management also opened a new, long-term course on training within industry (TWI), designed specifically to upgrade the quality of production workers.

5.8.5 Government Policies

There were three government actions that directly helped the growth of NGK. First, both the Japanese Army and Navy in the prewar decades provided testing devices in addition to procuring spark plugs for their own use in the early 1930s. However, in the early days their orders were minimal; the military did little to enlarge the size of the market until the advent of the war economy.

More importantly, the government encouraged the domestic production of machinery and introduced protective tariffs. Beginning in 1930, spark plugs were subject to ten percent ad valorem duties. The rate went up in 1932 to 35 percent. The govenment's emphasis on domestic content greatly encouraged domestic manufacture of spark plugs, since the market had until then been practically dominated by foreign brands such as Lodge (England), Bosch (Germany), Champion (U.S.A.) and AC (U.S.A.). This measure, in fact, led to the mushrooming of local

243

spark plug manufacturers, with a total of more than 20 new brands.

After World War II, tariff protection continued for some time. The importation of spark plugs was practically prohibited in April 1955. The ban was later lifted, but the tariff rate continued to be set at a 15 percent level in 1961 (to be more exact, the higher of the following was applicable: 15 percent ad valorem tariff or the lump sum of ¥18 per plug.).

NGK also benefitted from the government's general economic policies, which placed first priority on economic growth. For instance, the Special Tax Law (*Sozei tokubetsu sochi hō*) of 1957 stipulated that certain industrial machinery could be allowed accelerated depreciation, whereby the period of depreciation was reduced from 19 to 13 years.

Chapter 6

PARTS PROCUREMENT PRACTICES IN THE JAPANESE AUTOMOBILE INDUSTRY: SUMMARY AND INTERPRETATION

We have conducted in-depth interviews of selected firms in order to present concrete examples of ancillary firm development in the Japanese automobile industry. Two primary and eight ancillary firms is obviously a small sample in view of the size of the entire population, and it would be difficult to draw any conclusive judgments from the data collected from the interviews. Furthermore, the sample firms were not randomly chosen. Some ancillary firms were selected for the authors by one of the primary firms, while others were selected jointly by the authors and experts from the Japan Auto Parts Industries Association (JAPIA). Nonetheless, it is worth reviewing the survey. The in-depth investigation of the ten sample firms reveals several general features which seem fairly common in the development processes of ancillary firms in Japan. This chapter summarizes our major findings and presents an interpretation of the development process of the selected firms.

6.1. General Features

Most of these companies started business when there was either a notable growth of the product market or some other favorable economic condition, usually a move by the government to promote or protect the industry.

When Nishimura Bankin, the predecessor of Tokyo Radiator, was founded in 1905, there was an economic boom following Japan's victory in the Russo-Japanese War (1904–05). Similarly, Ezoe Magoemon, who conceived the local manufacture of spark plugs and later became president of NGK, in 1921 initiated the experimental production of spark plugs in the wake of the first significant growth of the Japanese automobile market. The 1918 Act to Aid the Production of Military Vehicles had stimulated truck makers and the economy was still enjoying favorable effects of World War I. Although the war boom had ended in 1919, the number of automobiles in use at that time exceeded seven thousand, a level sufficiently high to familiarlize the general public in big cities with the new product.

In 1928, Nippon Insulator (the mother company of NGK) began commercial production of spark plugs, following establishment of knocked-down assembly plants by Ford and GM. NGK was formally incorporated in 1936 as an entity separate from the parent company. In the same year, the government initiated a full-scale domestication program for the industry with the Automobile Industry Act, which brightened the prospects for local parts manufacturers as well as for local automobile producers.

In 1937, Kojima Press entered the industry primarily because Kojima Hamakichi, founder of the firm, had been encouraged by the 1936 Act. A year earlier, Nippondenso, then an integral part of Toyota Motor, established a pilot plant to produce various electrical auto parts. This laid the foundation for the formal founding of Nippondenso Company in 1949.

While these firms were established under favorable economic conditions, there were a few exceptions to the rule. First, although Aisan was incorporated in 1938, the company had formally started in 1924 in the midst of a recession brought about as a reaction to the post-World War I economic boom. The company began as Fujita Tatsujirō's privately-owned shop, making spindles for cotton spinning mills. Another example would be Yazaki Sadami's private business in wire harnesses, encouraged by Toyoda Sakichi, and started in 1931 when the economy was in a slump.

Active Expansion and Modernization of Production Facilities

There were three periods, each extending over several years, when all of the investigated firms made extensive investments in their production facilities. The first was the stretch of six years from 1936 to 1942. This corresponds to the period of growing militarism, when the government and the military tried to reinforce the industrial strength of the country, in particular, the motor vehicle (truck) and munitions industries. During this period, NGK and Kojima Press established new and larger plants while all the other firms expanded production facilities considerably to cope with the expected increase in demand.

The second period lasted for about five years, from 1951 to 1955. In 1950, the outbreak of the Korean War revived the Japanese economy, from the serious economic slump that accompanied the braking of postwar inflation. With this shot in the arm, the Japanese economy quickly got on a fast track to recovery from its wartime destruction. In particular, the motor vehicle industry benefited from large U.S. military special procurement orders and from the notable recovery of domestic demand for commercial vehicles. During the period, all the ancillary firms were actively engaged in investing to replace their old, worn-out equipment with imported modern machinery. The main focus of the investment was on "modernization" or "quality improvement" of the facilities rather than mere expansion of capacity.

The third period, the six years from 1960 to 1965, was during the National Income Doubling Plan announced by the government in 1960. The plan's objective was to double the real gross national product in ten years. During the decade, the Japanese economy accelerated its pace of growth to an average nominal annual rate of 15 percent. The automobile ancillary industry grew at an even faster pace, with special support from the government by way of extensions of the Provisional Act for the Promotion of the Machinery Industry. The Act offered the industry special low interest loans, accelerated depreciation of pro-

247

duction facilities, and encouraged industrial reorganization to strengthen the competitiveness of the industry.

Another driving force for extensive investment by ancillary firms came from their respective primary firms. As importation of passenger cars was scheduled to be liberalized in 1965, the primary firms were anxious to improve product quality and production efficiency both in their own factories and in their supporting industries (ancillary firms). In response to this appeal, the ancillary firms renovated their production facilities by extensively introducing automation and mass production systems to achieve higher productive efficiency and lower cost.

Exploitation of Imported Technologies

Like many other Japanese industries, the automobile industry was dependent on foreign technology as a basis for its development. Thus, in the 1930s, while Nissan inherited the locally designed DAT model, its initial development was assisted by a group of American engineers (headed by Gorham). The company's prewar production facilities relied extensively on foreign equipment and technological support.

In contrast to Nissan, Toyota developed, in 1935, its first vehicle (the A1) using a mixture of local and imported parts and components with no direct help from foreign engineers. However, its production facilities were largely imported, and the car's basic design was patterned after that of two American models: the power train and chassis of the Chevrolet and the body style of the DeSoto.

In the postwar development of the industry, some of the Japanese auto makers concluded multi-year technical agreements with European auto makers in order to improve their abilities to manufacture passenger cars.

Ancillary firms have also capitalized on foreign technologies. According to a survey by the Auto Trade Journal (1979, pp. 162–68), jointly undertaken with JAPIA, the number of technological agreements concluded between Japanese auto parts manufacturers and foreign firms, under which the former imported the latter's technologies, was 249 in 1979, with U.S. firms accounting for 142 (57%), West Germany

248

44 (18%), U.K. 33 (13%), France 10 (4%), and other European countries and Australia 20 (8%).

Of the eight sample ancillary firms, four had technological tie-ups with foreign firms. Among them, Aisan concluded a technological agreement with the Carter Carburetor Division of ICF of the United States in 1962. Aisan's main product then was the carburetor for Toyota vehicles, modelled after Carter products during World War II. According to Aisan's management, the arrangement was most profitable for the company in acquiring engineering and marketing information regarding product development, and was one of the most powerful driving forces for the subsequent rapid growth of the company. Later, in 1968, Aisan also introduced technology from General Motors relating to automatic control mechanisms of internal combustion engines.

Nippondenso underwent a comprehensive technological tie-up with Robert Bosch Company of West Germany in 1951. This agreement gave Nippondenso an opportunity to improve significantly its technological level, moving the company closer to being on par with western firms. The then president, Hayashi Torao, had been deeply impressed by the high technological standards of Bosch, and appealed to his employees with the slogan, "We shall catch up with Bosch in ten years!" He then declared ten major policies to attain the objective. Eventually, the target was realized with substantial improvement in product quality and the diversification of the company's product lines. Subsequently, Nippondenso also concluded technological agreements with Bendix for the manufacture of an electronic fuel injector, as well as with General Motors (air-pump, integrated circuit (IC) regulator, and others), General Electric (compressor and aluminum glazing), Texas Instruments (ICs), Western Electric (semiconductor manufacturing process), Fairchild (semiconductor manufacturing process), RCA (ICs), Sinclo (Flywheel and magneto), Eltra (ignition coil) and Honeywell (IC regulator)—all U.S. firms.

Yazaki introduced technologies on tachometer production from Kinzle Apparate of West Germany in 1959, while Topy introduced technologies on wheel manufacturing from Firestone (U.S.A.), and

GKN Kent Alloyes and Aibon (both England).

In addition to such formal arrangements, there were many other channels of technological information from various foreign sources to the ancillary firms. Product samples were one such form, as in the case of Yazaki. It first came to know about a specific product design known as the wire harness when the company received orders for them through Nissan in conjunction with repair work on GM jeeps in 1950.

Industrial tours in various forms were another important channel of technological information. In many industrial sectors of Japan, including the automobile industry, a great number of industrial tours were arranged through the 1950s and 1960s whereby advanced industrial practices in the United States and in Europe could be observed. Such tours were organized by either primary firms, ancillary firm associations, trade associations, the Japan Productivity Center, or other professional institutions. The tours exposed both engineers and management to new manufacturing technologies, modern machinery and equipment, and various production and management know-how, many of which were subsequently applied to their own firms either directly or with some modifications.

Technological Aptitude of Production Workers and Engineers

A point worth noting in the Japanese experience is the relatively high adaptability of both production workers and engineers to new machinery and technology. Both the ancillary and primary firms have relied heavily on sophisticated foreign machinery. The technology gap was naturally wider in the earlier days of their development. Nevertheless, workers at ancillary firms managed to master the operations of imported machinery with little outside help. In fact, for political or economic reasons, especially before and immediately after the war, it was almost impossible for ancillary firms to invite foreign engineers. With the guidance provided by simple instruction manuals attached to the imported machines, the workers soon achieved the required standard of performance, while machine troubles were adequately handled by the engineering staff (or sometimes by staffs of the primary firms).

Even when the firms such as Nippondenso and Aisan entered technological agreements with foreign concerns, there were only a few long foreign visits to their plants. Although the companies gained a lot from the technological ties, the major channels of technology transfer were published engineering information and several short visits to the foreign counterparts (usually lasting for only a few days) by the companies' management and engineering staff.

This suggests that the technological and technical levels of the production workers and the engineers of the industry were sufficiently high, even in the prewar days, to absorb (or adapt to) the engineering standards of the advanced countries. Herein possibly lies a key reason for the industry's success.

Stable and Close Relationship between Primary and Ancillary Firms

It is impressive that all of the sample ancillary firms continued to maintain stable business relationships with their primary firms over long periods of time. In fact, none of the sample ancillary firms ever experienced business interruptions with the primary firms once they started the regular supply of parts and components. Indeed, almost all of the nearly 200 ancillary firms in the Toyota group have experienced a continuous subcontracting relationship since the establishment of formal contacts with Toyota. Figures 6.1 and 6.2 show the distribution of the length of their business relationship with Toyota and the year of establishment, respectively, of the member firms of Kyōhō Kai (the association of Toyota-related, first-tier ancillary firms). One can readily find similar patterns of relationship between primary and ancillary firms in the other automobile manufacturing groups.

Alongside this stable relationship between primary and ancillary firms was the phenomenon of "groupism." In other words, most of the ancillary firms in the Japanese automobile industry belonged to some business group formed around the primary firms. Some ancillary firms dealt exclusively with their primary firms by supplying every piece of their output to the latter. Many others, while dealing with more than one primary firm, maintained an especially close relationship with the

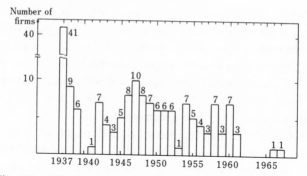

Fig. 6.1. Distribution of Kyōhō Kai Members by Year
Subcontracting Relationship with Toyota Started

Notes: Firms with incomplete information are omitted.
Sources: Adapted from Toyota Jidōsha 1967.

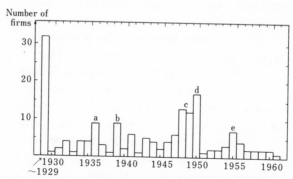

Fig. 6.2. Year of Establishment of Kyōhō Kai Member Firms,
1962

Notes: a) 1936 Act to promote local industry; new Toyota plant opened.
           b) GM and Ford forced out; Toyota's Koromo plant in operation.
           c) Many firms "established" in 1948–49 were successors to existing
              businesses.
           d) Korean War boom.
           e) First mass-produced Toyota.
Sources: Toyota Jidōsha 1967, and Nikkan Kōgyō Shimbun Sha 1980.

Table 6.1. Sales Distribution of Auto Parts Manufacturers in
the Toyota and Nissan Groups, 1967

(A) Toyota group

Category	No. of sample firms	Customers			
		Toyota Motor	Other firms in Toyota group	Other auto makers	Outside automobile industry
A	14	53.1%	8.4%	13.8%	24.7%
B	31	60.2	26.6	3.5	9.7
C	10	20.8	11.6	14.4	53.2
D	15	20.1	5.3	35.4	39.2
Total	70	44.1	9.9	17.6	28.4

Legends: A: Affiliated firms of Toyota Motor Co.
B: Subcontractors with exclusive relationship with Toyota.
C: Subcontractors with loose relationship with Toyota.
D: Independent auto-parts manufacturers.

(B) Nissan group

Annual sales (¥ bil.)	No. of sample firms	Customers			
		Nissan Motor	Other firms in Nissan group	Other auto makers	Outside automobile industry
– 0.2	14	38.0%	28.9%	19.3%	13.8%
0.2– 0.5	17	57.7	29.7	7.7	4.9
0.5– 1	22	33.1	26.8	25.0	15.1
1– 5	18	40.6	17.7	22.7	19.0
2– 5	21	50.9	19.5	25.0	4.6
5–10	5	46.6	23.1	28.9	1.4
10–	4	67.6	31.8	0.6	—
Total	101	54.6	25.3	15.4	4.7

Sources: Chūshō Kigyō Kenkyū Center (1968), pp. 60–61.

primary firm that was its largest customer.

Among our sample firms, Kojima Press and Maruyasu Industry supplied their products almost exclusively to Toyota and other firms in the Toyota Group. The same relationship held true between Tokyo Radiator (TRS) and Isuzu, although TRS products were sold to firms outside the automobile industry, such as makers of construction and agricultural machinery. While Aisan and Nippondenso no longer maintained the exclusive relationship they had with Toyota in their early days, Toyota was still their principal customer. The remaining three, Yazaki, Topy, and NGK, represented the independents whose products were supplied to several primary firms. However, it was widely known that Yazaki maintained a closer relationship with Toyota than with any other primary firm.

A survey taken in 1967 reported the sales distribution of the major suppliers to Toyota and Nissan (Table 6.1). The table clearly shows the cohesive association in the Toyota and Nissan Groups, although the share of sales to the principal primary firm varied significantly among the member firms. According to a later report, however, the cohesive groupism began to erode after 1961 (Nakamura 1976, pp.86–97).

Primary Firms' Extensive Support of Ancillary Firm Development

Another notable feature commonly observed between primary and ancillary firms was the primary firms' active interest in the growth of the latter. For instance, Toyota offered various forms of assistance to its ancillary firms, especially in their early stages of development, such as: (1) loaning or selling second-hand production facilities (machine tools and others) at nominal prices; (2) sending a group of experienced workers headed by a qualified engineer; (3) providing special programs for the training of production workers; and (4) supplying financial and other non-pecuniary help. Toyota was by no means an exception in this regard.

Obviously, the active interest and involvement by primary firms in the development of ancillary firms was based on the stable and continuous relation between primary and ancillary firms. Two channels were

254

generally utilized for such assistance: first, individual transactions between a primary firm and an ancillary firm; and second, collective transactions channelled through the ancillary firm's association. Of the four types of assistance stated above, (1), (2), and (4) are usually extended through the first method and (3) through the second.

Associations of Ancillary Firms

Ancillary firms' associations have played an indispensable role in the development of both ancillary and primary firms. They served not only as the primary firms' channel of assistance to ancillary firms, but also as an effective instrument for the cultivation of loyalty. Further, they fostered intra-group competition in productivity improvement.

The Toyota-related association was organized voluntarily in 1939 by some eighteen ancillary firms to promote the exchange of ideas and other cooperative activities for the improvement of product quality and efficiency. It was initially called the Toyota Kyōryoku Kai (Toyota Cooperative Circle), and was later transformed into a more integrated organization and renamed Kyōhō Kai. Toyota became a formal member in 1943, at the height of World War II when more unified production activities between primary and ancillary firms were demanded by the military. During the war, the association functioned as an instrument through which the primary firm (Toyota) not only coordinated production plans but allocated raw materials among ancillary firms. Subsequently, when Toyota faced serious financial and labor problems in 1949, the member firms cooperated with the primary firm by deferring the collection of receivables from Toyota.

Kyōhō Kai was split into three geographical divisions in 1948, Tōkai, Tōkyō, and Kansai. In the postwar decade, especially after 1950, it reinforced cooperative activities among its members in order to promote the rationalization of their production systems and management. By 1968 Tōkai Kyōhō Kai had established among its 114 members two committees in charge of quality control and value analysis (VA), and four product subdivisions (body parts, foundry and machining, pressed parts, and special parts). By 1979 Kyōhō Kai's total membership had grown to 225 (136 in Tōkai, 64 in Kantō, and 25 in Kansai).

In addition to Kyōhō Kai, Toyota-related ancillary firms formed two other associations. Seihō Kai, being composed of 21 firms manufacturing dies, gauges, tools, and fixtures, and Eihō Kai, with 36 firms, supplying auxiliary products services—such as construction, building of production facilities, etc.

Takara Kai, the largest association of Nissan-related ancillary firms, was first organized in 1954, shortly after Nissan started an active program of modernization and expansion of production system. By 1979, membership had reached 109, all either small- or medium-scale firms. Nissan held at least a 25 percent interest in each of these firms and appointed one or more member of senior management.

In addition to Takara Kai, the Nissan-affiliated ancillary firms formed two other associations: Shōhō Kai and Kōhō Kai. The former consisted (at the time of the survey) of 49 large-scale suppliers of parts and components to Nissan, which were either independent auto parts manufacturers, or specialized concerns catering to diversified industries and not necessarily maintaining close links with the primary firm (Nissan). Examples of the former were manufacturers of wheels and spark plugs (such as Topy and NGK); and examples of the latter were manufacturers of electrical parts and bearings (such as Hitachi and Tōyō Bearing). On the other hand, Kōhō Kai consisted of 21 member-firms supplying jigs and dies to Nissan or other member firms of the Nissan group.

The Nissan-related ancillary firms' association performed more or less the same types of cooperative activities as those of the Toyota group. At the same time, however, one could also discern differences betweeen the two. The survey undertaken by the Chūshō Kigyō Kenkyū Center reported that Nissan had adopted more direct involvement than Toyota in developing its ancillary firm network. According to the survey, in 1963 Nissan undertook to reform its ancillary firms according to the following three principles: (1) enlargement of production scale, (2) reduction in the number of ancillary firms, and (3) transfer of sub-assembly operations from Nissan to ancillary firms. With these policy directives, Nissan became the driving force for the merger or grouping of its ancillary firms, mostly the member firms of Takara Kai, and went actively into capital participation in them.

There was an acceleration in this regard when, at the government's urging, Nissan merged with the Prince Motor Company in 1966. By that time, Prince Motor had also developed its own ancillary network, numbering 320 firms. Immediately after the merger, Nissan moved to drastically decrease the number. For example, 56 suppliers of pressed parts were reduced to 8 and 86 suppliers of machine parts to 10 within a few years. The eliminated companies were either to merge with the surviving firms or to become ancillary to the latter (i.e., to become second-tier). This was called the "selection plan," whereby Nissan designated a limited number of firms on which it would henceforth concentrate its aid and support. These, in turn, were expected to look after their own suppliers, the second-tier firms including those that were downgraded.

To qualify as first-tier, the firm had to have: capital assets over 50 million yen, publicly held stock, an independent decision-making capacity to cope with technological as well as managerial requests from Nissan, the inclusion on the board of people who were not members of the principal owner's family, the capacity to competitively market unique products (50 percent or more of which were supplied to firms other than Nissan), and the technological capability to take over the subassembly operations of Nissan.

All but one Japanese primary firm has an asssociation of ancillary firms, although their size and specific features vary. Honda with 300 ancillary firms is the only exception. The names and member sizes of the associations are listed in Table 6.2 (based on Appendix Table A-18).

Fuji Heavy's associations are centered on the firm's two main plants, Nissan's are functional. Besides the three regional associations listed, Toyota also has two other functional associations.

Some ancillary firms developed their own organizations of second-tier ancillary firms, the pattern of which followed closely that of the first-tier ancillary firm associations. Among the eight ancillary firms included

SUMMARY AND INTERPRETATION

Table 6.2.   List of Ancillary Firm Associations, 1979[a]

Primary firms	Name of associations	Number of member firms
Daihatsu Motor Co.	Daihatsu Kyōyū Kai	143
Fuji Heavy Industries	Fuji Gunma Kyōryoku Kai	158
Fuji Heavy Industries	Fuji Mitaka Kyōryoku Kai	54
Hino Motors	Hino Kyōryoku Kai	247
Isuzu Motors	Isuzu Kyōwa Kai	269
Mitsubishi Motors Corp.	Mitsubishi Motors Kashiwa Kai	344
Nissan Diesel Motor Co.	Nissan Diesel Yayoi Kai	60
Nissan Motor Co.	Nissan Shōhō Kai	49
Nissan Motor Co.	Nissan Takara Kai	112
Suzuki Motor Co.	Suzuki Kyōdō Kumiai	104
Toyo Kogyo Co.	Tōyū Kai Kyōdō Kumiai	92
Toyota Motor Co.	Kansai Kyōhō Kai	25
Toyota Motor Co.	Kantō Kyōhō Kai	64
Toyota Motor Co.	Tōkai Kyōhō Kai	136

Notes: [a] See p. 67 for the 1968 list.

in the present study, three had their own associations: Aisan, Nippondenso, and Tokyo Radiator. The active involvement of both primary and ancillary firms in these organizations suggests that the member firms, and perhaps the primary firms in particular, reaped substantial benefits from these institutional arrangements.

Product Specialization by Ancillary Firms

A major feature in the business behavior of automobile ancillary firms is that a great number of them, at least those at the first tier, have pursued specialization by product item in preference to specialization by process. Furthermore, many of the ancillary firms seem to have consciously limited the range of their product lines at least until they reached a certain level of maturity. It is true that many once had, especially in their early stages, widened their product lines. But five of them had at one time or another retreated from other business lines to concentrate on the manufacture of limited types of auto parts. The following excerpts from our case studies illustrate the point.

In 1934, Nishimura Tsunetarō stopped accepting orders for various pressing jobs in order to concentrate his resources on radiator manufacturing. He then changed the name of his family business from Nishimura Bankin Kōjō to Nishimura Radiator Manufacturing. Similarly, in 1940, when Toyota expanded truck production, Kojima Press reluctantly gave up the manufacture of its original line of products, partly because of material shortages. In 1943, NGK was obliged to concentrate on the manufacture of spark plugs and to give up the production of other items (radio shields, ceramic filters, and acid-resistant cement), mainly because demand had reached an unprecedented peak because of the war. In 1951, Yazaki stopped the profitable production of electric wires for general use and confined itself to the wire-harness business. In 1957, the new chief executive sent to Aisan by the primary firm (Toyoda Loom) decided to discontinue the manufacture of parts for automatic looms. He then ordered the redirection of all the company's resources to the production of automobile parts.

Maruyasu Industry and Nippondenso illustrate a different method of product specialization because they were separated from their parent companies after World War II to concentrate on the manufacture of automobile parts (double-shielded tubes in the case of Maruyasu and electrical components and radiators in the case of Nippondenso).

Topy Industries is the only firm in our sample where product lines were broadly diversified in the 1950s. This exceptional behavior, however, may be explained by the special feature of Topy's development. The company was established only in 1964 after a series of mergers of several companies, each of which had specialized in a specific kind of operation.

The majority of the sample ancillary firms had, voluntarily or otherwise, experienced a narrowing of product lines, confining themselves to the manufacture of a limited number of auto parts. Many of the firms began to widen their product lines in the mid-1960s (or in the early 1960s at the earliest). The diversifications, however, were limited in most cases to production of other auto parts.

Vertical Integration

Along with product specialization, the ancillary firms generally pursued a policy of vertical integration, even as they increasingly resorted to subcontracting to second-tier ancillary firms for the manufacture of easy-to-produce parts, especially after the mid-1960s.

For example, NGK used to subcontract the supply of electric terminals to an outside firm. However, the company decided to internalize the production of all key parts in 1932, when the supplier went bankrupt. Metallic accessories were also transferred to in-house production in 1934 for a similar reason. It was only in 1961 that capacity limitation led NGK to establish an ancillary firm that specialized in the production of metallic parts for use in spark plugs; subsequently, four other ancillary firms were added.

Similarly, Yazaki decided in 1951 to establish its own smelting furnace in order to be self-sufficient in its supply of copper ingot even at the cost of terminating commercial relations with the bank that declined to support the venture. The founder and then president of the company was so eager to reinforce this backward integration that he persevered even though the operation consistently lost money. Indeed, twice he made substantial investments in new furnaces, embodying improved technology.

Aisan decided in 1957 to internalize die-casting and plating operations, for which it had previously relied on subcontractors. The introduction of the die-making process ensued in 1960. Such a move was suggested, and financially and technologically supported by the primary firm (Toyota), enabling Aisan's subsequent growth.

It is also notable that almost all of the investigated ancillary firms designed and manufactured considerable portions of their machinery and equipment, although the timing and extent of in-house manufacture varied from one company to another. Aisan had its own machine and tool manufacturing shop even in the prewar period, as did Tokyo Radiator. For example, several years before World War II, a senior engineer, who later became company president, converted two old lathes and developed two drawing benches for the manufacture of tubes. At the time of the interviews, the company manufactured a number of special-purpose machines for the production of radiators; some of the machines had been sold outside Japan.

On the other hand, Nippondenso, being an outgrowth of a production department of Toyota, had been accustomed to the in-house manufacture of machine tools even before its formal founding in 1949. Shortly thereafter, a policy was declared to promote in-house manufacturing of production facilities, placing the Production Engineering Section in charge of the task. The Section, which had been engaged in the improvement of production devices and other engineering services, afterwards began developing various special-purpose machines with the use of precision-machine tools it had acquired from arsenals. It was later expanded to form the Machine Tool Department, which played a significant role in the development of the mass production system for diversified products.

For Maruyasu Industry, the internal development and manufacture of production equipment was one of its major policies from its founding in 1951. In pursuance of the policy, the company management consistently encouraged acquisition of machine tools. In the mid 1970s, Maruyasu was even selling dies, gauges and machine tools to outside customers and it manufactured several automatic welding machines for the primary firm. In 1961 Yazaki established a section specializing in the supply of dies. The section became an independent corporation in 1965, named Yazaki Engineering, supplying various machine tools as well as metal dies and jigs to the other member firms of the Yazaki Group. Kojima Press began in-house manufacture of press dies in 1960, and set up a die-making section in 1963. By 1973 the section employed approximately 100 workers; later it was transformed into the Machine Tool Division.

We thus find that a great number of ancillary firms produced a portion of their production facilities. In many cases, however, the internally-supplied machines and equipment were designed for specific purposes and were comparatively small in size, whereas most of general-purpose and large-scale machinery were purchased from specialized machine tool makers.

Quality Improvement Prior to Cost Reduction

An interesting feature of the ancillary firms studied concerns the precedence of product quality improvement over explicit cost reduction.

Ezoe, the first president of NGK, was especially keen on maintaining the uniform quality of the company's products. While still at Nippon Insulators (NG), he surprised his colleagues by abolishing the traditional two-grade system by which the company had classified its products. He also standardized the operations in insulator production, which led to a significant reduction in the defect rate. In 1921, while still at NG, Ezoe argued that an electric generating company should base its purchase of insulators on nothing but quality. Pursuing this argument, he insisted that an experiment be undertaken whereby his company's insulators would be tested against U.S. as well as competing domestic brands. The experiment disclosed that, except for those impaired by the irregularity of ceramic bodies, NG's were superior in average strength to all others tested. The discovery of the defects seriously upset Ezoe, who then intensified his effort to make the quality of the company's products more uniform.

Nippondenso introduced statistical quality control (SQC) in 1950 when it supplied rifle parts to the U.S. Army. The practice was reinforced when it signed a technological agreement with Bosch, which entailed the standardization of the company's production operations and facilities. Seven years later, in 1957, the company set up QC activities, culminating in the adoption of a "total quality control" (TQC) system, which put greater emphasis on explicit cost aspects and advocated full involvement of all employees.

Tokyo Radiator also concentrated its efforts and available resources on improving product quality until around 1960, when it started to put more emphasis on cost reduction. In order to integrate the two objectives (quality improvement and cost reduction), the company started the TQC movement in 1964 with full involvement of all employees. The company also began active participation in the value analysis activity (VA) of Kyōwa Kai (the ancillary firms association of Isuzu Motor) from 1965.

Aisan's first attempt at systematic production management was the introduction of a statistical quality control system in 1953. Beginning around 1960, however, the emphasis shifted to the areas of production control and cost management as exemplified by the introduction of the just-in-time (*kanban*) system," Toyota's unique inventory and production control device, and VA (value analysis) and VE (value engineering).

Kojima Press also placed priority on quality. The company started to introduce the concepts and techniques of QC in 1961 and was awarded the Deming Prize in 1967. It was followed by the ZD (zero-defect) movement to further improve product quality by upgrading company-wide managerial controls. Starting in 1973, however, the main focus of improvement shifted to costs, when an annual target for cost economy was set and attained.

In the cases of Maruyasu, Yazaki, and Topy, there was no clear indication whether they had adopted such quality-first policies. However, the five cases cited are perhaps enough to suggest there was a tendency among ancillary firms to give first priority to product quality.

Strong Leadership by the Founders

Another impressive feature of many of the firms studied is the manifestation of strong entrepreneurship by their founders. For example, Kojima Hamakichi, the founder of Kojima Press, succeeded in getting a headstart with Toyota by knocking on Toyota's door persistently for nine months until he finally received his first order. He was also known among his employees and friends as a thrifty person. He directed his sons and every employee to make best use of even a small odd piece of metal sheet or a bent nail. He himself followed the discipline most strictly. When he moved his tiny old shop to a bigger site shortly after the establishment of formal contact with Toyota, he carefully dismantled every piece of the wooden structure of the old shop and utilized them in the construction of the new factory building. On the other hand, he was an active investor in the introduction of modern machinery to improve the production system of the company.

Similarly, Yazaki Sadami, the founder of the Yazaki Group, kept close contact with the primary firm by personally delivering his products (mostly wire harnesses), thus directly acquiring feedback information. Even after the growth of his business, he was always at the forefront of various other business activities. There were few holidays in his personal calendar and he was in the habit of saying "I will take rest in the grave." He died in August 1974 at the age of 64, while travelling in connection with a special marketing program for a new product.

The sample firms (both primary and ancillary) abound with similar stories about their founders (or their former chief executives). Anecdotes were inevitably told with a tone of pride, suggesting the basic philosophies of the forefathers were still alive among the present management and employees.

Whether this should be considered nationalism or entrepreneurism is open to debate, but one thing particularly striking about the early builders of the automobile and auto parts industry in Japan is their faith. They believed Japan would undergo motorization, like that of the United States. They believed that if the United States could produce cars and trucks, so could they, and the fact the United States had vastly more advanced technology and a wealthier market was irrelevant. That faith meant they persevered. The government may have provided support and a protected market, and foreign firms may have been willing to provide technological help, but those, we believe, would not have been sufficient conditions for the industry to progress as far as it did in the prewar period, or to prosper as it did in the postwar years.

6.2. An Interpretation
Alternative Policies in Parts and Procurement

An automobile consists of nearly 20,000 parts, each requiring many stages of manufacturing. Ancillary firms develop if (and only if) primary firms subcontract some manufacturing processes to them. Assuming final assembly is undertaken by a primary firm itself, one may then ask specifically how it would procure the necessary parts and components. Figure 6.3 depicts a series of policy alternatives open to the firm (note, however, that there are cases where final assembly is also subcontracted).

The first major decision is whether to rely on foreign or domestic sources.[1] If the firm chooses the latter, it must decide whether to produce those parts and components internally or buy them from outside suppliers, and so on. Needless to say, the last two decisions cannot be made by the primary firms alone, as the other end of the string is in the hands of each ancillary firm. But the bargaining position of the latter is often weak compared to that of the primary firm.

In the remainder of this section, an attempt will be made to summarize

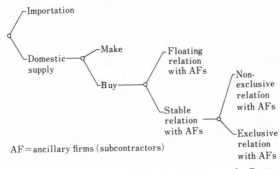

AF = ancillary firms (subcontractors)

Fig. 6.3. Alternatives in the Acquisition of Parts and Components

[1]   It may seem more natural to expect that a primary firm makes up its mind on the make-or-buy issue *before* deciding whether or not to procure the part domestically. However, in the Japanese historical context, domestication of parts production was given supreme importance, so that any importation was more from necessity than choice.

the actual policies adopted by Japanese primary firms in reference to the above classification (see Table 6.3).

The first phase of the industry's history (1902–16) saw only small scale, trial production of motor cars by a few inventors and the arsenals. Of these, the arsenals were the only factories engaged in the production of prototypes. The tiny family businesses, on the other hand, were hardly qualified to be called "primary firms." In fact, most of these pioneers tried to produce every necessary part and component, although some relied on the importation of certain difficult-to-make items (such

Table 6.3. Policies Adopted by Japanese Automobiles Makers[a]

	Phases of automobile development		
	I, II and III (–1945)	IV (1946–60)	V (1961–79)
(1) Importation or domestic supply	Domestic supply increasingly displacing imports	Domestic supply supplemented by imports	Overwhelmingly domestic, with a slight shift toward importation
(2) Make or buy	Major components made, other bought	Shifting of in-house production to ancillary firms	Make and buy
(3) Floating or stable	Stable	Stable	Stable
(4) Non-exclusive or exclusive	Exclusive	Exclusive	Moving toward non-exclusive

Notes: [a] See Figure 6.3 and text for additional explanation. Five phases correspond to sections 2.1–2.5 in Chapter 2.

as engines, electrical parts, and tires) as well as on local subcontractors for some processing operations, such as casting, forging, and milling (Kodaira 1968, pp. 27–37).

In the second and the third phases of development (1917–45), the principal primary firms (Tokyo Gas & Electric, Tokyo Motor, Nissan, and Toyota) devoted substantial effort to domesticizing the procurement of parts and components (mostly for trucks), trying simultaneously to promote both internal production and subcontracting. For various items, however, they initially had to rely on imports. In general, major functional components such as engines, transmissions, body assembly, and chassis frames were targeted for internal production, while efforts were concentrated on the search for possible local suppliers for other kinds of parts and components (Kodaira 1968, ch. 4, especially pp. 84–86 and 91–96). The primary firm chose in most cases to establish "stable" and "exclusive" relationships with the ancillary firms.

The switch from import to domestic supply was actually a necessity for the primary firms. International political tension was building up, and the Japanese Army was anxious to secure domestic sources for military trucks. Although the Automobile Industry Act of 1936 did not require any explicit level of domestic content, it must have been more than clear to all the primary firms that the essential objective of the government was the complete domestication of truck manufacturing. When Japan went to war against the United States, importation of parts and components of course completely stopped.

The reason for the simultaneous promotion of "make" and "buy" is easily understood. Under heavy pressure, the primary firms had to try every possible means to obtain numerous parts and components from Japanese sources. Fortunately for the primary firms, a certain number of local suppliers had already developed for each item, mainly among the manufacturers of spare parts, although a few were qualified to supply original equipment (OE).

The situation described above also explains the primary firms' preference for stable and exclusive relationship. While for many items the number of possible candidates as first-tier ancillary firms was not necessarily small, the primary firms often found them in need of financial or technological support for the improvement of product quality and production capacity. Consequently, careful selection was made and, once selected, the choice was adhered to. Although it took Kojima nine months to receive its first trial order, thereafter Toyota gave the company extensive and generous support.

From the primary firms' viewpoint, it was also beneficial to have as few parts suppliers as possible in order to realize some scale economies in the small market. To attain this objective while maintaining competition among the ancillary firms, the two-supplier principle was adopted, exemplified by the procurement guideline set in 1939 by Toyoda Kiichirō, the founder of Toyota Motor. He decreed that the number of suppliers for each item should be neither less nor more than two. With such intensive support extended by the primary firms, it seemed natural for the ancillary firms to develop "stable" and "exclusive" relationships with the former.

Similar development took place in many other industrial sectors. For example, the government's Guideline for the Development of Machinery and Steel Industries (*Kikai tekkō seihin kōgyō seibi yōkō*), issued in 1940 encouraged primary firms to develop their own ancillary firm networks. Control of the steel supply during the war further reinforced a stable and exclusive relationship between primary and ancillary firms. Following the spirit of the guideline, a special administrative directive was formulated to promote the concerted development of the auto parts industry, leading to the establishment of the Japan Auto Parts Traders Union (Nihon Jidōsha Buhin Kōgyō Kumiai; the predecessor of JAPIA).

In the period following World War II, the primary firms followed an almost uniform pattern in their choices along the decision tree depicted in Figure 6.3. Local parts and components makers had become well-established by the end of the war, so they were ready when the production of commercial vehicles resumed. The primary firms redeveloped their passenger car models in part utilizing technological skills acquired in truck production. Dependence on the ancillary firms was

268

further increased by the transfer of subassembly operations of various components (such as carburetors and brake units) from primary to ancillary firms. The late 1940s and the early 1950s saw the entry of new members into the auto parts business, mostly from the munitions industries. The stable and exclusive nature of the primary-ancillary relation was reinforced by the activities of the ancillary firm associations.

A main reason for the primary firms' choice of domestic supply rather than imports in the postwar period may be ascribed to the strict foreign exchange control and high tariff barriers imposed not only on auto parts but also on many other commodities because of the meager foreign currency reserves held by Japan.

The rationale of the primary firms' second choice (heavier dependence on subcontracting), as well as their third (stable relationship with the ancillary firms), and fourth (exclusive relationship) policy decisions may be explained as follows. The postwar development of the industry was characterized by the remarkable growth of the market, and the intensifying competitions among the primary firms. These firms vied in introducing improved models, resulting in the expansion and modernization of their production systems, especially after the Korean War (1950–51). Beginning around 1955 the manufacturers of passenger cars made strenuous efforts to excel others in the diversification of car models and the expansion of their dealership network. Given their limited financial and human resources, they sought desperately to find efficient ways to expand production capacity to capture the ever-growing market of increasingly diversified products.

The rapid growth of demand and the severe competition prompted the primary firms to restructure their ancillary firms network and to reinforce the exclusive nature of their relationships with them, which in turn warranted the stability of the primary-ancillary relations. While extensive technical and financial support was extended from the primary to the ancillary firms, the latter accomplished, on their own initiative, considerable technological upgrading between 1945 and 1955. The heavier reliance on subcontracting arrangements was further encouraged by the substantial wage differentials between the larger (primary) and the smaller (ancillary) firms, which put the latter in a relatively more advantageous position in the manufacture of labor-intensive items.

In the fifth phase (1960 and after), the primary firms made two slight changes in their policy. The first was the relaxation of the exclusiveness in the primary-ancillary relationship. Many (especially large-scale) ancillary firms gradually widened the range of their customers—a move supported by the primary firms. Toyota, for example, directed its ancillary firms to decrease its share in their sales to below 60 percent (Nakamura 1976, pp. 86–97).

The policy changes by the primary firms were partly rooted in the continuous technological transformation in the manufacturing process of parts and components, effecting greater economies of scale on the part of the ancillary firms. Given the possibility of further reductions in costs, the primary firms were obliged (perhaps reluctantly) to allow the ancillary firms to receive more orders, even from rival assemblers. In any event, economized operations were imperative as the primary firms faced the liberalization of trade and capital.

At the same time, however, the primary firms counterbalanced the policy change by increased equity participation in the ancillary firms, thus reinforcing their influence on them. Note, however, that despite these changes, the stable nature of the primary-ancillary relationship has never been shaken. In fact, the primary firms could no longer afford to change their parts suppliers, as many auto parts producers had acquired oligopolistic power over the market (see Table 6.4). The primary firms' heavy dependence on subcontracting was established more firmly than ever.

Another change took place in the traditional policy of domestic sourcing of parts and components. From around the mid-1970s, some primary firms again began to purchase parts and components from foreign producers (mostly European and American). Among the then-existing eleven primary firms, Honda was the most active along this regard, followed by Toyota and Nissan. The items procured from abroad

Table 6.4. Market Shares of the Three Top Manufacturers of
Selected Parts and Components (1960)

Item	Share (%)	Item	Share (%)
Piston	90.0	Bearing metal	74.4
Piston ring	100.0	Bush	60.2
Cylinder liner	84.0	Electrical parts	81.6
Valve	83.0	Ignition coil	65.9
Fuel pump	94.3	Steering wheel	91.9
Carburetor	78.0	Clutch	84.0
Air cleaner	88.4	Coil spring	68.4
Oil filter	86.0	Chassis spring	75.6
Radiator	68.0	Brake lining	76.7
Meters	86.7	Sheet metal	92.6
		Shock absorber	95.5

Sources: Nakamura (1976), p. 88.

were glass; tire, cloth and leather for seats and carpets; and headlamps, most of which were incorporated into vehicles for.export to Europe and the United States. However, overseas procurement was progressively expanded in terms of both volume and variety as time went on.

By the mid-1960s, many Japanese auto parts manufacturers had attained international standards both in product quality and price, as reflected by the rapid increase in their overseas sales (Figure 6.4). The growing dominance of Japanese motor vehicles in the export market resulted in trade conflict with the United States and some European countries, thus compelling the primary firms to import foreign-made parts and components for the assembly of export models. Foreign-made parts and components were expected to be adopted eventually in the domestic models after the yen's appreciation following abolition of the fixed exchange rate system on 28 August 1971.

In the late 1970s, Japanese auto parts manufacturers began to show active interest in setting up manufacturing operations outside Japan. It

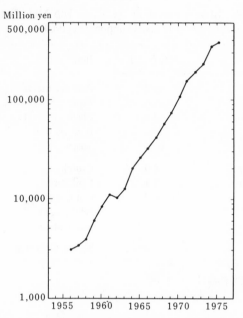

Fig. 6.4.   Exports of Automobile Parts and Components

Notes: Vertical axis is on logarithmic scale.
Sources: Appendix Table A-14.

seemed natural that local procurement of parts and components would increase in many developing economies as they pushed domestic content programs.

Policies on Product Specialization

The majority of the ancillary firms studied had, at one time, narrowed their product lines and confined themselves to the manufacture of limited kinds of auto parts. Diversification of their product lines came later, especially after the mid-1960s. How should we interpret this product specialization? In answering the question, it is pertinent to reflect on the contrast between two policies: "specialization by product" versus "specialization by process."

A basic policy decision for an ancillary firm is whether it should specialize in manufacturing certain items (such as wheels, carburetors, and the like) or in certain kinds of operations (such as pressing, casting, machining, etc.) applied to diversified products. In the automobile industry, most of the first-tier ancillary firms have adopted, not only in Japan but also in other countries, specialization by product.

In the Japanese experience, one finds some instances of ancillary firms starting their business as specialists of certain kinds of processing and later switching to specialization-by-product when they joined the automobile industry. But it is hard to find a reverse case. For example, Tokyo Radiator originated in a tiny sheet metal workshop established in 1905 by Nishimura. Named after its founder, Nishimura Bankin Kōjō (literally, sheet-metal workshop) accepted various job orders ranging from installation and repair of tin roofs, to manufacture and repair of simple machine parts, all of which required metal-forming operations only. Subsequently, several years after it began the manufacture of radiators for Isuzu, Nishimura decided to restructure the business into a firm specialized in radiator manufacture. Accordingly, it was renamed Nishimura Radiator Seizō.

Why did the first-tier ancillary firms specialize by product rather than by process? The main reason may be found in the unique nature of machine products: they consist of a great number of parts and components. Figure 6.5 illustrates the characteristic features of machine production under the two systems. Specialization by process (pattern B) surpasses that by item (pattern A) in attaining higher economies of scale; all the operations in a family of processing activities (e.g., pressing) may be performed efficiently by one of the m firms, each of which is assigned to just one kind of processing. On the other hand, however, the primary firm must carry a heavier burden under pattern B in order to ensure the same flow of materials as under pattern A.

Under the system of specialization by process, material has to be transferred up to $m-1$ times among the ancillary firms before it eventually reaches the primary firm as a part. To check and control the

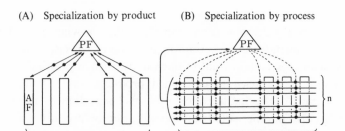

(A) Specialization by product   (B) Specialization by process

Fig. 6.5. Two Basic Patterns of Specialization

quality and delivery schedule of the part supply, the primary firm generally has to inspect m times, including the last move to the primary firm and excluding the initial in-flow to the bottom-tier ancillary firm, for each item. The total number of check points amounts to m times n in case of pattern B, while it is only n in pattern A.

In the case of pattern A, moreover, it is easier for the primary firm to attribute the responsibility for any quality defect or delivery failure to a particular ancillary firm. Thus, pattern A has the advantage of a lesser burden of production control, although it has to sacrifice scale economies to some extent. The primary firm may be able to reap additional benefits from pattern A such as shorter lead time in the supply of parts and components, and more concerted efforts by the ancillary firms to improve the quality and cost performance of their products. The total lead time for the production of a part or component is much shorter under pattern A because fewer physical inter-firm movements are involved.

In general, the more vertically integrated a production system (in our case, pattern A in comparison with pattern B), the much wider will be the range of control variables available to management for improving the quality of their products. But to achieve this flexibility, which is good for upgrading product quality, the firm has to abandon the opportunities to grow by diversifying its product line.

The policy of vertical integration by the ancillary firms may be

274

understood along the same line. Most of the ancillary firms under investigation were active in vertical integration, both forward and backward, and they came to produce various production equipment and machinery for themselves. Obviously, such extensive vertical integration of the production systems must have made the firms even more capable and flexible in controlling product designs and manufacturing methods, which eventually affected product quality. Applying this vertical integration policy also entailed a certain cost for the firm, however. The firm might suffer scale diseconomies in the production of some materials (such as smelting in Yazaki's case). The in-house manufacture of production equipment often may have turned out to be more costly than just purchasing similar equipment from specialized manufacturers.

Quality-First Policy

Finally, it should be recalled that priority was placed on product quality over simple cost considerations. It is worthwhile reflecting briefly why this was the case.

Many of the firms studied, both primary and ancillary, had their major focus on product quality improvement rather than cost reduction in their production management activities at least until around the mid-1960s. In fact, the concept and method of modern quality control (QC) was introduced much earlier than the techniques of industrial engineering (IE), comprising both value analysis (VA) and value engineering (VE). IE's main concern centers around improved efficiency and cost reduction. But why did the industry give so high a priority to product quality?

One may interpret the phenomenon in the following manner: first, the sequence was logical, as the application of QC formed the basis for effective introduction of IE. IE could not be applied effectively without first having stable production operations characterized by uniformly low defect rates, few machine troubles, and error-free operations by production workers. Most of these could usually be attained by appropriate application of QC. Furthermore, previous application of statistical quality control (SQC) provided IE with valuable data on the production

275

processes and their operations.

Second, the introduction of QC would face less resistance from the workers compared with other techniques of modern production management, especially techniques directly oriented toward cost reduction. QC could be justified by an unassailable and worthwhile objective, which was to supply the customers with products of better and uniform quality.

Third, the reduction of defect rates was in fact the most effective measure for lowering the cost of production in the postwar Japanese economy, which had been endowed with relatively cheap labor but with scarce raw materials.

The keen quality consciousness observed in both ancillary and primary firms under study may be ascribed also to the specific historical circumstances surrounding the industry. At the very early stage of its development, the market was occupied by a limited number of wealthy people who vied with each other in driving a better car but cared little about cost. The development of the local automobile industry was afterwards directed and supported by the Army, which eventualy acted as the patron of the industry in the prewar decades. What this generous buyer wanted was a better (or more durable) vehicle even if at a higher cost.

Immediately after World War II, the most important customer of the industry turned out to be the U.S. Army as well as the newly established National Police Reserved, both of which relieved the industry of serious financial difficulties arising from the Dodge Plan recession (1949). In the 1950s, taxi and car rental companies were major customers. Time and again the clients were oriented more to product quality than mere initial cost. In sum, in the beginning, the consumers were consistently more conscious of quality than cost, until around 1960 when the industry saw, for the first time in its history, the emergence of another type of consumer: those more concerned with cost.

Given market conditions, the most effective strategy for a firm to survive and grow was to concentrate its resources and effort on improving product quality. The disadvantage of high costs arising from the policies of "specialization by product" and "vertical integration," as well as lost opportunity for diversification as a result of the "product specialization" policy, were all offset by the customers' generous attitude toward cost and the high growth rate of the industry.

It was only in early and mid-1960s, when the product quality of the first-tier ancillary firms approximated contemporary international standards and customers grew cost-conscious, that many of the firms shifted emphasis from quality to cost. More specifically, it was around this period that many first-tier ancillary firms resumed diversification, and began to be more active in utilizing second-tier subcontractors.

Chapter 7

CONCLUSION

Although the manufacture of automobiles started in the Meiji period, full-fledged development of the industry did not begin until Ford and General Motors established assembly plants in the mid 1920s. But they were forced out of the country by 1940 because of the government's desire to establish domestically-controlled production facilities. What would have been the fate of the industry had the Automobile Industry Act of 1936 not been enacted remains an object for speculation. However, judging from the prevailing standard of the country's machinery industry in the prewar decades, it would have been extremely difficult for domestic assemblers to have competed with their foreign counterparts.

Harder still is to know what would have been the fate of ancillary firms if the market had been dominated by foreign-controlled corporations. Both Ford and GM bought local original equipment parts to a limited extent, but without the government's measures to encourage this, survival might have been tough.

The Japanese machinery industry was not mature enough in the 1930s to start mass production of durable goods. Nevertheless, it had accumulated sufficient skills to engage in the small-lot production of made-to-order items such as steel ships, and also in the manufacture of relatively simple consumer durables such as bicycles and sewing machines. The successful fabrication of automatic looms for the cotton textile industry stood at the top end of the technological spectrum that Japan had achieved in the period. Just as significant as this was the presence of a goodly number of educated engineers as well as scientists capable of transmitting advanced foreign technologies into domestic application.

In any event, it seems reasonably certain that the probability of indigenous development of production by both primary and ancillary firms would have been quite low without some form of public assistance. In this sense, the experience of Japan's automobile industry is a textbook example of the infant-industry thesis in action. Both the assemblers and the parts makers were shielded from foreign competition until they were strong enough to stand on their own.

Even though direct measures, such as import quotas, duties, price controls, etc., were gradually abolished, the industry was the beneficiary of highly effective, *de facto* protection: tight foreign-exchange controls, which were in place for macroeconomic reasons. Furthermore, the government successfully preserved an atmosphere favorable to the growth of the industry through such institutional devices as the Provisional Act for the Promotion of Machinery Industries.

But it would be totally erroneous to ascribe the successes to policy guidance alone. There were at least two additional factors that functioned as basic, promoting agents of the industry's development: relatively concomitant growth of other sectors of the economy, and the backlog of mechanical and related engineering know-how. Protection may have been necessary, but it was far from a sufficient condition for growth.

First and foremost, the growth of the domestic market owed much to the technological and economic transformations in agricultural production, whereas the activities of light industries earned necessary foreign exchange while creating effective demand that encouraged further expansion of the industrial sector. Also, one should not overlook the timely growth in the raw-materials processing sector, especially the steel industry, that lay a cornerstone for the postwar economic growth of Japan in general.

The critical nature of an ambitious marketing strategy to cope with the ever-changing market demand deserves special mention. Sales promotion, coupled with the increase in income, resulted in structural

CONCLUSION

changes in demand, shifting it from three wheelers to small trucks, and then to passenger vehicles. The nature of the purchasers also changed from being nearly 100 percent business corporations to being predominantly the general public.

To further expand the market and upgrade the quality of parts and components, standardization and commonization of makes and models have been highly effective and conducive to achieving scale economies. It is also possible that such national projects as the prewar "Standard Models" and the postwar "Citizens' Cars," coupled with protection policies, inspired intensified attempts by parts and components manufacturers to improve their technology and quality.

For any firm to grow, there must be a market for the product. In the context of the present study, the size of the market for ancillary firms depends not only on the growth of the market for the final product but also on the policy of the primary firms with regard to the acquisition of necessary parts and components.

The most important aspect of the technological development of the Japanese automobile industry lies in the timely choice of appropriate technologies and appropriate products. In prewar days, this was necessary to bridge the gap between the sophisticated technology required for automobile production and the generally low level of industrial technology available in the country. Appropriate choices of technology and product would enable the indigenous sectors to fully utilize their production capacity, leading to an efficient manufacturing system in terms of economic endowment.

Thus, relatively less capital-intensive methods of production were generally adopted. When Toyota built the Koromo plant, for instance, its capacity was considerably scaled down, compared with that of the standard U.S. plant, in order to match the small Japanese market. At the early stage of ancillary firm development, numerous cases can be cited where second-hand production equipment was extensively utilized. With regard to appropriate product, it is important to note that three-wheelers and small-sized vehicles preceded and influenced the development of the passenger car market.

When it comes to the diffusion of technology, the important role played by the arsenals in transmitting sophisticated technology to the private sector indicates the desirability of establishing a public research institute or experimental station to assume such a role. Because of the high risk and cost involved in such activities, the government shared responsibility in creating external economies of this nature.

For an ancillary firm taking the first step in its growth (especially in a developing country), there are two difficulties to overcome. The first is the "battle for survival," in which the firm has to establish and defend a foothold in the market in competition with imports, primary firms' in-house production, and other domestic ancillary firms including those associated with foreign counterparts. The second is the "competition for growth," in which competition with foreign manufacturers becomes increasingly important. But the ancillary firm often has to start without sufficient financial, technological, and managerial resoures. In other words, its competitive position is likely to be much weaker than its major rivals, primary firms and foreign manufacturers.

To realize substantial development of ancillary firms in the follower countries of modern economic growth, some measure of protection and assistance seems essential for a certain period. In the Japanese case the primary firms and the government jointly assumed this role. The primary firms extended financial, technological, and managerial assistance to their ancillary firms on the basis of the stable and exclusive relationships between them. On the other hand, the government, including its armed forces in the prewar decades, offered persistent and comprehensive support to both the primary and ancillary firms through various kinds of policy instruments. The Japanese motor vehicle industry was fostered in its infant stage by the military's demand for trucks. This caused the rapid growth of truck manufacturing but a conspicuously slow development of passenger car production.

Note, however, that both the government and the primary firms supported ancillary firm development for their own interests. In the prewar decades, the government and the Army had a keen interest in developing the industry (both primary and ancillay firms) in order to secure a sufficient domestic supply of military vehicles. From the primary firms' view point, quick domestication of vehicle manufacturing by developing an extensive network of affiliated suppliers (ancillary firms) was the most effective, and perhaps the only, strategy they could pursue for their own survival and growth under the circumstances.

In the postwar days, the government, more specifically MITI, designated the automobile industry as one of the strategic industries in Japan's economic reconstruction. MITI saw in the industry a great dollar-earning potential. The rapid growth of the domestic market, initiated by the special procurement demands of the Korean War, and later encouraged by the government's promotional and protectionist policies, gave strong impetus to the profit motive of the primary firms, which then felt the need to expand and modernize their production capacity as fast as possible. Again the extensive utilization of subcontracting was the most suitable method to perform the task, and the need drove the primary firms to assist the ancillary firms to develop.

Finally, but not least, one should not underestimate the role of the ancillary firms themselves. In order to survive and grow, they have made extensive efforts over the years under often entrepreneurial leadership of key executives, continuously adapting themselves to the strenuous competitive environment. All the favorable conditions described in the previous chapters for the development of ancillary firms would have been useless without this.

In summary, therefore, sufficient growth of the product market, persistent (but gradually fading) support by the government, appropriate assistance by the primary firms, and the ancillary firms' own efforts to develop, were four essential elements for the successful development of ancillary firms. They may be likened to four wheels of a four wheeler; missing any one of them would have hampered the steady development of the ancillary firms in the Japanese automobile industry.

APPENDIX

APPENDIX

Table A-1. A Comparison of Productivity Indicators of Selected Automobile and Automobile Parts and Components Manufacturers, Fiscal Year 1967

	Name of company	Size of employment (thousand)	Gross value added per employee (thousand yen)	Gross value added per tangible fixed asset (%)[c]	Country
Automobile manufac- turers	Toyota and Nissan[a]	34	2,885	114.72	Japan
	VW and Benz	118	1,930	136.85	W. Germany
	GM, Ford and Chrysler[b]	462	4,705	171.20	U.S.A.
Automobile parts and components manufac- turers	Nippondenso, Nihon Hatsujō and Kayaba Kōgyō[b]	9	1,702	145.69	Japan
	Fichtel & Sachs	10	1,667	158.64	W. Germany
	Borg-Werner	43	3,969	173.34	U.S.A.
	Joseph Lucas[d]	70	1,095	256.05	U.K.
	Bendix	76	3,599	455.45	U.S.A.

Notes: [a] Average of two corporations.
  [b] Average of three corporations.
  [c] Fixed asset is expressed in book value (at year's end), and net of depreciation.
  [d] As of 1968.
Sources: Tsūshō Sangyō Shō (MITI), *Sekai no kigyō no keiei bunseki, kokusai keiei hikaku* [Survey on Financial Statements of Major Corporations in the World], 1970 ed., pp. 116–26.

APPENDIX

Table A-2. Growth of Capital Intensity in Terms of the Number of Lathes per Employee, Automobile Parts and Components Industry[a]

Year	Number of lathes (A)	Number of employees (B)	$\dfrac{(A)}{(B)}$
1939	1,379	37,817	0.0365
1940	1,455	43,985	0.0331
1957	15,330	70,779	0.2166

Notes: [a] Inclusive of parts and components for two wheelers. The data cover establishments (1939, 1940) or firms (1957) with more than five employees.

Sources: Shōkō Shō (Ministry of Commerce and Industry), *Kōjō tōkeihyō* [Census of Manufacturers], 1939, 1940 and Tsūshō Sangyō Shō (MITI), *Chūshō kigyō sōgō kihon chōsa* [Basic Survey on Medium- and Small-scale Firms], 1957.

Table A-3. Total Factor Productivity in Automobile Parts and Components Production

A. Company-based data, classified by size of capital asset

Total asset (million yen)	1955			
	Gross value added per employee (thousand yen)	Gross value added per tangible fixed asset	Share of labor (%)	Index of total factor productivity
– 1.9	319.1	2.25	53.2	123.4
2– 4.9	342.4	2.27	43.0	134.7
5– 9.9	337.0	1.41	47.3	102.6
10– 49.9	398.4	1.43	43.9	112.8
50– 99.9	443.3	1.44	42.9	119.2
100–499.9 ⎱ 500–999.9 ⎰ 1,000–	448.5	1.03	48.9	100.0
Average	378.2	1.32	46.2	—

APPENDIX

Table A-3. (continued)

Total asset (million yen)	1966			
	Gross value added per employee (thousand yen)	Gross value added per tangible fixed asset	Share of labor (%)	Index of total factor productivity
− 1.9	1,059	1.71	61.0	102.6
2− 4.9	869	1.38	60.6	83.8
5− 9.9	671	1.30	66.5	68.1
10− 49.9	738	1.11	60.4	69.5
50− 99.9	898	1.21	56.9	81.7
100–499.9	1,004	1.09	51.3	84.3
500–999.9	1,085	1.04	47.2	86.6
1,000–	1,938	0.83	44.4	100.0
Average	1,644	0.89	47.2	—

Sources: Jidōsha Buhin Kōgyō Kai and Nihon Kikai Kōgyō Rengō Kai (1957).

APPENDIX

Table A-3. (continued)

B. Factory-based data, classified by size of employment[a], 1957

Size of employment	Gross value added per employee (thousand yen)	Gross value added per tangible fixed asset	Share of labor (%)	Index of total factor productivity
1– 3	424	4.98	28.3	121.8
4– 9	371	6.40	37.8	128.1
10– 19	315	5.54	48.7	102.4
20– 29	321	4.79	46.0	96.7
30– 49	330	4.60	50.1	93.1
50– 99	391	4.33	43.3	100.3
100–199	479	3.40	38.6	95.2
200–299	448	3.70	49.3	93.4
300–499	597	3.28	37.4	100.9
500–999	629	2.65	42.9	88.4
1,000–	907	2.61	30.2	100.0

Notes: [a] Inclusive of factories manufacturing two wheelers' parts and components.
Sources: Tsūsho Sangyō Shō (MITI), Chūshō kigyō sōgō kihon chōsa hōkoku [Basic Survey on Medium- and Small-scale Firms], 1957.

Table A-4. Age of Machinery and Equipment in the Automobile Parts and Components Industry, 1955–69

(In percent)

Type of machinery	Less than 5 yrs old				Less than 10 yrs old			
	1955	1960	1965	1969	1955	1960	1965	1969
Machine tools	23.1	43.7	47.6	45.4	36.8	57.5	74.0	78.8
Metal fabricating machinery	36.0	55.5	54.7	54.9	56.3	71.7	82.2	84.4
Testing equipment	65.7	74.5	66.7	62.0	79.5	90.4	90.2	89.0
Others	33.9	61.1	61.4	60.4	49.4	75.7	88.3	91.1
Total	30.3	52.4	55.7	53.7	45.3	66.6	81.9	84.7

Sources: Nihon Jidōsha Buhin Kōgyō Kai (JAPIA), Jigyō hōkoku sho [Annual Report of Activities], 1970, pp. 334–36.

Table A-5. Number of Existing Machine Tools per Establishment, Automobile and Automobile Parts and Components Manufacturers

Size of establishment in terms of employment	Machine tools[a]				Secondary metal forming and cutting machines and equipment[b]				Total of two types listed herein and all others			
	1960	1963	1967	1973	1960	1963	1967	1973	1960	1963	1967	1974
30– 49	20.9	25.6	25.5	—	5.3	6.3	8.6	—	26.3	31.9	34.2	—
50– 99	29.8	33.9	39.5	—	7.6	10.0	12.7	—	37.4	43.8	52.2	—
100–299	55.1	64.3	68.3	112.6	15.9	16.0	17.9	23.2	71.1	80.3	86.2	112.0
300–499	161.3	108.3	115.0	154.1	29.5	38.1	39.2	34.9	190.8	146.4	154.1	154.1
500–999	247.8	223.3	196.3	254.7	35.7	42.7	53.1	78.0	283.4	266.0	249.5	332.7
1,000–	800.3	849.0	788.6	877.9	86.9	95.2	122.7	171.0	887.2	944.1	911.2	1,048.9
Average	63.7	76.9	87.3	233.3[c]	12.3	15.8	21.1	53.0[c]	76.0	92.7	260.6	276.3[c]

Notes: [a]   Consisting of lathes, drilling machines, boring machines, milling machines, planers, grinding machines, gear cutting and finishing machines, etc.
  [b]   Consisting of bending machines, hydraulic presses, mechanical presses, shearing machines, forging machinery, wire forming machines, manual presses, etc.
  [c]   Average of establishments with 100 employees or more.

Sources: Tsūshō Sangyō Shō (MITI), Kōsaku kikai setsubi tō tōkei chōsa hōkoku [Statistical Survey on Machine Tools], various issues.

291

APPENDIX

Table A-6. Distribution of Establishment by Size, Automobile Parts and Components Production, 1947–1974 (Two, Three and Four Wheelers)

Size of establishment by employment	Proportion measured by	Annual average of:				
		1947–1954	1950–1959	1955–1964	1960–1969	1965–1974
4–49	Total employment	42.7%	40.5%	33.8%	28.5%	25.5%[a]
	Number of establishments	89.6	87.8	85.3	86.4	89.0[a]
500–	Total employment	13.9[b]	16.1[c]	20.6	29.5[d]	38.0[e]
	Number of establishments	0.2[b]	0.2[c]	0.3	0.3	0.4

Notes: [a] Excluding 1970.
　　　　[b] Excluding 1948–1950.
　　　　[c] Excluding 1950.
　　　　[d] Excluding 1969.
　　　　[e] Excluding 1969, 1972 and 1974.
　　　　The data for above computation cover two, three and four wheelers.
Sources: Computed from Tsūshō Sangyō Shō (MITI), *Kōgyō tōkei hyō* [Census of Manufacturers], various issues.

Table A-7. Size Distribution of Automobile Parts and Components Manufactures[a] in Terms of the Number of Employees, 1956–1972

Size of employment	1956		1960		1965		1970		1974	
	Number of firms	%	Number of firms	%	Number of firms	%	Number of firms	%	Number of firms	%
– 49	118	37.8	71	21.3	41	12.1	27	8.4	16	5.3
50– 99	58	18.6	62	18.6	47	13.9	28	8.7	27	8.9
100–299	85	27.2	102	30.6	103	31.9	98	30.4	85	28.1
300–499	22	7.1	37	11.1	44	13.0	45	14.0	41	13.5
500–999	18	5.8	34	10.2	50	14.7	62	19.3	69	22.8
1,000–	11	3.5	27	8.1	49	14.5	52	19.2	65	21.4
Total	312	100.0	333	99.9	339	100.1	322	100.0	303	100.0

Notes: [a] First-tier ancillary firms only.
Sources: Nihon Jidōsha Buhin Kōgyō Kai (JAPIA), *Jigyō hōkoku sho* [Annual Report of Activities], various issues.

APPENDIX

Table A-8. Median Size of Ancillary Firms: Automobile Parts and Components
Manufacturing (Two, Three and Four Wheelers)[a]

Year	Chassis and bodies	Parts and accessories
1948	880	57
1949	279	47
1950	?	86
1951	?	67
1952	121	70
1953	266	68
1954	403	83
1955	232	76
1956	282	95
1957	191	82
1958	216	90
1959	570	108
1960	336	141
1961	191	152
1962	476	370
1963	531	144
1964	386	168
1965	706	176
1966	595	233
1967	788	225
1968	?	267
1969	?	191
1970	?	395
1971	?	230
1972	?	266
1973	?	260
1974	?	175

Notes: [a] In terms of the number of employees.
Sources: Estimated from Tsūshō Sangyō Shō (MITI), *Kōgyō tōkei hyō* [Census of Manufacturers], various issues.

294

Table A-9. Cost Structure of the Automobile Parts and Components
Production[a]

(In percent)

Items	1956	1957	1958	1959	1960
Raw materials	39.6	39.3	35.6	36.8	34.4
Purchased parts	14.5	14.8	15.3	14.6	17.6
Subcontracted works	9.3	9.6	9.3	9.3	9.5
(Subtotal)	(63.4)	(63.7)	(60.2)	(60.7)	(61.5)
Labor	12.4	12.5	13.1	12.7	13.6
Depreciation	2.4	2.8	3.6	3.4	3.8
Administrative & sales	12.6	12.2	12.9	11.8	11.0
(Subtotal)	(27.4)	(27.5)	(29.6)	(27.9)	(28.4)
Others	9.2	8.8	10.2	11.4	10.1

Notes: [a] JAPIA member firms only.
Sources: Nihon Jidōsha Buhin Kōgyō Kai (JAPIA), *Jigyō hōkoku sho* [Annual
Report of Activities], 1961, p. 234.

Table A-10.   Investment in Government-Designated Machine Tools in the
Automobile Parts and Components Industry

(Million yen, except for last column)

Year	Total annual investment	Investment financed through the Provisional Act (*Kishin hō*)[a]			
		Total	Through the Japan Development Bank[b]	Through the Small Enterprise Loan Corporation[c]	Number of Corporations financed
1956	920	434	434	—	16
1957	1,650	473	473	—	17
1958	1,080	367	367	—	17
1959	1,380	310	310	—	19
1960	1,910	—[d]	—	—	—
1961	8,700	2,917[e]	1,215	187	43[f]
1962	7,400	1,602	1,348	254	44
1963	11,000	3,272	2,450	822	66
1964	12,500	4,108	3,423	685	66
1965	9,700	2,800	2,460	340	38
1966	20,000	2,794	2,420	374	35
1967	42,954	4,679[g]	4,165[g]	514[g]	42

Notes: [a] *Kikai kōgyō shinkō rinji sochi hō* [The Provisional Act for the Promotion of Machinery Industries].

[b] Nihon Kaihatsu Ginkō.

[c] Chūshō Kigyō Kinyū Kōko (Medium- and Small-scale Firm Financing Corporation).

[d] The Provisional Act could not be extended in time for execution.

[e] Inclusive of a loan extended by the Export-Import Bank of Washington, amounting to 1,515.08 million yen.

[f] Not inclusive of the company that received the Export-Import Bank loan.

[g] Planned figures.

Sources: Nihon Jidōsha Buhin Kōgyō Kai (JAPIA), *Jigyō hōkoku sho* [Annual Report of Activities], 1967, pp. 5 and 323.

Table A-11. Rationalization Projects in the Automobile Parts and Components Industry

Parts and components designated in the projects	(1) Annual investment plans (× indicates a projected expenditure for the year) 1955 · · · 1960 · · · 1965	(2) Rate of decline in cost, 1960–65 (1960=100)	(3) Proportion of replacement goods in total production of parts and components (%) 1960ᵃ	(3) 1965ᵃ	(4) Market share of three largest producers, 1966 (%)
Engine parts					
Pistons	× × × × × × × × × × × ×	71.6	41.1	23.1	66.4
Piston pins	× × × ×	?	13.7	3.0	?
Piston rings	× × × × × × × × × × × × × ×	76.3	59.8	45.3	10.0
Cylinder liners	× × × × × × × × × × × ×	80.3	40.3	37.9	70.6
Gaskets	× × × ×	?	58.8	29.9	64.1
Intake & exhaust bulbs	× × × × × × × × × ×	78.5	36.1	11.9	81.9
Fuel pumps	× × × × × × × ×	63.0	16.3	15.4	68.3
Fuel pump screens		?	27.0	?	?
Carburetors	× × × × × × × × × ×	?	13.5	7.4	61.8
Fuel injection systems	× × × × × × × ×	76.0	21.6	12.4	94.5
Fuel strainers	× × × × × ×	?	24.4	54.0	56.2
Air cleaners	× × × × × × × ×	?	11.9	23.0	71.0
Oil filters	× × × × × ×	?	28.0	63.0	78.0
Water pumps	× × × × × × × × × × ×	} 75.3	12.3	11.9	81.2
Oil pumps	× × × × × × × ×		1.0	2.4	84.7
Coil springs	× × ×	?	0.5	9.2	?

Table A-11. (continued)

	Production period (1955 · 1960 · 1965)	(1)	(2)	(3)	(4)
Radiators	× × × × × × × × × × × × × × × ×	75.3	5.3	6.7	77.3
Thermostats		?	9.7	41.5	?
Connecting rods	× × × × × × × × × × × × × × ×	65.0	30.5	26.3	76.5
Fan belts		?	85.4	?	?
Timing chains		?	0	?	?
Timing gears		?	27.6	0.6	?
Transmission and steering systems					
Steering wheels	× × × × × × × × × × × × × ×	?	1.8	1.6	94.7
Power steering systems	× × × × × × × × × ×	?	4.5	7.4	99.4
Clutch systems	× × × × × × × ×	?	24.3	35.3	80.5
Clutch disks		?	45.6	67.3	88.5
Clutch linings	× × × × × × × × ×	?	31.1	43.1	86.5
Pressure plates		?	?	?	?
Clutch covers		?	?	?	?
Clutch springs	× × ×	?	6.6	2.5	?
Release levers		?	?	?	?
Oil seals	× × × × × × × × × × × × ×	65.7	36.2	23.3	80.0
Needle roller bearings		?	0	11.2	?
Hub bolts & nuts	× × × × × × × × × × × ×	?	15.1	11.0	?
Wheel discs	× × × × × × × × × ×	76.8	14.7	6.8	71.3
Steering systems	× × × × × × ×	?	?	?	88.8

Suspension and brake systems

	1955 — 1960 — 1965	(1)	(2)	(3)	(4)
Chassis springs	× × × × × × × × × × × × × × ×	90.0	41.9	24.6	78.4
Shock absorbers	× × × × × × × × × × × × × × ×	64.0	24.0	15.2	96.2
Brake system	× × × × × × × × × × ×	?	?	?	71.0
Brake linings	× × × × × × × ×	74.0	63.5	59.5	85.8
Brake cylinders	× × × × × × ×	?	34.7	10.8	76.0
Brake discs		?	?	?	?
Brake shoes		?	?	22.2	39.2
Brake return springs		?	?	?	?
Brake hoses	× × × × × × × × × × × × × × × × ×	?	10.9	8.0	?
Power brakes	× × × × × × × × × × ×	?	29.1	13.3	100.0
Air brake systems	× × × × × × × × × × ×	?	8.7	17.3	92.4
Air compressors		?	?	?	?
Brake chambers		?	?	?	?
Brake pipes	× × × × × × × × × ×	?	?	?	?

Body parts

	1955 — 1960 — 1965	(1)	(2)	(3)	(4)
Lamps	× × × × × × × × × × × × × × ×	71.5	18.4	18.8	82.7
Switches	× × × × × × × × × × × × × × ×	?	27.9	20.1	75.5
Speedometers & other meters	× × × × × × × × × × × × × × ×	?	9.1	7.9	70.4
Winkers		?	93.7	—	?
Windshield wipers	× × × ×	?	27.2	9.0	80.6
Horns	× × × × × × × × × × × × × × ×	60.5	30.2	35.7	87.7
Cable casings	× × × × × × × × × × × × × × ×	?	22.9	19.0	79.8

Table A-11. (continued)

	1955 · 1960 · 1965 (×)	(1)	(2)	(3)	(4)
Wire harnesses	× × × × × × × ×	?	17.2	2.2	?
Tools		?	?	?	?
Jacks		?	67.6	3.9	?
Grease pump	× × × ×	?	84.3	55.5	?
Spanners		?	93.7	—	?
Window regulators	× × × × × × × × × ×	?	2.1	3.5 ⎫	?
Door handles & door locks	× × × × ×	?	6.5	4.6 ⎭	62.0
Electric bulbs		7	62.7	54.5	?
Hinges		?	0.1	0.4	?
Seats	× × × × × × × ×	?	1.5	0.2	70.0
Car coolers		?	63.6	83.5	?
Car heaters		?	60.4	19.8	?
Tire bulbs	× × × × × × × × × × ×	76.5	76.9	32.8	100.0
Electrical components					
Batteries		?	?	?	?
Generators	× × × × × × × × × × × ×	?	6.7	11.7	?
Starters	× × × × × × × × × × ×	?	8.0	12.0	?
Regulators	× × × × × × × × × ×	?	18.2	32.1	?
Distributors	× × × × × × × × × ×	?	7.2	15.1	?
Spark coils	× × × × × × × × × × × ×	?	32.6	28.5	64.1
Spark plugs	× × × × × × × × × ×	68.5	94.2	94.5	100.0

Note: The brace joining Window regulators (3.5) and Door handles & door locks (4.6) in column (3) corresponds to the combined value 62.0 in column (4).

	(1) 1955 · 1960 · 1965	(2)	(3)	(3)	(4)
Heater plugs	· · · · · · · · ·	?	60.4	75.0	?
Pressed parts					
Pressed parts in general	× × × × × × × × ×	?	?	?	43.1
Frames & axle housings	× × × ×	?	0.0	3.2	?
Oil pans		?	?	?	?
Engine gear cases		?	?	?	?
Miscellaneous parts					
Window frames	× × × × × × × × × × × × × ×	72.0	0.9	26.7	88.1
Window-glass weather-strip rubbers		?	?	?	?
Vibration-proof rubbers	× × × × × × ×	5.5	54.6	1.1	89.3
Rubber bushes	× × ×	?	31.1	12.2	67.7
Bumpers		?	2.4	22.8	?
Ornaments & steering handles		?	?	?	?
Radio shields		?	?	?	?
Exhaust pipes and mufflers	× × × × × × × × × ×	?	7.8	23.7	70.8
Related products					
Automobile clocks		?	?	?	?
Internal sealings		?	?	?	?
Ornaments		?	?	?	?
Curbed window glasses	· · · · · · · · · · · ·	?	?	?	?

Notes: ^a Figures relating to the second half of the fiscal year.

Sources: Nihon Jidōsha Buhin Kōgyō Kai (JAPIA), *Jigyō hōkoku sho* [Annual Report of Activities], various issues.

301

Table A-12. Domestic Production, Export and Import of Automobiles
(Three and Four Wheelers)

(In thousands)

Calendar year[a]	Domestic production	Of which number of three wheelers	Total export	Total import	Total domestic holdings[c]
1930	0.8	0.3	—	—	—
1931	1.0	0.6	—	—	—
1932	2.4	1.5	—	—	—
1933	4.1	2.4	—	—	—
1934	6.2	3.4	—	—	—
1935	15	10	—	—	—
1936	25	13	—	—	—
1937	33	15	—	—	—
1938	35	11	—	—	—
1939	43	8	—	—	—
1940	54	8	—	—	—
1941	51	5	—	—	—
1942	41	4	—	—	—
1943	28	2	—	—	—
1944	23	1	—	—	—
1945	9[b]	0[b]	—	—	—
1946	18	3	—	—	—
1947	19	7	—	—	—
1948	37	17	—	—	—
1949	55	27	—	—	—
1950	67	35	—	—	—
1951	82	44	7	—	—
1952	101	62	1	—	358
1953	147	97	1	6	434
1954	168	98	1	0.4	554
1955	157	89	1	1	707
1956	216	105	4	1	813
1957	297	115	7	1	922
1958	287	99	11	1	1,087
1959	421	158	21	1	1,430
1960	760	278	50	2	1,751

Table A-12.   (continued)

(In thousands)

Calendar year[a]	Domestic production	Of which number of three wheelers	Total export	Total import	Total domestic holdings[c]
1961	1,038	225	59	6	2,176
1962	1,135	144	71	12	2,868
1963	1,401	117	100	12	3,633
1964	1,783	80	152	13	4,642
1965	1,919	43	196	13	5,782
1966	2,320	33	258	16	6,983
1967	3,173	26	364	15	8,495
1968	4,108	22	622	16	10,501
1969	4,692	17	865	16	12,871
1970	5,303	14	1,094	20	15,444
1971	5,822	12	1,786	19	17,826
1972	6,298	3	1,967	25	20,061
1973	7,086	3	2,071	38	22,576
1974	6,553	1	2,619	44	25,136
1975	6,942	—	2,677	46	26,901
1976	7,841	—	3,710	41	28,139
1977	8,515	—	4,353	42	30,111
1978	9,269	—	4,601	55	32,044
1979	9,636	—	4,563	66	34,152
1980	11,043	—	5,967	48	36,255
1981	11,180	—	6,048	33	37,874
1982	10,732	—	5,591	36	39,632
1983	11,112	—	5,670	38	41,346
1984	11,465	—	6,109	45	42,939
1985	12,271	—	6,730	53	44,530

Notes: [a] The years 1930–44 refer to fiscal years (March–April).

[b] April through December.

[c] As of December of the previous year.

Sources: Nihon Jidōsha Kōgyō Kai [Japan Automobile Manufacturers Association], *Jidosha tōkei nempō (nempyō)* [Automobile Statistical Yearbook], various years.

Table A-13. Labor Efficiency in Automobile Production

Calendar year[a]	Production of two, three and four wheelers			Production of small passenger vehicles with four wheels	
	Domestic output in thousand units (A)	Employment (thousands) (B)	Average labor productivity[c] $\frac{(A)}{(B)}$	Time required for engine production (hours/unit)	Time required for chassis production (hours/unit)
1930	2	—	—	—	—
1931	2	—	—	—	—
1932	4	—	—	—	—
1933	5	—	—	—	—
1934	8	—	—	—	—
1935	17	—	—	—	—
1936	26	—	—	—	—
1937	36	—	—	—	—
1938	38	—	—	—	—
1939	45	23	1.9	—	—
1940	57	28	2.0	—	—
1941	54	12	4.5	—	—
1942	43	33	1.3	—	—
1943	30	n.a.	n.a.	—	—
1944	24	n.a.	n.a.	—	—
1945	9[b]	7[b]	1.2	—	—
1946	18	50	0.4	—	—
1947	21	67	0.3	—	—
1948	45	56	0.8	—	—
1949	65	44	1.5	—	—
1950	75	45	1.7	—	—
1951	106	53	2.0	—	—
1952	180	53	3.4	—	—
1953	314	63	5.0	—	—
1954	333	66	5.0	53.25	102.86
1955	416	62	6.7	40.97	107.16

APPENDIX

Table A-13. (continued)

Calendar year[a]	Production of two, three and four wheelers			Production of small passenger vehicles with four wheels	
	Domestic output in thousand units (A)	Employment (thousands) (B)	Average labor productivity[c] $\frac{(A)}{(B)}$	Time required for engine production (hours/unit)	Time required for chassis production (hours/unit)
1956	549	59	9.2	35.20	93.67
1957	707	69	10.2	36.62	73.19
1958	789	70	11.2	31.56	75.40
1959	1,301	82	15.9	24.89	50.76
1960	2,232	81	27.6	19.77	46.08
1961	2,843	116	24.6	17.55	39.26
1962	2,810	121	23.3	16.29	21.08
1963	3,328	131	25.4	12.89	19.97
1964	3,893	150	26.0	10.99	19.76
1965	4,131	157	26.3	11.08	15.58
1966	4,767	163	29.2	11.09	12.20
1967	5,415	183	29.7	9.97	11.85
1968	6,359	197	32.2	9.66	10.65
1969	7,269	213	34.2	7.96	8.43
1970	8,251	213	38.8	7.72	6.92
1971	9,223	230	40.0	6.61	6.16
1972	9,863	229	43.1	6.04	5.58
1973	10,849	241	45.0	5.45	4.64
1974	11,062	231	47.8	5.18	4.64
1975	10,744	220	48.8	4.59	4.60
1976	12,077	220	54.9	4.02	4.27
1977	14,092	226	62.4	3.92	4.11
1978	15,269	227	67.3	3.34	3.59
1979	14,112	230	61.4	3.16	3.27
1980	17,477	236	74.1	3.18	3.20

305

Table A-13. (continued)

Calendar year[a]	Production of two, three and four wheelers			Production of small passenger vehicles with four wheels	
	Domestic output in thousand units (A)	Employment (thousands) (B)	Average labor productivity[c] $\frac{(A)}{(B)}$	Time required for engine production (hours/unit)	Time required for chassis production (hours/unit)
1981	18,593	238	78.1	3.49	3.64
1982	17,795	240	74.1	3.17	3.10
1983	15,919	242	65.8	2.77	3.12
1984	15,491	245	63.2	n.a.	n.a.
1985	16,807	n.a.	n.a.	n.a.	n.a.

Notes: [a] The years 1930–44 refer to fiscal years (March-April).
[b] April through December.
[c] The computation has been done with the original figures and may not agree with the ratios computed on the basis of rounded numbers reported herein.

Sources: Production: Nihon Jidōsha Kōgyō Kai [Japan Automobile Manufacturers Association], *Jidōsha tōkei nempō* [Automobile Statistical Yearbook], no. 4, 1976 and no. 14, 1986. Employment: Shōkō Shō [Ministry of Commerce and Industry], *Kōjō tōkei hyō* [Census of Manufacturers], various issues and Tsūshō Sangyō Shō (MITI), *Kōgyō tōkei hyō* [Census of Manufacturers], various issues. Production time: Rōdōshō (Ministry of Labour), *Rōdō seisansei tōkei chōsa hōkoku* [Report on Statistical Survey on Labor Productivity], various issues and *Shōwa 27–40 nendo rōdō seisansei tōkei shiryō* [Statistical Source Book on Labor Productivity, 1952–65], 1966.

APPENDIX

Table A-14. Domestic Production and Export of Automobile Parts and
Components (in Current Values)

(In million yen)

| Year[a] | Parts production by JAPIA member firms for | | | | | (Reference) |
| | Two, three and four wheelers | | | Three and four wheelers | | Import of parts for two, three and four wheelers *excluding* electrical components |
	Domestic production	Domestic production *excluding* electrical components	Export	Domestic production (for use by domestically produced cars)	Of which replacement goods	
1953	27,782	—	—	—	—	1,174
1954	28,214	—	—	—	—	2,646
1955	34,511	22,637	—	29,393	6,613	2,435
1956	58,922	40,609	3,096	56,209[b]	15,839[b]	2,005
1957	73,838	52,816	3,443	65,331	27,458	1,669
1958	72,202	50,091	3,987	62,184	16,814	891
1959	107,026	73,115	6,074	89,967	21,623	1,034
1960	165,218	111,773	8,351	137,783	28,010	1,017
1961	206,879	143,738	11,038	178,754	36,017	1,111
1962	221,497	154,443	10,234	197,654	38,511	1,360
1963	285,464	201,603	12,780	256,685	44,484	1,517
1964	364,616	264,276	20,521	329,938	59,380	1,454
1965	391,555	282,752	26,197	350,779	64,210	2,115
1966	501,109	365,786	32,871	458,892	81,905	3,321
1967	667,537	493,612	41,782	629,299	97,156	4,604
1968	832,952	617,674	57,858	791,815	110,770	4,762
1969	986,604	714,338	75,160	937,639	143,041	5,754
1970	1,161,289	835,450	108,579	1,094,577	161,826	8,586

307

Table A-14. (continued)

| Year[a] | Parts production by JAPIA member firms for | | | | | (Reference) |
| | Two, three and four wheelers | | | Three and four wheelers | | Import of parts for two, three and four wheelers *excluding* electrical components |
	Domestic production	Domestic production *excluding* electrical components	Export	Domestic production (for use by domestically produced cars)	Of which replacement goods	
1971	1,315,330	938,855	154,809	1,233,599	173,171	8,823
1972	1,534,212	1,081,731	190,744	1,441,198	212,091	6,716
1973	2,006,702	1,429,472	230,299	1,888,065	276,432	7,176
1974	2,247,410	1,598,928	347,721	2,071,407	309,616	12,877
1975	2,495,310	1,761,280	386,462	2,347,514	432,164	15,740
1976[c]	2,943,512	2,072,567	406,634	2,783,314	271,959	19,787

Notes: [a] First five columns refer to fiscal years (April-March), whereas the last column refers to calendar years.

[b] Data for the first half year (April-September) are missing; the figures for the second half year have been multiplied by two.

[c] Data after 1976 are not readily available.

Sources: Columns 1-5 are based on Jidōsha Buhin Kōgyō Kai (JAPIA), *Jigyō hōkoku sho* [Annual Report of Activities], various issues; the last column is based on Tsūshō Sangyō shō (MITI), *Kikai tōkei nempō* (Year Book of Machinery Statistics), various issues.

Table A-15.   Labor Efficiency in the Production of Automobile Parts and Components

Year[a]	Total shipment in current values (in million yen)	Parts production for two, three and four wheelers			Parts production for three and four wheelers. JAPIA member firms only	
		Employ-ment	Number of factories	Average labor produc-tivity in 1960 yen[b] (in million yen)	Employ-ment	Average labor produc-tivity in 1960 yen[b] (in million yen)
1939	126	37.817	1,571	0.759	—	—
1940	225	43,985	1,755	1.138	—	—
1941	363	61,964	1,752	1.287	—	—
1942	167	38,496	1,487	0.877	—	—
1943	n.a.	n.a.	n.a.	n.a.	—	—
1944	n.a.	n.a.	n.a.	n.a.	—	—
1945	238	26,577	661	1.364	—	—
1946	1,223	47,355	862	0.607	—	—
1947	2,731	41,152	908	0.713	—	—
1948	4,126	21,803	625	0.863	—	—
1949	5,041	19,235	709	0.837	—	—
1950	8,535	25,042	858	0.725	—	—
1951	16,235	29,304	1,065	0.593	—	—
1952	24,405	33,793	1,179	0.793	—	—
1953	37,010	54,217	1,773	0.793	—	—
1954	50,313	57,925	1,908	1.075	—	—
1955	49,681	65,034	2,139	0.967	—	—
1956	96,302	81,239	2,168	1.316	—	—
1957	106,462	91,122	2,689	1.161	72,387	1.002
1958	107,080	98,271	2,747	0.906	73,724	0.701
1959	148,881	126,880	3,059	1.051	88,998	1.105
1960	258,554	171,349	3,887	1.509	104,139	1.323

Table A-15. (continued)

Year[a]	Parts production for two, three and four wheelers				Parts production for three and four wheelers. JAPIA member firms only	
	Total shipment in current values (in million yen)	Employ- ment	Number of factories	Average labor produc- tivity in 1960 yen[b] (in million yen)	Employ- ment	Average labor produc- tivity in 1960 yen[b] (in million yen)
1961	347,918	191,229	4,016	1.830	129,263	1.387
1962	399,715	203,214	4,332	1.899	129,152	1.477
1963	471,965	235,010	7,527	2.057	137,705	1.836
1964	612,333	252,232	7,494	2.521	171,162	2.002
1965	688,491	259,187	7,557	2.955	168,653	2.313
1966	863,186	292,629	8,284	3.175	184,344	2.680
1967	1,098,363	318,563	9,126	3.645	204,929	3.246
1968	1,426,308	340,915	9,111	4.256	221,411	3.638
1969	1,665,856	348,013	9,492	4.855	227,099	4.187
1970	2,034,073	367,328	10,124	5.381	236,307	4.501
1971	2,136,157	344,421	10,425	5.753	246,992	4.633
1972	2,480,787	378,200	11,492	6.012	238,229	5.545
1973	3,127,502	393,250	11,830	6.803	254,422	6.348
1974	3,873,575	383,330	11,521	7.541	256.435	6.028
1975	4,294,851	381,555	12,129	7.752	248,530	6.505
1976	5,315,544	401,992	12,357	8.699	248,762	7.361
1977	5,705,066	403,721	12,516	9.352	256,231	n.a.
1978	6,431,965	401,104	9,248	10.246	n.a.	n.a.
1979	7,354,347	412,506	9,193	10.924	n.a.	n.a.
1980	8,815,277	437,347	9,510	11.767	n.a.	n.a.
1981	9,798,145	462,405	9,744	11.884	n.a.	n.a.
1982	9,682,048	456,156	9,840	11.891	n.a.	n.a.
1983	10,018,109	456,205	10,333	11.877	n.a.	n.a.
1984	11,325,565	477,227	10,024	11.121	n.a.	n.a.

Table A-15.   (continued)

Notes: a   Data for the first four columns refer to calendar years (employment is as of 31 December), whereas the last two column refer to fiscal years (April–March).

b   Average labor productivity is the value of shipment (or output) divided by the number of workers (employment). In converting the nominal values into real terms, the price index for parts and components given in Table A-16 (column 6) has been used except for the period prior to 1951. For the pre-1951 period, the Bank of Japan's wholesale price index of metal products and machinery has been used. The two indexes are linked in 1954.

Sources: First four columns from Shōkō Shō [Ministry of Commerce and Industry], *Kōjō tōkei hyō* [Census of Manufactures] and Tūshō Sangō Shō (MITI), *Kōgyō tōkei hyō* [Census of Manufacturers], various issues and the last two columns from Nihon Jidōsha Buhin Kōgyō Kai (JAPIA), *Jigyō hōkoku sho* [Annual Report of Activities], various issues.

APPENDIX

Table A-16. Price Data

Cal- endar year	Automobile prices (thousand yen per unit)			Wage earnings in the automobile industry (thousand yen/month; production and office workers)[c]	Price index of parts and com- ponents and steel sheets (1960 = 100)	Price index of parts and com- ponents (1960 = 100)	Consumer price index (1975 = 100)
	Passenger vehicles (four wheelers)	Trucks (four wheel- ers)	Trucks (three wheel- ers)				
1951	—	672[b]	224	14	—	14.0	26.1
1952	796	773[b]	274	17	—	36.6	27.4
1953	820	846[b]	313	18	—	54.2	29.2
1954	834	761	345	20	82.1	80.8	31.1
1955	771	764	373	18	80.1	79.0	30.8
1956	724	664	403	21	92.8	90.1	30.8
1957	715	589	441	21	102.0	100.6	31.8
1958	709	606	430	21	117.5	120.3	31.6
1959	674	586	324	23	110.1	111.7	32.0
1960	584	538	284	24	100.0	100.0	33.2
1961	565	476	311	27	99.4	99.7	34.9
1962	552	450	349	29	102.2	103.6	37.3
1963	560	418	331	33	100.3	101.5	40.1
1964	521	407	342	36	95.5	96.3	41.7
1965	486	396	344	39	88.8	89.9	44.5
1966	478	386	360	44	93.1	92.9	46.8
1967	438	395	387	48	94.4	94.6	48.6
1968	442	400	376	55	97.4	98.3	51.2
1969	443	422	417	65	97.9	98.6	53.9
1970	449	503	441	76	101.8	102.9	58.0
1971	472	487	378	86	105.9	107.8	61.5
1972	504	471	516	98	107.6	109.1	64.3
1973	524	496	510	119	116.0	116.9	71.9
1974	618	600	511	146	132.0	134.0	89.4
1975	661	624	—	170	143.0	145.2	100.0

Table A-16. (continued)

Cal-endar year	Automobile prices (thousand yen per unit)			Wage earnings in the automobile industry (thousand yen/month; production and office workers)[c]	Price index of parts and components and steel shets (1960 = 100)	Price index of parts and components (1960 = 100)	Consumer price index (1975 = 100)
	Passenger vehicles (four wheelers)	Trucks (four wheel-ers)	Trucks (three wheel-ers)				
1976	719	672	—	193	151.6	152.0	109.3
1977	762	707	—	210	152.4	151.1	118.1
1978	790	743	—	228	158.7	156.5	122.6
1979	807	777	—	250	164.9	163.2	127.0
1980	814	759	—	270	173.3	171.3	372.2
1981	871	771	—	285	180.0	178.3	143.9
1982	954	835	—	297	180.7	178.5	147.8
1983	999	859	—	312	187.0	184.9	150.5
1984	1,031	857	—	326	208.6	209.4	153.8
1985	1,050	889	—	337	212.1	213.4	157.0

Notes: [a] Value output divided by the number of automobile units produced.
[b] Based on the data provided by Kikai tōkei nempō (Year Book of Machinery Statistics).
[c] Assemblers and parts suppliers inclusive.

Sources: Automobile prices are estimated by using the data provided in Nihon Jidōsha Kōgyō Kai (Japan Automobile Manufacturers Association), Jidōsha tōkei nempō (or nempyō) [Automobile Statistical Year Book], various issues. Wage earnings are taken from Tsūshō Sangyō Shō (MITI), Kōgyō tōkei hyō [Census of Manufactures], various issues. Price indices of parts and components have been estimated on the basis of the data from Tsūshō Sangyō shō (MITI), Kikai tōkei nempō (Year Book of Machinery Statistics) and Bank of Japan, Bukka shisū nempō (Price Indexes Annual), various issues, and cover the following items: battery, springs (three kinds), spark plug, starter motor, distributor, carburetor, piston, piston ring, and meters. Finally, CPI is taken from Sōrifu Tōkeikyoku (Prime Minister's Office, Bureau of Statistics), Shōhisha bukka shisū nempō [Year Book of CPI] 1976.

Table A-17. Investment Ratios in the Automobile Parts and Components Manufacturing (for Two, Three and Four Wheelers)

Calender Year	(I) Investment in tangible assets in current prices (million yen)^c	(Y) Net value added in current prices (million yen)^a	$\dfrac{I}{Y}$ (percent)
1955	2,525	22,168	11.39
1956	6,492	33,833	19.19
1957	8,532	37,260	22.90
1958	8,836	40,488	21.82
1959	11,987	53,077	22.58
1960	28,597	99,770	28.66
1961	40,263	121,251	33.21
1962	41,095	149,004	27.58
1963	39,262	187,815	20.90
1964	49,385	210,299	24.53
1965	60,323	226,806	23.48
1966	71,082	264,582	26.87
1967	119,792	350,614	34.17
1968	174,190	461,310	37.76
1969	201,480	532,195	37.86
1970	253,169	655,998	38.59
1971	164,066	681,878	24.06
1972	165,804	818,843	20.25
1973	274,664	1,013,404	27.10
1974	331,241	1,129,813	29.32
1975	212,633	1,324,572	16.05
1976	236,171	1,755,794	13.45
1977	371,552	1,856,987	20.01
1978	397,684	2,044,001	19.46
1979	362,369	2,358,519	15.36
1980	559,467	2,640,434	21.19

APPENDIX

Table A-17. (continued)

Calender Year	(I) Investment in tangible assets in current prices (million yen)^c	(Y) Net value added in current prices (million yen)^a	$\dfrac{I}{Y}$ (percent)
1981	731,999	2,719,230	26.92
1982	736,101	2,535,485	29.03
1983	647,180	2,719,969^b	23.79
1984	694,835	3,191,740	21.77

Notes: [a] Covering establishments with four or more employees (through 1962), and establishments with 10 or more employees (1963–1974).

[b] Interpolation was necessary for groups having with 10 or fewer employees.

Sources: Tsūshō Sangyō Shō (MITI), *Kōgyō tōkei hyō* [Census of Manufacturers], various issues.

Table A-18. Number of First-Tier Ancillary Firms Classified by Their
Primary-Firm Related Associations

Association of ancillary firms	Year[a]	Number of		
		1976	1977	1978
Daihatsu Kyōyū Kai		138	142	141
Fuji Kyōryoku Kai (Gunma region)		133	133	161
Fuji Kyōryoku Kai (Mitaka region)		54	54	54
Hino Kyōryoku Kai		247	236	242
Honda[b]		n.a.	n.a.	345
Isuzu Kyōwa Kai		275	272	272
Mazda Yōkō Kai[c] (Western Japan region)				
Mazda Yōkō Kai[c] (Kansai region)		94	94	94
Mazda Yōkō Kai[c] (Kantō region)				
Mitsubishi Motors Kashiwa Kai		338	347	351
Nissan Diesel Yayoi Kai		62	62	60
Nissan Shōhō Kai		47	47	48
Nissan Takara Kai		112	109	112
Suzuki Kyōdō Kumiai		102	102	102
Toyota Kyōhō Kai (Kansai region)		25	25	25
Toyota Kyōhō Kai (Kantō region)		65	65	65
Toyota Kyōhō Kai (Tōkai region)		133	135	136
Gross total[d]		1,825	1,823	2,208
Net count[e]		n.a.	n.a.	1,494

Table A-18. (continued)

first-tier ancillary firms

1979	1980	1981	1982/83	1984	1985	1986
143	142	143	145	150	152	167
158	160	160	157	159	157	157
54	55	69	69	73	73	73
247	243	243	243	240	240	239
348	342	344	314	364	287	287
269	275	278	277	279	279	281
		60	56	58	59	59
92	91	56	56	57	57	57
		56	60	61	62	62
344	340	333	332	328	333	337
60	60	59	59	60	56	56
49	49	50	53	54	56	58
112	110	110	108	109	105	105
104	101	101	101	102	98	97
25	25	25	25	25	25	25
64	63	63	63	63	62	62
136	137	137	136	135	136	136
2,205	2,193	2,287	2,254	2,317	2,237	2,258
1,624	1,678	1,699	1,730	1,775	1,758	1,751

Notes: [a] Reference date is either middle or end of respective calendar year.

[b] Number of ancillary firms with business dealings with Honda Motor Company (no formal association existed for Honda-related ancillary firms).

[c] Formerly Tōyō Kōgyō Tōyūkai Kyōdō Kumiai (through 1980).

[d] A single ancillary firm may be counted twice or more, as it may deliver its products to more than one primary firm.

[e] Estimated from the index of the names of (first-tier) auto parts suppliers; not necessarily exhaustive.

Sources: Nihon Jidōsha Buhin Kōgyō Kai (JAPIA), *Nihon no jidōsha buhin kōgyō* [Auto Parts Supplier Industries in Japan], Tokyo: Auto Trade Journal, various years.

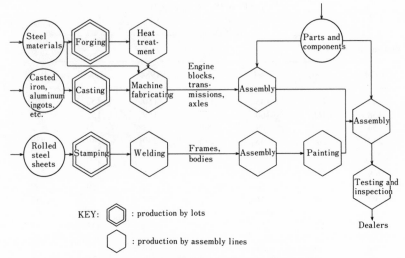

KEY: ⬡ : production by lots

       ⬡ : production by assembly lines

Fig. A-1.   Automobile Production Processes

Sources: Jidōsha Gijutsu Kai (1976), p. 13-1.

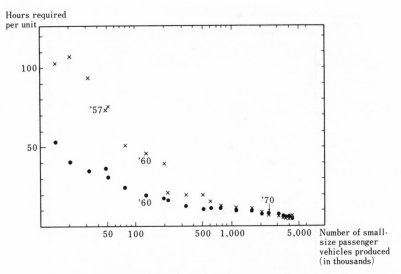

Fig. A-2. Growth of Efficiency in Automobile Production (Japan, 1954–1975)

KEY   ×: chassis production
          ●: engine production
          (both relating to the manufacture of small passenger vehicles)

Notes: The data indicate hours spent on *direct* operations only. Horizontal axis is on logarithmic scale.

Sources: Appendix Table A-13.

Average labor productivity (●)
and monthly wage earnings (⊙)

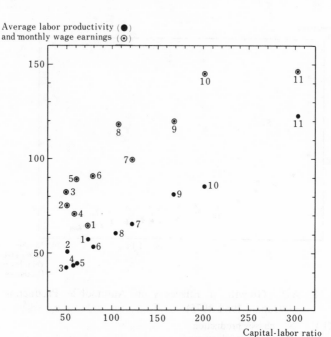

Fig. A-3. Capital–Labor Ratio, Average Labor Productivity
    and Monthly Wages in Automobile Parts and
    Components Production, 1957

KEY   (Size of company in terms of employment)
       1: 1– 3   7: 100–199
       2: 4– 9   8: 200–299
       3: 10–19   9: 300–499
       4: 20–29   10: 500–999
       5: 30–49   11: 1,000–
       6: 50–99

Notes: 1) All the figures are expressed in index numbers, where respective average
           values have been equated to 100; i.e., average capital labor ratio=115
           thousand yen per company, average labor productivity=736 thousand
           yen per company, and average monthly wages=15.5 thousand yen per
           regular employee.
        2) It should be noted also that the data for this figure are inclusive of two,
           three and four wheelers.

Sources: Tsūshō Sangyō Shō (MITI), *Chūshō kigyō sōgō kihon chōsa Hōkoku* [Basic
           Survey on Medium- and Small-scale Firms], 1957.

320

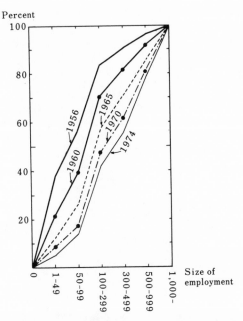

Fig. A-4. Cumulative Distribution of Automobile Parts and Components Manufacturers, by Size of Employment, 1956–1974

Notes: First-tier ancillary firms only.
Sources: Appendix Table A-7.

BIBLIOGRAPHY

Aisan Kōgyō Kabushiki Kaisha (Aisan Industry Company) 1973. *Aisan Kōgyō sanjūgo nen shi* [The Thirty Five Year History of Aisan Industry]. Ōbu City, Aichi Prefecture.

Amagai Shōgo 1982. *Nihon jidōsha kōgyō no shiteki tenkai* [Historical Development of the Japanese Automobile Industry]. Tokyo: Aki Shobō (a revised version of Kokuritsu Kokkai Toshokan 1978).

Arrow, Kenneth J. 1974. *The Limits of Organization.* N.Y.: W.W. Norton.

Auto Trade Journal 1979. *Nihon no jidōsha buhin kōgyō* [The Automobile Parts and Components Industry of Japan]. Tokyo.

Bain, Joe S. 1956. *Barriers to New Competition, Their Character and Consequences in Manufacturing Industries.* Cambridge: Harvard University Press.

Baranson, Jack 1967. *Manufacturing Problems in India—The Cummins Diesel Experience.* N.Y.: Syracuse University Press.

──────── 1969. *Automotive Industries in Developing Countries,* World Bank Staff Occasional Papers No. 8. Baltimore: The Johns Hopkins Press.

──────── 1976. "Enterprise to Enterprise Technology Transfer to Small Industries." In Asian Productivity Organization, *Intra-National Transfer of Technology.* Tokyo, 1976, pp. 19–34.

Blair, John M. 1972. *Economic Concentration, Structure, Behavior and Public Policy.* N.Y.: Harcourt Bruce Jovanovich.

Chūshō Kigyō Chō (Small Enterprise Agency) 1969. *Shōwa yon'jū-yo nendo chūshō kigyo hakusho* [The 1969 White Paper on Medium- and Small-scale Enterprises]. Tokyo.

BIBLIOGRAPHY

Chūshō Kigyō Kenkyū Center [Medium- and Small-scale Firms Research Center] 1968. *Jidōsha buhin kōgyō no jittai chōsa hōkokusho* [The Status and Problems of the Automobile Parts and Components Industry—A Survey Report], processed. Tokyo.

Cohen, Jerome B. 1949. *Japan's Economy in War and Reconstruction*. Minneapolis: University of Minnesota Press.

Culliton, James W. 1942. *Make or Buy*. Cambridge: Harvard University Graduate School of Business Administration.

Daiyamondo Sha 1966. *Sangyō frontier monogatari: tenka plug—Nippon Tokushu Tōgyō* [The Industrial Frontier Series: Spark Plugs—A Story of the NGK Spark Plug Company]. Tokyo: Daiyamondo Sha.

————— 1969a. *Pocket shashi: Tokyo Radiator Seizō* [Pocket-sized Company History of Tokyo Radiator Manufacturing]. Tokyo: Daiyamondo Sha.

————— 1969b. *Pocket shashi: Nihon Radiator* [Pocket-sized History of Nihon Radiator Company], Tokyo: Daiyamondo Sha.

Duncan, William Chandler 1973. *U.S.-Japan Automobile Diplomacy, A Study in Economic Confrontation*. Cambridge, Mass.: Ballinger Pulishing Company.

Fukushima Kyōtarō, ed. 1929. *Jidōsha nenkan* [Automobile Almanac]. Tokyo.

Hoshino Yoshiō 1966. *Nihon no gijutsu kakushin* [Technological Innovations in Japan]. Tokyo: Keisō Shōbō.

————— 1978. *Gijutsu shi* [History of Technology], vol. III. Tokyo: Keisō Shobō.

————— and Sakisaka Masao 1960. "Kikai kōgyō no shiteki tenkai [Historical Development of the Machine Building Industry]." In Arisawa Hiromi, ed., *Gendai Nihon sangyō kōza V, kikai kōgyō* [Japanese Industries Today V, Machine Building Industry]. Tokyo: Iwanami Shoten, pp. 11–65.

Industry Research System 1977. *Chōsa shiryō: Nissan group no zembō* [Research Material Series: A Comprehensive Profile of the Nissan Group]. Nagoya.

BIBLIOGRAPHY

Ishikawa Shigeru 1979. "Appropriate Technologies: Some Aspects of Japanese Experience." In Austin Robinson, ed., *Appropriate Technologies for Third World Development.* London: Macmillan, pp. 75–132. (Reprinted with a new appendix note in his *Essays on Technology, Employment and Institutions in Economic Development,* Tokyo: Kinokuniya Co., 1981, ch. 4).

——————— and Konosuke Odaka 1979. "Technology, Management and Market Factors in the Development of Machinery Industry in Asia: Selected Issues for Further Research on Ancillary Firm Development." Discussion Paper No. 14, Institute of Economic Research, Hitotsubashi University.

Isuzu Jidōsha (Isuzu Motors), ed. 1957. *Isuzu Jidōsha shi* [The History of Isuzu Motors]. Tokyo.

———————, ed. 1977. *Isuzu yonjūnen no ayumi* [The Forty Year History of Isuzu Motors]. Tokyo.

Iwakoshi Tadahiro 1968. *Jidōsha kōgyō ron* [Automobile Industry]. Tokyo: Tokyo Daigaku Shuppan Kai.

Japan Auto Parts Industries Association 1978. *A Review of the Japanese Automotive Parts Industry.* Prepared for the Second Asian Meeting on the Automotive Parts Industry, Manila, 10 May 1978.

Japan External Trade Organization and Japan Auto Parts Industries Association 1979. *A Review of the Japanese Automotive Parts Industry,* processed, Tokyo (contentwise identical as JAPIA 1978).

Jenkins, Rhys Owen 1977. *Dependent Industrialization in Latin America, The Automotive Industry in Argentina, Chile and Mexico.* N.Y.: Praeger.

Jidōsha Buhin Kōgyō Kai (Japan Auto Parts Industries Association; see also under Nihon Jidōsha Buhin Kōgyō Kai) and Nihon Kikai Kōgyō Rengō Kai [Japan Machine Industries Association] 1957. *Jidōsha buhin kōgyō no jittai* [A Survey on Automobile Parts Industries], 2 vols. Tokyo.

Jidōsha Gijutsu Kai (Society of Automotive Engineers of Japan) 1976. *Shimpen jidōsha handbook* (Automotive Engineers' Handbook), 5th edition. Tokyo: Tosho Shuppan Sha.

Jidōsha Kōgyō Kai (Japan Automobile Manufacturers Association) 1965 and 1967. (see also under Nihon Jidōsha Kōgyō Kai). *Nihon jidōsha kōgyō shi kō (1) & (2)* [A History of Automobile Production in Japan—A Provisional Manuscript, Parts (1) & (2)]. Tokyo.

BIBLIOGRAPHY

Jidōsha Kōgyō Shinkō Kai [Society for the Promotion of Automobile Industry] 1973–79. *Nihon jidōsha kōgyōshi kirokushū* [Documents on the History of Automobile Industry in Japan], processed. Tokyo.

Jidōsha Mondai Kenkyūjo [Automobile Research Institute] 1940. *Jidōsha keizai nenkan* [Economic Almanac of Automobiles]. Tokyo.

Kikai Shinkō Kyōkai, Keizai Kenkyūjo (Economic Research Institute, Japan Society for the Promotion of Machine Industry) 1968. *Gijutsu kakusa no kenkyū* [A Study on Technological Gap], processed. Tokyo.

———— 1975. *Nichibei kikai kōgyō ni okeru nai-gaisei mondai ni kansuru chōsa kenkyū—nichibei jidōsha kōgyō ni okeru nai-gaisei mondai* [A Report on Research Findings on the "Make-or-Buy" Issue in the Automobile Industry, A Comparison of Japan and the U.S.A], processed. Tokyo.

Kimoto Shōji 1968. *Hangyaku no sōro: shōsetsu Toyoda Kiichirō* [The Road of Rebellion: A Biographic Novel of Toyoda Kiichirō]. Tokyo: Mainichi Shimbun Sha.

Kodaira Katsumi 1968. *Jidōsha* [Automobile]. Tokyo: Aki Shobō.

Koide Tanehiko 1961. *Ezoe Magoemon, kindai tōgyō-shi jō no ichi ningen zō* [Ezoe Magoemon, A Portrait of a Man Who Contributed to the Development of the Modern Ceramic Industry]. Nagoya: Ezoe Magoemon Denki Sanshū Kai.

Kojima Press Kōgyō Kabushiki Kaisha (Kojima Press Manufacturing Company) 1975. *Sōgyōsha Kojima Hamakichi* [Kojima Hamakichi, A Biography of the Founder]. Toyota City.

Kokuritsu Kokkai Toshokan, Chōsa Rippō Chōsa Kyoku (Research and Legislative Department, National Diet Library) 1978. *Wagakuni jidōsha kōgyō no shiteki tenkai* [The Development of the Automobile Industry in Japan]. Tokyo (an earlier version of Amagai 1982).

Komiyama Takuji 1941. *Nihon chūshō kigyō kenkyū* [A Study on Medium- and Small-scale Firms in Japan]. Tokyo: Chūō Kōron Sha.

BIBLIOGRAPHY

Kōsai Yutaka 1986. *The Age of High-speed Growth*. Tokyo: University of Tokyo Press.

Lalkaka, Rusi 1974. "Acquiring Technology for Manufacturing Agro-equipment." *Agricultural Mechanization in Asia* (Tokyo), V., No. 1 (Summer Issue 1974), pp. 59–67.

Mainichi Shimbun Sha, ed. 1971. *Ikiru Toyoda Sakichi, Toyota group no seichō no himitsu* [Living Toyoda Sakichi: the Secret of the Growth of the Toyota Group]. Tokyo: Mainichi Shimbun Sha.

Maxy, George and Aubrey Silberston 1959. *The Motor Industry*. London: George Allen and Unwin.

Nakamura Shūichirō 1976. *Chūshō kigyō ron* [A Study on Medium- and Small-scale Firms]. Tokyo: Tōyō Keizai Shimpō Sha.

Nakamura Takafusa 1981. *The Postwar Japanese Economy: Its Development and Structure*. Tokyo: University of Tokyo Press.

Naruse Masao 1976. *Haguruma to watashi* [Gears and I]. Sagamihara City, Kanagawa Prefecture: Naruse Sensei Kiju Kinen Shuppankai [Publication Project Commemorating the 77th Birthday of Teacher Naruse].

NHK, "Document Shōwa" Shuzai Han [NHK, "Documentary Showa" Project Team], ed. 1986. *America sha jōriku o soshiseyo, gijutsu shōkoku Nihon no ketsudan* [Deterring the American Vehicles' Landing: A Crisis Decision by a Technology-dependent Nation], "Document Shōwa" vol. 3. Tokyo: Kadokawa Shoten.

Nihon Jidōsha Buhin Kōgyo Kai (Japan Auto Parts Industries Association) 1956, 1959, 1961, 1968. *Jigyō hōkoku sho* [Annual Report of Activities], processed. Tokyo.

Nihon Jidōsha Kōgyō Kai (Japan Automobile Manufacturers Association) 1969 (see also under Jidōsha Kōgyō Kai). *Nihon Jidōsha kōgyō shi kō (3)* [A History of Automobile Production in Japan—A Provisional Manuscript (3)]. Tokyo.

Nihon Kagaku-shi Gakkai [Japan Society for the Study of the History of Science], 1966. *Nihon kagaku gijutsu-shi taikei* [Science and Technology in Japan: A Collection of Annotated Historical Documents], vol. 18, *Kikai gijutsu*, [Machine producing technology]. Tokyo: Dai-ichi Hōki Shuppan.

BIBLIOGRAPHY

Nihon Kikai Kōgyō Rengō Kai [Japan Machine Industries Federation] 1983. *Kikai jōhō sangyō ni kansuru ichiren no rippō sochi no gaiyō to unyō* [A Summary of Enactment and Administration of the Acts for the Promotion of Machine and Information Industries], processed. Tokyo, September 1983.

Nihon Tokushu Tōgyō Kabushiki Kaisha (NGK Spark Plug Company) 1957. *Nihon Tokushu Tōgyō Kabushiki Kaisha nijū nen shi* [The Twenty Year History of the NGK Spark Plug Company]. Nagoya.

———— 1967. *Nihon Tokushu Tōgyō Kabushiki Kaisha sanjū nen shi* [The Thirty Year History of the NGK Spark Plug Company]. Nagoya.

———— 1977. *Nihon Tokushu Tōgyō Kabushiki Kaisha yonjū nen shi* [The Forty Year History of the NGK Spark Plug Company]. Nagoya.

Nikkan Kōgyō Shimbun Sha (The Daily Industry Journal) 1980. *Toyota o sasaeru kigyō gun* [The Firms Supporting Toyota Motor Company]. Tokyo: Nikkan Kōgyō Shimbun Sha.

Nippondenso Kabushiki Kaisha (Nippondenso Company) 1959–60. "Densō kaiko roku [Memoirs on Denso], nos. 1–16." *Densō jihō* [Denso Journal], Jan. 1959-Aug. 1960.

———— 1974. *Nippondenso nijūgo nen shi* [The Twenty Five Year History of Nippondenso], Kariya City.

———— 1984. *Nippondenso sanjūgo nen shi* [The Thirty Five Year History of Nippondenso], Kariya City.

———— 1984. *Nippondenso sanjūgo nen shi* [The Thirty Five Year History of Nippondenso], Kariya City.

Nissan Jidōsha Kabushiki Kaisha (Nissan Motor Company) 1965. *Nissan Jidōsha sanjū nen shi* [The Thirty Year History of Nissan Motor Company]. Yokohama.

———— 1975. *Nissan Jidōsha shashi 1964–1973* [The History of Nissan Motor Company, 1964–1973]. Tokyo.

Odaka Konosuke, ed. 1983. *The Motor Vehicle Industry in Asia, A Study of Ancillary Firm Development.* Singapore: Singapore University Press.

328

———————— 1984. *Rōdō shijō bunseki* (Dual Labor Markets in Japan, A Historical Inquiry). Tokyo: Iwanami Shoten.

———————— 1985. "Is the Division of Labor Limited by the Extent of the Market? A Study of Automobile Parts Production in East and Southeast Asia." In Kazushi Ohkawa and Gustav Ranis, eds., *Japan and the Developing Countries*, Oxford: Basil Blackwell, pp. 389–425.

Ohkawa Kazushi and Henry Rosovsky 1965. "A Century of Japanese Economic Growth." In W.W. Lockwood, ed., *The State and Economic Enterprise in Japan, Essays on the Political Economy of Growth*, Princeton: Princeton University Press, pp. 47–92.

Okumura Hiroshi, Hoshikawa Jun'ichi, and Matsui Kazuo 1965. *Jidōsha kōgyō* [Automotive Industry]. Tokyo: Tōyō Keizai Shimpō Sha.

Okumura Shōji 1960. "Jidōsha kōgyō no hatten dankai to kōzō [Development Stage and the Structure of the Automobile Industry]." In Arisawa Hiromi, ed., *Gendai Nihon sangyō kōza V, kikai kōgyō* [Japanese Industries Today V, Machine Building Industry], Tokyo: Iwanami Shoten, pp. 239–362.

Osaka Shi, Keizai Kyoku (Economic Bureau, City of Osaka) 1964. *Osaka shi jidōsha buhin kōgyō sōgō shindan hōkolusho* [Auto Parts Manufacturing Industry in the City of Osaka: Report of Integrated Diagnostic Research]. Osaka.

Ōshima Taku 1973. "Nihon jidōsha sangyō kenkyū josetsu (An Introductory Inquiry into the Automobile Industry in Japan)." *Kikai keizai kenkyū* (Engineering Economics Review), no. 6 (Aug. 1973), pp. 2–33.

———————— 1980. *Jidōsha sangyō* [Automobile Industry]. Tokyo: Tōyō Keizai Shimpō Sha.

Ozaki Iwao 1976. "The Effects of Technological Changes on the Economic Growth of Japan, 1955–1970." In Karen R. Polenski and Jiri V. Skolka, eds., *Advances in Input-output Analysis*, Cambridge: Ballinger Publishing Company, pp. 93–111.

Ozaki Masahisa 1955. *Jidōsha Nihon shi* [A History of Automobiles in Japan], 2 vols. Tokyo: Jiken Sha.

———————— 1966. *Kokusan jidōsha shi* [A History of Domestic Production of Automobiles]. Tokyo: Jiken Sha.

329

Rosenberg, Nathan 1963. "Technological Change in Machine Tool Industry." *The Journal of Economic History*, XXII, no. 4 (December 1963), pp. 414–46. (Reprinted in his *Perspective on Technology*, Cambridge: Cambridge University Press, 1976).

Satō Seichū 1975. *Otoko no shinikata, aru sōgyō sha no shōgai yori* [How a Man Ought to Die, A Biography of a Business Pioneer]. Tokyo: Keizai Kai.

Saxonhouse, Gary and Gustav Ranis 1985. "Technology Choice and the Quality Dimension in the Japanese Cotton Textile Industry." In Kazushi Ohkawa and Gustav Ranis, eds., *Japan and the Developing Countries*, Oxford: Basil Blackwell, 1985, pp. 155–76.

Selzer, Lawrence H. 1928. *A Financial History of the American Automobile Industry, A Study of the Ways in Which the Leading American Producers of Automobile Have Met Their Capital Requirements*. Boston and N. Y.: Houghton Mifflin.

Sharin Kōgyō Kabushiki Kaisha (Japan Motor Wheel Company) 1964. *Sharin to tomoni sanjū nen* [Thirty Years with Wheels]. Tokyo.

Shimokawa Kōichi 1977. *Beikoku jidō sha sangyō keiei-shi kenkyū* [The Automobile Industry in the U.S.A., A Study in Managerial History]. Tokyo: Tōyō Keizai Shimpō Sha.

Smith, Adam 1776/1950. *An Inquiry into the Nature and Causes of the Wealth of Nations*. Edited by Edwin Cannan, 6th ed., London: Methuen.

Stigler, George 1951. "The Division of Labor Is Limited by the Extent of the Market." *Journal of Political Economy*, LIX, no. 3 (June 1951), pp. 185–93.

Suzuki Ryūichi 1959–60 "Densō kaiko roku (1)–(16)" [My Memoir of the Denso]. *Denso jihō* [Denso Journal], No. 78 (May 1959)–No. 93 (Aug. 1960).

Tokyo-to, Keizai Kyoku (City of Tokyo, Economic Bureau) 1963. *Tokyo To jidōsha buhin kōgyō no jittai bunseki* [An Empirical Analysis of the Auto Parts Manufacturing Industry in Tokyo]. Tokyo.

Tomiyama Kazuo 1973, *Nihon no jidōsha sangyō–kuruma wa dō kawaru ka* [Automobile Industry in Japan, Its Future Prospects]. Tokyo: Tōyō Keizai Shimpō Sha.

Topy Kōgyō Kabushiki Kaisha (Topy Industries) 1971. *Gojū nen shi* [The Fifty Year History of the Topy Industries]. Tokyo.

Toyota Jidōsha Kōgyō Kabushiki Kaisha (Toyota Motor Co.) 1958. *Toyota Jidōsha nijūnen shi* [The Twenty Year History of Toyota Motor Company]. Toyota City.

——————— 1967. *Toyota Jidōsha sanjū nen shi* [The Thirty Year History of Toyota Motor Company]. Toyota City.

Tsūshō Sangyō Shō, Jūkōgyō Kyoku (Heavy Industries Bureau, Ministry of International Trade and Industry) 1960. *Nihon no kikai kōgyō, sono seichō to kōzō* [Machine-building Industry of Japan, Its Growth and Structure]. Tokyo.

Ueno Hiroya, ed. 1970. *Jidōsha sangyō no model to yosoku* [An Econometric Model of the Automotive Industry, with Forecast for Its Future]. Tokyo: Nihon Keizai Shimbun Sha.

——————— and Mutō Hiromichi 1970. "Jidōsha kōgyō ron—hogo seisaku no jittai to hyōka" [Automobile Industry—Reality and Evaluation of the Protection Policy]. *Chūō kōron, keiei mondai* [Chūō Kōron Magazine, Special Issue on Managerial Issues]. June 1970, pp. 412–50.

Wada Hidekichi 1937. *Nissan konzern dokuhon* [A Reader on Nissan Concern]. Tokyo: Shunjū Sha.

White, Lawrence J. 1971. *The Automobile Industry since 1945*. Cambridge: Harvard University Press.

——————— 1979. "Appropriate Factor Proportions for Manufacturing in Less Developed Countries: A Survey of the Evidence." In Austin Robinson, ed., *Appropriate Technologies for Third World Development*, London: Macmillan, pp. 300–41.

William R. Gorham-shi Kinen Jigyō Iinkai [Committee to Commemorate Mr. William R. Gorham], ed. 1951. *William R. Gorham den* [A Bibliography of William R. Gorham]. Tokyo.

Williamson, Oliver E. 1975. *Markets and Hierarchies: Analysis and Antitrust Implications, A Study in the Economics of Internal Organization*. N.Y.: The Free Press and London: Collier Macmillan.

Yamamoto Tadashi 1978. *Toyota yonjūnen no kiseki* [A Forty Year Record of Toyota Motor]. Tokyo: Daiyamondo Sha.

INDEX

INDEX

INDEX